D0492625

Madonna

To Lynne, Ali and Lyds

MADONNA
ANDREW MORTON

Michael O'Mara Books Limited

First published in Great Britain in 2001 by
Michael O'Mara Books Limited
9 Lion Yard, Tremadoc Road
London sw4 7nq

A CIP catalogue record for this book
is available from the British Library

isbn 1-85479-888-X

1 3 5 7 9 10 8 6 4 2

Designed and typeset by Martin Bristow

Printed and bound in England by The Bath Press, Bath

Contents

Acknowledgments

Considering that this is a book about an all-American girl, it seems curious that my research began and ended in a typically English fashion – with a cup of tea and home-made cake. It began with a discussion about the family tree of her husband, Guy Ritchie, at the North London home of one of his relatives, Gavin Doyle. It ended, some months later, with a short journey south to the Thames-side study of Sir Tim Rice. There, surrounded by *Evita* memorabilia, as well as cricketing gear assembled for an impending match in Berlin, the Oscar-winning lyricist talked about the singer he came to know. Even in New York, the home of fast food and filter coffee, it was hard to escape English tea. This time, though, it was served with kosher milk and biscuits in a Greenwich Village apartment, as a rabbi meditated on Madonna's interest in the Jewish mystical teachings known as the Kabbalah.

For the most part, given the singer's nocturnal lifestyle in the clubs of New York and Los Angeles, research was perforce undertaken long after afternoon tea had ceased to be served. Her former boyfriend Mark Kamins gave an erudite discourse on different tequilas in a Cuban bar in Tribeca; Scottish friends explained the character of folk in Dornoch, where Madonna married, over a glass or two of malt whisky; while back in SoHo, the film director Abel Ferrara waxed lyrical about the efficacious properties of Budweiser beer, brewed in nearby New Jersey. As he talked about one of the world's brightest showbiz stars, outside in the street a placard-carrying evangelist denounced the modern cult of celebrity.

Yet, as those who were interviewed made abundantly clear, Madonna is far more than a run-of-the-mill celebrity. By dint of enterprise, creativity and dynamism, the very qualities that helped to make America, she has established herself as a towering figure not only in the world of popular entertainment, but in modern culture. My thanks, then, to all those who shared their insights and observations to help me chart her trajectory and gain a fix on a personality that has, in spite of the thousands of articles about her, remained as elusive as it is enigmatic.

I am indebted to Jim Albright; Lucinda Axler; Arthur Baker; Camille Barbone; Erika Belle; Fred Brathwaite aka Fab Five Freddie; Vito Bruno; Gary Burke; Norris Burroughs; Nick Ciotola and Kerin Shellenbarger at the

Acknowledgments

Senator John Heinz Regional History Center, Pittsburgh; Mary Anne Dailey; Professor Gay Delanghe, the University of Michigan; Mark and Lori Dolengowski; Gavin Doyle; Abel and Nancy Ferrara; Katherine Fortin; Vince Gerasole; Dan and Ed Gilroy; Stuart Graber; Linda Alaniz-Hornsby; Virginia Humes; Geneva College, Beaver Falls, Pennsylvania; Mark Kamins; Peter Kentes; John Kohn; Celeste LaBate; Jimi LaLumia; Pearl Lang; Jeff Lass; Robert Leacock; Sir Michael Leighton, Bt; Andrew Lownie; Jock McGregor; Colonel William McNair; Patrick McPharlin; Curt Miner; Coati Mundi; Michael Musto; Claire Narbonne-Fortin; Sioux Nesi; Rabbi Julia Neuberger; Bert Padell; Andy Paley; Tommy Quon; Sir Tim Rice; Mira Rostova; Whitley Setrakian; Bobby Shaw; Peter Sibilia; Ed Steinberg; Carol Steir; Steve Torton; Dr Nick Twomey; Robert Van Winkle aka Vanilla Ice; Bonnie Winston; Ruth Dupack Young; Curtis Zale; Fred Zarr. Those mentioned above who lent me their rare and fascinating photographs are also acknowledged separately on page 9.

My thanks also to my researchers, Lizzie Clachan, Will Hartley and Tania McKeown, for tackling the mountain of paper that has been produced about Madonna, and to my editors, Jacquie Wines and Toby Buchan, for making sense of my additional molehill, as also to their colleagues at Michael O'Mara Books – Gabrielle Mander, Helen Cumberbatch, Karen Dolan, Diana Briscoe, Rhian McKay, Nessa Williams and Athene Chanter. I am also indebted to the people at St Martin's Press, New York, and especially to my editor there, Hope Dellon, and her assistant, Kris Kamikawa. Martin Bristow worked his usual miracle on the design and setting of the book, on a very tight deadline, and Andrew Armitage compiled the index with great skill. As ever, my publisher and friend Michael O'Mara encouraged me when I was flagging and, more important, kept me up to date with the progress of my soccer team, Leeds United, during the weeks spent across 'the Pond.' And finally, to my wife Lynne and daughters Lydia and Alexandra, who cheered me on. I have made a lot of new friends and had a lot of fun, and I can only hope that readers will enjoy reading my book about Madonna as much as I enjoyed researching and writing it.

ANDREW MORTON
Highgate, London, September 2001

Photograph Acknowledgments

More than half the photographs in this book have been provided by people who know or have known Madonna over the years; the majority of these are published in this book exclusively and for the first time. The author and publishers are deeply indebted to all the people, listed below, who so kindly provided these rare photographs, as also to Zooid Pictures Limited, and to the individual agencies who supplied images; they too are listed below.

Page 1, Arlett Vereecke/MOV/London Features International; page 4, Splash News and Picture Agency; page 5, L. Alaniz; pages 6 and 7, photography by Peter Kentes; page 8 (*upper and lower*), L. Alaniz; pages 9, 10 (*upper and lower*), and 11, © Mark D.; pages 12–13, 14 and 15 (*upper and lower*), photography by Dan Gilroy; page 16 (*upper and lower*), photography by Curtis Zale; pages 17 and 18, L. Alaniz; page 19 (*upper and lower*), photography by Gary Burke; pages 20 (*upper and lower*), 21 (*upper and lower*), 22 (*upper and lower*), 23 and 24, courtesy of Camille M. Barbone, from her private collection; page 25 (*upper and lower*), © Stephen Torton, courtesy PictureShow Gallery, Berlin; pages 26, 27, 28, 29, 30, 31 and 32, courtesy of Camille M. Barbone, from her private collection; page 33, Rex Features; page 34, Big Pictures; page 35 (*upper*), John Bellissimo/Corbis UK Ltd; page 35 (*lower*), Corbis UK Ltd; page 36 (*upper*), P. Ramey/Corbis Sygma; page 36 (*lower*), London Features International; page 37 (*upper*), Ken Friedman/Retna Pictures; page 37 (*lower*), Rex Features; page 38 (*upper*), SIPA/Rex Features; page 38 (*lower*), Nick Elgar/London Features International; page 39 (*upper*), Corbis/Sygma; page 39 (*lower*), Corbis/Sygma; page 40 (*upper*), R. Galella/Corbis Sygma; page 40 (*lower*), Charles Sykes/Rex Features; page 41 (*upper*), Rex Features; page 41 (*lower*), Splash News and Picture Agency; page 42 (*upper*), SIPA/Rex Features; page 42 (*lower*), Faroux/SIPA/Rex Features; page 43, Rex Features; page 44, Rex Features; page 45 (*upper*), London Features International; page 45 (*lower*), Richard Young/Rex Features; page 46, SIPA/Rex Features; page 47 (*upper*), Marion Curtis/Rex Features; page 47 (*lower*), SIPA/Rex Features; page 48 (*upper*), ACT/Rex Features; page 48 (*lower*), Rex Features.

Chapter One

All-American Girl

ARRIVING AT JFK AIRPORT, a glance at the snaking line for taxis – longer than for the average Disney ride but without the thrill at the end – banishes any lingering hesitation about accepting an offer that would normally be refused. After a seven-hour flight from London, 40 dollars seems like a very good deal for a ride into Manhattan in the back of a white stretch limo, albeit unlicensed. The motley group of fellow travelers, from Canada, France and New York, think so too. 'Help yourself to drinks,' offers the moonlighting chauffeur magnanimously.

Soon there's a party going on – the roof open, the sparkling, flashing neon interior lights twinkling brighter than the early-evening stars. In the setting sun the striking skyline glitters, alight with promise, dripping with possibilities. A couple of decades before, on such a journey, on such an evening, in such a limo, an aspiring young singer called Madonna Louise Veronica Ciccone had reclined, like a punk mistress of the universe. She had told her friend Erika Belle: 'One day I'm going to own this town.' The former cheerleader from the American Midwest had not always been so certain.

Our limo glides past Lincoln Center, where the lonely teenager once sat by the fountain and wept, despairing that she would ever make it in the Big Apple. We drive by the imposing West 64th Street apartment building where she now lives, testament to her success, past the restaurant that makes a special Caesar salad just for her, and by Central Park where she met the father of her first child. After this impromptu whistlestop tour of Madonna's life, the limousine driver kicks us out at Columbus Circle. From the top of a brown brick apartment building a red neon sign, advertising a TV show, blazes one word into the night sky: 'BIOGRAPHY.'

A biographer is a personality detective, a literary gumshoe searching for clues, testing alibis and gathering evidence that will help illuminate a character who has made an impression on our world. Initial house-to-house – or rather bar-to-bar – inquiries in New York reveal a perplexing picture of Madonna. In preliminary questioning, few witnesses mention her singing or acting career. Under duress, artist Brent Wolf confesses he dreamed of her every night for five years. Then he blurts out, 'But my friend Rob was worse than me.' A mature student from Arizona, who really should know better, testifies that when she has to make a tough decision, she asks herself, 'What would Madonna do?' Even though it's a common occurrence – in India Knight's novel, *My Life on a Plate*, a girl who accidentally gets pregnant asks the same question – it merely serves to accentuate the riddle of Madonna. Typically, cultural forensics are no help; all those college lecturers endlessly debating her impact on racial and gender relations in post-modern society, are still, after twenty years, desperately seeking Madonna.

One thing is certain. We are not dealing with one of your average one-hit wonders of the pop world here. Our girl's got a staggering record of success: more number-one singles than The Beatles and Elvis Presley, sixteen films, fourteen albums and five sell-out concert tours, more than 100 million records sold to date. Not to mention enough gold and platinum records to cover entire walls and a fortune in Grammy awards and other baubles. She even has a Golden Globe for her performance in the musical *Evita* stashed away in one of her homes – New York, London or Los Angeles.

The fact that she is the most wanted woman in the world means that there is a high price on her head. Big-time 'fences' like Sotheby's and Christie's this year auctioned off her cultural castoffs – her signature sold for $200 while a Jean-Paul Gaultier bra from her Blonde Ambition Tour went for over $20,000. Then there are the bounty hunters: there were offers of $350,000 for the first picture of her daughter Lourdes, while one enterprising chap hid in the rafters of Dornoch Cathedral in Scotland in an attempt to film the christening of her son Rocco last year.

A look through her file shows clearly that since childhood Madonna dreamed single-mindedly of becoming a celebrity. 'I've been provoking people since I was a little girl. I'm very interested in being alluring,' she once confessed. As with so many showbiz divas, it started with the small stuff: a show of exhibitionism at family gatherings, hogging the spotlight at school concerts, always being the center of attention at college dance performances. By the time she moved to New York, she was on the slippery slope, rapidly moving from recreational self-absorption to flirting with the hard stuff, avidly sniffing success. Pretty soon she had pawned her dance career for a hit of fame, never really coming down from the high of seeing her first single go to number one in the charts. From then on she was hooked, utterly addicted to fame, mainlining on mass adulation, graduating from one-hit wonder to singing and acting sensation, celebrity superstar and, finally, universal icon.

Of course, as always in these cases, there were victims. In the global village, she outraged neighborhood elders by going round half-dressed and encouraging other girls to do the same, scandalized the closed minds within the Catholic Church with her open sexuality, and was always provoking the stuffier contributors to the parish magazine. As a serial controversialist, she had, however, many supporters in the community, especially among blacks, gays and young women. For all the years she has spent stirring up trouble and scandal, it remains difficult to draw an accurate portrait of the real Madonna. A consummate mistress of disguise, she has always cleverly hidden behind an assortment of masks, cloaking herself in the mystery of her mythology. 'If she were a painting, she would be an abstract by Picasso,' says one former lover, the rap star Vanilla Ice. 'She has so many faces.'

When people got really affronted at her behavior, as when she published the controversial *Sex* book, she always had an explanation. She claimed she was being criticized because she was a woman, or that what she had done was meant to be ironic, or that no one quite got it. If one of the escapades she was involved in went wrong – one of her films failing, for example – she always blamed someone else, usually the director. For two decades she's been causing mischief and mayhem and getting away with it. Equally, she has not done badly out of her years of cultural agitation. The girl who once sprayed graffiti on the walls of the Establishment now owns one of the biggest houses in the neighborhood. Yet, even though she seems to have undergone a metamorphosis from iconoclast to institution, Madonna likes to think she is still a rebel at heart. And maybe she still is.

A glance around her New York apartment yields a few signposts in the quest to pinpoint her personality. As she sits curled up on her elegant sofa, Madonna cuts an unlikely figure as the individual at the center of the longest cultural manhunt in history. At 5 foot 4½ inches tall – the half-inch is important to her – she is of average height, with striking, indeed mesmerizing hazel eyes, an insolent set to her mouth, a slight gap between her two front teeth and fine alabaster skin. Her much photographed face ranges in expression from sexy to intelligent, bored to amused – and every permutation in between – in a moment. Even though she may be casually dressed in $20 sweatpants from the discount chain Kmart, and a pair of cheap flip-flops, she holds herself in a way that suggests command and control, that she is a woman used to being in charge of herself and others.

A conversation merely reinforces that feeling. Madonna goes straight to the point, discarding the irrelevant and unfocused. 'OK, Bert, what have you got? Are we doing good?' she used to say to her former business manager Bert Padell, mocking his Brooklyn inflections. With no time for, nor interest in, small talk, she would get directly down to business, nibbling on a ricecake as she fired a thousand questions at him. It is much the same in other encounters – pleasant, matter-of-fact, to the point. 'There's an intensity about her,' recalls former lover Dan Gilroy, the man who first introduced her to music. 'She asks a question to get a reaction, not just for a chat.'

Questions, questions, questions; Madonna, ever the creative detective, searching for clues to the new and the ground-breaking. Even when she is quietly listening to music – the sounds of Ella Fitzgerald, Eastern music and electronic sampling all waft round her home – she is never simply relaxing, but analyzing the sound and the lyrics for a fragment of an original idea, jotting down her thoughts in a notebook bound in marbled paper. Creatively, she is never off duty, pillaging her daily life for ideas and raiding the minds of others for inspiration.

Her bestselling single, 'Vogue', for example, came about through a chance conversation with her best friend, actress Debi Mazar, a pal from her days in New York when they were hitting the clubs every night. It was Debi who spotted the dance craze, voguing, which swept the New York gay and Latino scene in the late 1980s. When she told Madonna about this cool, posing dance with its hypnotic hand movements, the singer homed in on its creative and commercial potential, collaborating with producer Shep Pettibone to write the song, which integrated the latest dance style with lyrics expressing Madonna's own homage to Hollywood stars of a bygone era.

As producer Ed Steinberg, who made her first video says, 'She is very clear about what she wants but at the same time she accepts the creative input of other people. That is one reason why she is so successful – she is not a total egotist.' The resulting single, with its accompanying stylish black-and-white video, had perhaps the greatest popular appeal of any of her songs, all the result of a chance conversation, a creative mind and artistic collaboration. Michael Musto of the *Village Voice* commented, 'That is her genius. She takes something that is totally over with the in-crowd in New York and then brings it to Iowa. Her talent is picking something that is bubbling under the surface and making it her own.'

While her ability to pick over the bones of modern culture and her successful collaborations with other artists are the hallmarks of her career, a constant source of admiration is the way she can effortlessly switch the focus of her attention, moving seamlessly from discussing a merchandising deal to framing the 'hook' for her latest song. Songwriter Andy Paley, who has worked extensively with Paul Simon and Brian Wilson, went to her Los Angeles home on numerous occasions while they were working on the soundtrack for *Dick Tracy*, the 1990 film directed by her lover, Warren Beatty. For four hours at a stretch she would focus entirely on the creative process, waving away her secretary and others. 'She puts the blinkers on when she is working,' he says. 'All outside distractions are forgotten. We sat at the piano and she would tap out the rhythm. She wants to feel that she can dance to any song she records. That's her test.' Paley and other writers, including her first producer Mark Kamins, reckon that Madonna is one of the best in the business, a much underrated musician and lyricist. 'She is the easiest person I know to write songs with,' Paley says. 'She has a very clear vision, the most direct person you will ever work with.'

While that vision has been clouded by the controversy, much of it self-generated, which has enveloped Madonna's career, artistically her song-writing is often overshadowed by the striking appeal of her pop videos. Several of her films have been exhibited in museums around the world, notably the Pompidou Center in Paris, as modern works of art.

This stunning visual sense is no accident; Madonna has spent a lifetime studying photographs, black-and-white movies and paintings. 'She is the perfect example of the visual artist,' notes graffiti artist and cultural commentator Fab Five Freddie, who watched her blossom during her years in New York. 'These days you cannot have longevity in the pop game without a firm understanding of the image. She has that and goes so much deeper than people give her credit for. How many pop singers have ever heard of Frida Kahlo, for example, let alone wanted to make a movie about her?'

It is the Mexican artist's striking work *My Birth* that greets visitors to Madonna's New York apartment, a painting which she uses as a kind of social litmus test, stating that if a guest fails to appreciate the work she could never consider him or her a friend. Her art collection, carefully chosen over twenty years, means so much to her that she would rather be remembered as a modern-day Peggy Guggenheim than as a singer and actress. 'Paintings are my secret garden and my passion. My reward and my nice sin,' she says, the works in her collection acting as indicators to the many paradoxes of her complex personality.

So, for example, in Kahlo's *My Birth*, the painter imagined her own birth without male intervention, an image that not only undercuts the traditional notion of the female as womb but presents woman as self-reliant, independent and strong, themes which have informed both artists' work. As she was to show more fully with her roles as an actress, particularly as Eva Perón in *Evita*, Madonna only seems to understand the world around her in terms of herself. So, she not only appreciates Kahlo's paintings, but personally identifies her own life with that of the tragic artist who saw herself as existing outside conventional society. 'I worship Frida Kahlo paintings because they reek of her sadness and her pain,' says Madonna, who admires strong beauties like Georgia O'Keefe, Marlene Dietrich and Greta Garbo. Similarly, the singer empathizes with the lifestyle of Art Deco artist Tamara de Lempicka, whose erotic portraits of stylish sybarites adorn her apartment. She shares Lempicka's biographer's view that the painter's place in the pantheon of modern artists has been denied because, bisexual and libidinous as she was, she was seen as being sexually and politically incorrect. Inevitably perhaps, Madonna sees her own life reflected in the painter's resistance to conformation with sexual norms.

Madonna, whose unrepentant exploration of traditional gender roles has helped, for example, to make lesbianism acceptable to mainstream society, also identifies with other groups and individuals who were at one time voices in the wilderness. So an Irving Penn photograph of the black champion boxer Joe Louis, the grandson of a slave who hailed from the city she calls home, Detroit, and a small bronze bust of heavyweight champion Muhammad Ali reveal the veneration and association she feels with oppressed races of America. She was thrilled when Ali, whom she associates with the fight by American blacks for civil rights, came to her apartment one evening. Similarly, she reveres the memory of Elvis Presley, who died on her birthday. She sees in his early career, when he outraged moral America with his hip-shaking stage routine during the 1950s, a reflection of her own struggle to express the view that women could be feminine, sexual and empowered. That she calls her own multimedia company Maverick underlines her belief that she is a rebel in the face of convention, an outsider who at times has stood proudly independent of her family, church, school and society.

Yet, paradoxically, the same woman who, rather romantically, sees herself as beyond the mainstream, a misunderstood artist, is in reality a living, breathing example of the all-American girl, the perfect embodiment of modern Main Street USA. Thus her creative success has been characterized by her genius for making the avant-garde acceptable to the general public. At the same time, while the vaudeville of her sexual politics, particularly her trademark conical bra and bold crotch-grabbing, owes much to the European tradition displayed in shows – admittedly, American shows – like *Cabaret* and the *Ziegfeld Follies*, Madonna's knowing, winking suggestiveness and sly humor is in the mold of Mae West, the American film actress, who believed that a woman's place was on top.

Even the trajectory of her career – a cheerleader from the Midwest who came to the Big Apple to find fame and fortune and then tried to join the Hollywood elite to pursue her acting career – is as traditional as the Stars and Stripes. Her greatest disappointment is that while she considers herself more an actress than singer, her thespian skills have yet to be fully appreciated by the world of theater. Despite this, just how far Madonna has risen in the firmament of stars is demonstrated in the fact that, while she wanted a 'Grace Kelly style' for her first wedding, at her second she actually wore a tiara that had belonged to the late Princess. While her appeal lies in the fact that she can be presented as the ultimate girl-next-door, she truly is one in a million, a living archetype, an embodiment of the radical sexual and social changes in modern America over the last twenty years.

While her place as a sexual revolutionary is assured, her dynamism, ambition and life-affirming philosophy would not be out of place in the corporate boardroom. Ironically, of all the many faces Madonna presents to the world – dancer, impresario, producer, singer, actress, entertainer and artist – the one she tries most assiduously to disguise is that of successful businesswoman. She is quoted as having once said, 'Part of the reason I'm successful is because I'm a good businesswoman, but I don't think it necessary for people to know that.' 'Get OUT', she ordered director Alex Keshishian when his camera crew tried to film a business conference during the infamous *Truth or Dare* documentary (released as *In Bed With Madonna* outside the USA), which recorded her Blonde Ambition Tour in 1990.

The girl who arrived in New York with a fistful of dollars is, and has been, a publisher, music mogul, TV executive, merchandising magnate and film producer and one of the richest women on the planet, estimated to be worth between $300 and $600 million. 'She's a great businesswoman,' says Seymour Stein, the record company mogul who first signed her. 'She's very smart and she trusts her instincts, which are great.'

Her success has certainly impressed the business community. While politicians, feminists and other moral commentators debated the graphic sexual content of her 1992 book, *Sex*, senior professors at Harvard Business School beat a path to her door. They wanted to know the secret of selling 1,500,000 copies of a $50 book in a matter of days. She considered, but eventually turned down, their invitation to address students and faculty. If she had given a lecture, as she originally intended, they would have learned that, once the hype and controversy of her artistic career is stripped away, Madonna is just like them, an embodiment of the drive, enterprise and can-do culture that has powered the American dream.

She is every inch the conventional self-made tycoon: cautious in her investments, conservative in her spending, controlling every part of her multi-million dollar empire. 'Sometimes,' says Sir Tim Rice, the co-creator of the musical *Evita*, in which she played the lead role in the film version, 'it was as if you were dealing with General Motors.'

Indeed, Madonna is a classic capitalist, conforming to all the rules, never putting a foot wrong, running her life like clockwork. Like a typical cigar-chomping company chairman, she is the first to arrive and the last to leave, her schedule full, her day disciplined, while every evening she religiously sits down and lists her goals for the next day. The engineered controversy and deliberate chaos she causes in her artistic life contrast with the order and regimentation of her business routine. However, the bottom line always shadows her creative effort. 'She is not just a businesswoman but an innovator and creator,' observes Bert Padell. 'Money comes second, creation comes first.'

Even her joshing sense of humor would not be out of place in the executive washroom. 'I'll give you sixty,' she told Padell during an early morning phone conversation. As he launched into an explanation of a financial issue, the phone suddenly went dead. When he redialed, she laughingly told him, 'See? I told you sixty seconds. My time is valuable.'

The girl who lived off popcorn and dressed in hand-me-downs has no intention of squandering her fortune, keeping well clear of the extravagant and the speculative. 'She is exactly the same way now as she was when she first came into my office without a nickel,' recalls Padell. 'It doesn't matter if it's a dollar or $10,000, she wants to know about it.' Unlike her adventurous public image, Madonna is a prudent investor who has eschewed the stock market for the safety of interest-bearing government bonds.

She was not one of those who got their fingers burnt in the Internet bubble – indeed, she was so slow out of the starting blocks that she had to sue for the rights to her domain name, Madonna.com. – preferring to keep her other assets in property and art. While paintings may be her 'sin,' as she says, 'Financially it is an excellent investment, as well as something sumptuous to admire every day.' However, her shrewd approach has led her to lose numerous paintings because she refused to pay the asking price. It is now the same with property. When she first came to live in London, she was so shocked by the high prices that on several occasions she lost out on homes she liked because her offers were unrealistically low. Frugal as she is in her financial dealings, if there is one song she would withdraw from her catalogue it is 'Material Girl'; Madonna has always regretted the decision to record a song that defined her as a consumer rather than an artist. As far as she is concerned, money is a means to an end, usually artistic, rather than an end in itself.

Like other self-reliant and self-made millionaires, Madonna believes that work has its own dignity, a belief underpinned by her recent interest in the Kaballah, a mystical text of Judaism. Thus, although she sends her maternal grandmother Elsie Fortin money every month and has bought her and other elderly relatives televisions and other home comforts, Madonna is reluctant to featherbed family and friends.

She likes to present a hard-boiled, sassy image, but her maternal and compassionate instincts are much in evidence, and not only in the way she dotes on her two children, Lourdes and Rocco. When fashion guru Gianni Versace was murdered, Madonna was the first person to phone his sister Donatella to console her. She has also quietly paid for drug rehabilitation therapy for numerous friends and family members, to help them stand on their own two feet. Indeed, much of her charity work is discreet and unshowy. A well-known supporter of AIDS charities, she is also a so-called 'quiet donor' to a charity for breast cancer, the disease which killed her mother. Every Friday after Thanksgiving the singer enjoys an annual ritual, visiting the children's wards of hospitals in Manhattan and Harlem and distributing hats, pictures and small gifts.

On one occasion she was accompanied by Sean Penn, on another by her friend Debi Mazar. There is only one condition – that the hospitals concerned ensure that her visits are absolutely private. Seeing these children struggling to cope with life-threatening illnesses like AIDS and leukemia, leaves her drained and deeply moved. During one visit she walked into a ward where a young boy, in the late stages of leukemia, simply refused to get out of bed. Depressed and upset, he seemed to have given up the fight for life. The boy's father was beside himself, unable to convince his son to battle on. So Madonna went into his room and joshed: 'Hey, get out of bed. Who do you think you are?' Then, for the next thirty minutes she sat quietly talking and playing with him until, finally, he gingerly climbed out of bed and joined the other children. 'Everyone was moved to tears,' recalls one eyewitness.

While she may be a compassionate capitalist, she is also a competitive millionaire, her financial ambitions conforming to the dreams of the super-rich American male. For several years she harbored the notion of owning her own basketball team. While she is a fervent supporter of the New York Knicks, her financial advisors sounded out several other teams. Her heart, however, was set on the Knicks but her offer to take a share in the team was turned down. Typically, she wanted to be an active investor, involved in the day-to-day decision-making. The current owners didn't want that, preferring instead a sleeping partner. In the end, discussions came to nothing.

Now able to pay millions of dollars for a painting or a home she likes, Madonna has effortlessly taken on the mindset of the super-rich. 'But I'm broke,' is a remark heard all too frequently from the queen of pop, who, like the British monarch, never carries money. Her bodyguard or chauffeur is given a $300 float to take care of daily expenses. For while she may employ bodyguards, chauffeurs, maids and cooks, old habits die hard. The girl who survived by bumming meals from friends and acquaintances has not changed overmuch. When she is out with a group of friends, Madonna is rarely the one to reach for the check. She will wait to see if someone else is going to pick up the tab and then, as a last resort, she will break down the bill, so that everyone pays their share. Jimmy Albright, her former bodyguard and lover, remembers how he would often end up paying for everyone – even though he was the poorest guy at the table. As he observes, 'I used to tell her that she was so tight she squeaked. She thinks that because people know she has a lot of money they will try and take advantage of her. But she's on top of everything.'

Her penny-pinching approach startled her Australian-born butler at her Notting Hill home in London. When he splashed out $600 for flowers, including her favorite tiger lilies, she reprimanded him severely for his extravagance. In New York she uses a modest car service rather than stretch limos, to save money, and keeps an eagle-eye out for those who feel that, because she is now wealthy, she can be ripped off. On tour she will personally haggle with hotels for cut-price rates and she checks every bill, refusing, for example, to pay excessive phone or fax charges.

This obsessive need for control goes way beyond the parameters of a typical business manual. Even on the rare occasions she takes a holiday – she has had only a handful in her adult life – she has an organized schedule to work on lyrics and future projects. She is literally never still for a moment, a musical poet in motion. This was the woman who refused to perform 'The Star-Spangled Banner' at the Superbowl, not through lack of patriotism, but because she could not control the light and sound systems.

Indeed she clearly demonstrated her patriotism and concern when she became the first celebrity to make a donation to charities helping the victims of the World Trade Center and Pentagon attacks in September 2001. She gave around $1 million – the proceeds from three Los Angeles concerts – to children orphaned by the disaster, the singer leading her audience of 20,000 in prayer.

Her frequent response to any opposition is 'This is not a democracy.' Strict with herself, she is as demanding of her staff and those with whom she works. Madonna is the boss, able to reduce to tears her one-time secretary Caresse Henry-Norman, now her manager, in the search for a missing pair of shoes in her New York apartment, or to snap at her publicist Liz Rosenberg, whom she calls 'Momola,' when she brought out her school year-book in the green room just before she was due to appear on the comedy show, *Saturday Night Live*. Apparently, she didn't like to be reminded of a past life while she was psyching herself up for a TV performance.

A picture by her bed gives another clue to her deep-rooted need for control, to contain what she calls 'the ickiness' of life. The black-and-white photograph, illuminated day and night, is of her mother, also christened Madonna, who died of breast cancer when her eldest daughter was just five years old. Her tragic death took away the implicit sense of security in Madonna's life. One consequence of this is that Madonna has endless nightmares about death and, despite regular health checks, particularly for breast cancer, sees herself in a race against time, desperate to achieve as much as she can. She says: 'I've got to push myself so hard because I have demons. I won't live forever and when I die I don't want people to forget I existed.'

At the same time, her mother's untimely death snatched from her perhaps the one person she could rely on for unconditional love and affection. Has this resulted in lasting emotional damage? Madonna seems to have spent a lifetime searching for love, yet continually rejecting or discarding those who have loved her, always afraid of being hurt once more.

Although she is in control of her artistic and business life, she has all too often lost control of her love life. In contrast to her supremely self-confident public image, the private Madonna is often uncertain and unsettled in her relationships. 'She can stand before 80,000 people in a stadium and hold them in the palm of her hand. Yet off the stage she is the most insecure woman I have ever met,' says her ex-lover Jim Albright.

While the picture of her mother offers a glimpse at the paradox that is Madonna, so, too, does another old black-and-white photograph that hangs on the wall in her children's nursery – this is a portrait of her father, Tony Ciccone, and a young Madonna. Just as she has spent a lifetime looking for unconditional love, so, too, has she spent years seeking her father's approval. She remains at heart the little girl continually trying to win over her father, searching for love and acceptance, while rejecting his conformist lifestyle, as a company man working in the defense industry. She is also repelled and attracted by Roman Catholicism, and her father remains a devout Catholic.

While shock and sensation have been Madonna's handmaidens in her success as a cheerleader for controversy and hedonism, her father has always lived by the rules and regulations, either of his company or his church. Nowhere was this divide between them better expressed than in the publication of her controversial *Sex* book in October 1992. She said it was an act of rebellion against her father, the church and the world in general. Yet, predictably, when they celebrated Christmas together that year at the family home in Rochester, Michigan, it was never once mentioned.

It is not surprising, then, that her father, the man who gave Madonna the values of self-help, independence and thrift, has steadfastly refused the gifts she has offered, be it buying him a new house, a car, or the 50 acres of land in north Michigan where he now tends his award-winning vineyard. 'He didn't want any part of the money because of the way she made it,' explained Madonna's former schoolfriend Ruth Dupack Young, who worked with Tony

Ciccone for ten years at General Dynamics. 'That was definitely the impression he gave. He made everything on his own and he didn't want to be part of her money. He is a strict Catholic who followed the rules and he found it tough when his daughter didn't. It was difficult for him at work being ragged by the other engineers. He is proud of her, but also dismayed by her. There comes a point in life when you ask yourself how much do you do just for success.'

Yet it is the dynamic of her personal life, the loss of her mother, the conflict with her father, sin and religion, eroticism and romance, love and loneliness, which have informed her work and formed the bedrock of her success. More than for any other artist, her life is her art, Madonna both the painter and the canvas of that unique creation – herself.

She is the girl who wanted to rule the world but not to change it. She ended up doing a little of both. This is her story.

Chapter Two

The American Dream

Unshaven, rumpled and weary, Gaetano Ciccone cut an unprepossessing figure as he emerged, blinking in the May sunshine, from the bowels of the passenger ship, *Presidente Wilson*, moored in the Hudson River not far from the Statue of Liberty. But so did the 1,230 other passengers who had been crammed with him in the cheapest third-class or steerage quarters of the ship, which earned her keep ferrying human cargo across the Atlantic, arriving every two months at Patras, Naples and Trieste to pick up her quota of Greeks, Italians and Eastern Europeans, all heading for a fresh start in the New World.

On April 19, 1920, Gaetano Ciccone had been one of several hundred, mainly young, men clutching pathetic bundles of possessions, patiently waiting on the quayside at Naples harbor as the rather ungainly outline of the 12,500-ton steamer came into view. Some were returning to America after visiting their families. Most, like Gaetano, were making their first journey; the anxious excitement of embarking on a new life anchored by the sobering recognition that few would ever see their loved ones again.

Gaetano was little different from his fellow passengers. At nineteen he was perhaps a little younger, at 4 foot 10 inches in his stocking feet a little shorter, but he felt similar mixed emotions at leaving those he loved for an uncertain future. He had only been married a short while, inevitably to a girl from his village, dark-haired Michelina di Ulio. Her parents, Carmen and Constantine, were friends of the family, while Michelina, a year younger than Gaetano, was his childhood sweetheart. His parents, Nicola Pietro and Anna Maria, had not only blessed their union but also encouraged their teenage son to leave Pacentro, a dusty village of some 1,800 souls in the Abruzzi region of Italy, north-east of Rome, knowing that his future there was as stony as the soil.

For centuries the Ciccone clan had eked out a hand-to-mouth existence as peasant farmers or farmhands, for a long time exploited by the feudal rule of the Caldora family whose fifteenth-century castle dominated the valley. With the most recent wave of calamities – notably a severe drought, persistent crop failures, the flu epidemic of 1918, as well as the privations of the First World War – many of the Ciccone clan had made up their minds to head west. Most of the able-bodied men in the village left, some lured by the stories, invariably exaggerated, of the wonders and possibilities of the New World. There were in any case enough reports in letters and even joyful visits from family members who had already settled out there, all testifying to the abundance of work in the steel mills around Pittsburgh and the coalmines of West Virginia. Many a young girl, anxious to escape the grinding poverty of home, persuaded her parents to let her travel to the United States on the dubious premise that a potential husband was awaiting her over the water.

Just three months after Gaetano embarked on the *Presidente Wilson*, his uncle and aunt, Michele and Maria, and his cousin Giustinao also made the long journey to Naples, where they boarded the steamship *Giuseppe Verdi* for the two-week voyage to America. They and Gaetano, whatever their personal hopes and misgivings, were, however, only statistics in the greatest organized migration in the history of mankind. Between 1880 and 1930, more than twenty-seven million people entered the United States, up to seventeen million of them passing through Ellis Island, the principal US immigration reception center in New York, during the years 1892–1924. Many, like Gaetano were defined as 'chain migrants' – young men coming to find work first, then sending for wife and family to join them.

Like so many immigrants, Gaetano's first impression of America was a fleeting glimpse of the fabled New York skyline before he was crammed with five or six thousand others into the seething, stifling hubbub of the huge, red-brick reception hall on Ellis Island. The huddled, anxious mass of humanity shuffled slowly toward a row of immigration officers, standing, like unforgiving schoolteachers, behind a series of wooden desks, waiting to vet the new arrivals.

As Gaetano, speaking through an interpreter, answered the questions of the immigration officer, William Geder, he could see nearby the short splay of wooden steps leading to the exit. They beckoned him to freedom, acceptance and, he hoped, the welcoming arms of his uncle Ciccarelli, who had planned to travel from Aliquippa in Pennsylvania, where lodgings in a boarding house and perhaps even a job were waiting for young Gaetano

First, however, he had the hurdle of Officer Geder's questions to get over. Gone were the days when virtually everyone, bar the diseased and mentally incompetent, gained entry to America. The hostilities aroused by the First World War and the ongoing Communist revolution in Russia had led, in much of the United States, to a fetid climate of hostility and xenophobic suspicion towards new arrivals.

After he had confirmed that he could read and write – most Italians of his background couldn't do either, even in their own language – Gaetano shook his head when asked if he was an anarchist or advocated the overthrow of the government by force or revolution. These were not idle questions – a wave of race riots, strikes and anarchist bombings the previous year had placed America on red alert. Indeed, the Attorney-General, Mitchell Palmer, had hysterically announced that the Communist revolution was due to start in America on May Day 1920 – just forty-eight hours before Gaetano arrived – with a wave of bombings and assassinations.

At the end of his interview, Gaetano pulled out a grubby wad of bills, as evidence that as well as having paid for his passage he had saved enough to bring with him $40 for board and lodging until he could find work. A skeptical officer, Geder ordered a recount and penciled in the arrival document that Gaetano had in fact only brought $30. In the haste of officialdom, Michelina, his wife who had been left behind, was renamed 'Michela' on his entry papers.

Finally, Gaetano was free to leave, after a nerve-racking if unexceptional admission to the nation of hope, enterprise and freedom. Like millions of others, he soon discovered that he had exchanged one kind of servitude for another. His story, at once prosaic yet heroic, was repeated hundreds of thousands of times in dozens of American towns and states during this period.

Aliquippa in 1920 was a classic company town: the steel company, Jones and Laughlin, owned and controlled virtually everything – from the houses, water, gas and electricity, to banks, buses and everyday shops. Its history was recent; in 1907 the company, wanting to expand its operations from Pittsburgh's South Side, bought the site of the former Woodlawn amusement park and built a huge modern mill and housing for a projected 30,000 people. Eventually the name was changed from Woodlawn to Aliquippa (after a local Native American princess) – although, because of its isolation and the iron rule of the company, the locals knew it by another name: Little Siberia.

Gaetano Ciccone, however, viewing Aliquippa for the first time, could be forgiven for thinking he had arrived not in an Arctic prison camp but in an industrial version of Dante's Inferno. Once described as 'hell with the lid off,' Aliquippa's burning smokestacks belched out a steady stream of grey and black that shrouded the horizon as far as the eye could see, while the sky directly above the town glowed with fiery oranges, reds and murky yellows from the steel mills. The pervasive rotten-egg smell of sulfur was one Gaetano would soon get used to.

This corruption of the landscape was mirrored by the rawness of daily life. Pittsburgh had the world's highest mortality rate for typhoid, and tuberculosis was rampant; there was more space for cemeteries in the city than for recreation, while the destitute and immigrants like Gaetano were crowded in a squalor unsurpassed by the Old World.

It is unclear whether Gaetano and others of his clan had been brought over by the notorious *padroni*, or bosses – Italians already in America who acted as employment brokers and operated a form of indentured servitude. It is more likely, though, that he had to bribe the mill foreman with some of his carefully saved dollars to secure a hot and dirty job on the floor of the blast-furnace shed. Certainly, it was not long before he joined the streams of fellow steelmen, metal lunch pail in hand, traveling to the J and L mill, where he was officially described as a 'wire worker.' For the first few months he doubtless shared a bed with another worker on an opposite shift in his boarding house in West Aliquippa, where the 4,200 Italian immigrants were clustered. After a while he settled into the mute industrial rhythm of the community, the hardships of the field exchanged for the iron rigors of the foundry.

The local newspaper – controlled, needless to say, by the boss of J and L, Tom Girdler – regularly ran editorials denouncing union organizers as 'bloodsuckers' and 'mad dogs,' who should be met with violence. During the 1892 'battle' of the Homestead Steel Works (part of the Carnegie Steel Company), near Aliquippa, sixteen people had been killed and hundreds injured when steel bosses sent in 300 Pinkerton detectives to break a strike organized by the Amalgamated Association of Iron, Steel and Tin Workers. As a result of the strike non-union labor was brought in, and the steel industry was not unionized until the mid-1930s. During the national steel strike of 1919, a year before Gaetano arrived, union organizers had been turned away by police waiting at Aliquippa train station, and on one occasion a union organizer was spirited away by the police and committed to a state mental hospital.

The company deliberately sought to recruit immigrants, knowing that they would have arrived with no notions of joining unions, and, partly for that reason, would be easy to control and willing to do the hard, dirty work in the mill. Newly arrived Slovaks, Greeks, Italians, Irish and Eastern Europeans all worked alongside one another, the lack of a common language in this polyglot community a convenient barrier to communication, and thus to fraternization and organization. Furthermore, every ethnic group was assigned to a different housing area and discouraged from straying into other neighborhoods.

Within the cowed immigrant workforce there was a pecking order based on nationality and race. One Italian carpenter, for example, was told he could not have a more skilled job because 'he had the map of Italy all over his face'. Indeed, the Italians were the bottom of the heap, and Italian peasants like

Gaetano the lowest of the low. In the shadow of the Mafia, they faced dis-
crimination not just from the authorities but from other ethnic groups, who
referred to them as 'dagos,' a corruption of the common Spanish name
Diego, but often held to be derived from 'day laborer.'

In America between 1874 and 1915, some thirty-nine Italian Americans
had been lynched for alleged offenses, and it was not uncommon for the
police, faced with a crime, to round up as many Italians as possible. Such was
the climate of hatred that Italy at one point broke off diplomatic relations.
A comment in the *New York Times* was typical of the temper of the period.
'Those sneaking and cowardly Sicilians, the descendants of bandits and assas-
sins . . . are to us a pest without mitigation.'

The Ciccones, like millions of other Italians, refused to be cowed by the
bellicose and the belligerent. They stayed rather than ran, worked hard, and
lived on to fight another day. It is as though Gaetano Ciccone absorbed
whole the advice from an immigration guidebook, written in 1891, on how to
survive in America – and then passed it on to future generations. 'Hold fast,
this is most necessary in America. Select a goal and pursue it with all your
might . . . You will experience a bad time, but sooner or later you will achieve
your goal . . . Do not take a moment's rest. Run.' One view might certainly be
espoused by Gaetano's famous granddaughter: articulating America's can-do
ethic, the guidebook's author wrote: 'A final virtue is needed in America –
called cheek . . . Do not say: "I cannot, I do not know."'

The rampant racism of the time, coupled with company policy, ensured
that Gaetano kept to his own people. By 1925 records show that his young
bride Michelina had now joined him and they had started a family. In all they
had six boys; first born was Guido, followed by Rocco, Neilo, Pete, Guy, and
Silvio, born on June 2, 1931. (Silvio later anglicized his name to Tony.) This
large, bustling family of boisterous boys crammed into a modest house at 420
Allegheny Avenue, a stone's throw from Saint Joseph's Roman Catholic
church, where Gaetano, his wife and boys, as well as the three other Ciccone
families who lived on the same street, worshiped.

Day-to-day life was a struggle, the local women taking in washing and
ironing to make ends meet. The Ciccones grew vegetables in their backyard,
while Gaetano brewed homemade wine, a skill his son Silvio would one day
turn into a business. Whether Michelina was one of the many indomitable
Italian wives who met the pay train at the mill for fear that their husbands
might drink it away at the local tavern remains a moot point – Madonna has
said that her paternal grandparents were alcoholics.

Not just wine was brewing in the community, however. On the night of
May 12, 1937, the workforce finally rebelled against years of ruthless

exploitation. In July 1935, the historic National Labor Relations Act was made law. Commonly known as the Wagner Act, its general objective was to guarantee to employees 'the right to self-organization, to form, join, or assist labor organizations, to bargain collectively through representatives of their own choosing, and to engage in concerted activities for the purpose of collective bargaining or other mutual aid and protection.' Unsurprisingly, it was resisted by many large companies, and when a landmark Supreme Court ruling ordered J and L to reinstate workers fired for daring to organize a union, the company chairman, Horace E. Lewis, stonewalled in applying it. At this, almost the entire population, including the women and children, gathered in grimly quiet protest at the long tunnel that marked the main entrance to the giant J and L plant. The hissing, clanking, roaring mill was stilled, and for the first time in memory the valley did not glow brilliant red that night.

It was a short-lived strike. Within forty hours, the company capitulated and the action was called off. It was a moment that changed the lives of everyone in Aliquippa for ever. 'We were really happy, really happy!' recalled one elderly woman in a TV documentary commemorating this historic victory. 'We had a parade; I tell you that street was loaded with people, celebrating, hollering and screaming.' (They were fortunate; a similar union rally in Chicago on Memorial Day 1937 led to the police massacring men, women and children after indiscriminately firing on the unarmed crowd.)

Those fateful hours in Aliquippa genuinely transformed the lives of those who took part, and the story of how the people took on the might of the company, and won, was passed on from generation to generation. A decade after union recognition, the whole town was transformed, the community redefined. As the industrial historian Lynn Vacca, has noted: 'For the first time, the immigrant workers who made up the majority of Aliquippa's population began to think of themselves as authentic American citizens, with real recourse to the civil and economic rights they had up until then only heard about.'

Gaetano himself took an active part in the strike, and, young as he was, Silvio is bound to have absorbed, consciously or unconsciously, the change in the communal climate. Like thousands of other children of immigrants, he was imperceptibly and inevitably growing apart from his parents. Born in America, he spoke Italian at home but learned English at school; he took part in the traditional Italian festival celebrating San Rocco's feast day in August, but he played baseball in the street with his friends.

A devout Catholic boy, bright, studious yet conformist, Silvio went to Saint Joseph's church every day and, with his brothers, attended the Catholic school on the church grounds. Like many sons of steelworkers, Silvio had an aptitude for sciences, mathematics and engineering. Yet within the close-knit Italian community, education was seen as a curse as well as a blessing. While few steelworkers wished for their sons to follow in their own footsteps, they felt that education was a dangerous source of cosmopolitan ideas threatening traditions and ethnic values, and it was with reluctance that they recognized that only through education could their offspring escape the iron demands of the foundry floor.

Indeed, it is an extraordinary achievement in men like Gaetano Ciccone that they triumphed against all the odds. Most learned English after a fashion, they worked hard, taught their children, nourished their churches, helped to build the labor movement and kept faith in the American dream, which eventually most realized in the careers of their children and grandchildren. How far Silvio's ambition to stay in school, rather than work full-time, created conflict within the family is difficult to judge. Madonna has articulated her father's dreams and desires. 'It's not that he was ashamed, really, but he wanted to be better,' she has said. 'I think he wanted us to have a better life than he did when he was growing up.'

The reality was not quite so sharply defined. With the Korean War looming, and with it the promise that the military would take care of a young man's education, Silvio signed up to the Air Force Reserve. As a teenager living through the Second World War and seeing his brothers go off to fight – his brother Peter served with the US Navy – he was eager to do his bit. He rose through the ranks to become a sergeant and, after a short period stationed in Alaska, was sent to the huge Goodfellow airbase outside San Angelo in Texas, where he worked in the control tower overseeing pilots learning to fly jet fighters. He used his time wisely, and while waiting for his discharge studied at the nearby San Angelo Junior College. After completing his military service in 1952 he returned to his hometown in Pennsylvania, commuting from his parents' home to Geneva College, a Christian institution founded in 1848, located not far away in Beaver Falls.

Earnest and steadfast, he remained deeply committed to his Catholic faith, going to church every day and attending Bible classes as he actively integrated his Christian faith and values with the more practical demands of a three-year degree course in physics. He and the other five physics majors were a rather anonymous bunch, contributing little to extra-curricular activities at the college. It was entirely understandable. In those days the college catered to young men and women who were working their way through school. Silvio was no exception, taking on a variety of jobs in Aliquippa to pay his college fees. His graduation photograph, taken in June 1955, reveals a young man, just twenty-four, with a cool, steady, intelligent stare, a down-turned, rather cruel, mouth, and the dark, brooding good looks of a 1950s matinée idol.

A little over three weeks after the photograph was taken he traveled north to Bay City in Michigan, where he married a girl three years his junior, Madonna Louise Fortin.

The Fortins were one of the pioneering families of North America, boasting a pedigree that went back three centuries. In 1650 Julien Fortin, then twenty-nine, went on a great adventure, sailing from Le Havre in his native France for a new life in what was then known as New France. Three months after setting out he arrived in the small port of Quebec, where he quickly found work and went on to become a butcher and a prosperous businessman. His wife, Geneviève Gamache, whom he married on February 11, 1652, had twelve children by him, four girls and eight boys. Their offspring settled throughout Canada, these sturdy folk becoming the solid working backbone of the fledgling nation. Stoical, tenacious and resolute, the Fortins have a name for the family's dominant characteristic. They call it 'Fortintude.' 'It's a combination of determination and stubbornness to get to where they want to go,' says Claire Narbonne-Fortin. 'In essence, to achieve their dreams. So nothing Madonna Junior does ever surprises us.'

Down the generations their jobs have ranged from steamboat captain to policeman, saloonkeeper to machinist. For the most part, though, the Fortins made their way in farming and lumber. Their lives revolved around the land, so it was entirely normal that when Elsie Fortin was born, on June 19, 1911, it should be in the upstairs bedroom of her grandfather Nazaire's wooden farmhouse at Standish, Arenac County, in northern Michigan. She was brought up in Bay City where her father Guillaume Henri, a sometime shipyard laborer and farmhand, and her mother Marie-Louise had moved to in search of work. It was here she met and married Willard Fortin, the son of a lumberjack and later a successful manager in a Bay City construction company.

Staunch Catholics, Willard and Elsie sent their eight children, two girls and six boys, to the local Visitation Church school and later to Saint Joseph's high school. It was here that their eldest son Dale first saw eight-year-old Katherine Gautier, the daughter of French-Canadian parents. He excitedly told the nuns at the school and his younger sister, Madonna, that one day he was going to marry the dark-haired schoolgirl. He was true to his word.

So it was that, in April 1951, Katherine Gautier and her mother, Dale's mother – the indomitable Elsie Fortin – and his sister Madonna all crammed into the car of Dale's friend and best man Leonard Beson for the long, dusty ride to Goodfellow airbase in Texas, where Dale, a veteran of the fighting in Korea with the rank of sergeant in the USAF, was stationed. There he had become friendly with Silvio Ciccone, now known as Tony, whom he invited to the marriage service. It was a fateful decision.

Tony, in his smart blue USAF uniform, watched the bride and groom intently as they took their vows before Chaplain Carlin in an intimate Roman Catholic service at the small chapel on the airbase. But he only had eyes for the maid of honor, seventeen-year-old Madonna Fortin, whose dark, radiant beauty was perfectly complemented by the pale yellow lace dress and matching organdy cape that she was wearing that day. 'Oh, she was a real beauty,' recalls Katherine. 'He was the one who fell for her.'

Shortly afterwards, Dale was discharged from the service and returned to Bay City, where he set up home and took a job as a lumber salesman. Tony Ciccone visited as frequently as Air Force leave would allow, and it was clear to everyone that in Dale's sister Madonna he had found the woman of his dreams. 'They were both quiet,' recalls Katherine. 'She was attracted to him because he was a nice, decent man, very handsome, who treated her well.' The fact that Madonna had been engaged for a few months to a besotted young man from Monroe, Michigan, proved no hindrance to the budding romance. Within weeks of meeting Tony she ended her other relationship, and for the next three years they conducted a long-distance courtship while he took up his studies at Geneva College in Pennsylvania and she started work as an X-ray technician for two Bay City radiologists.

They were married on July 1, 1955, by Pastor George Deguoy at the Visitation Church in Bay City, where the Fortin family regularly worshipped. This time Dale Fortin was the best man, Madonna's lifelong friend Geraldine 'Chicky' Sanders her maid-of-honor. Naturally both sets of parents were present, and it is worth noting that on the marriage certificate Gaetano Ciccone was named as Guy. The gradual process of assimilation, re-creation and reinvention, which is at the heart of the American story, was finding, and would continue to find, its perfect expression in the Ciccone family.

The newly married couple seemed to represent the dreams and values of the Eisenhower years, an era of full employment, rigid convention and cultural conservatism, yet also of an unbounded optimism and unquestioning faith in the American dream. Not only had Tony shaken off his given name, but he had left behind the gritty blue-collar life of Aliquippa and had taken an office job as an optics and defense engineer with Chrysler. He was to spend his career in the defense industry, eventually earning a substantial six-figure salary with General Dynamics, working with the Hughes Corporation on tank design.

In those early days, though, the college graduate was at the bottom of the white-collar ladder. After a short stay in Alexandria, Virginia, where Tony worked on a defense contract, the Ciccones moved into a cramped bungalow on 443 Thors Street in the suburb of Pontiac, Michigan, about twenty-five miles north-west of Detroit. They had barely unpacked the Catholic statuary, crucifixes, and other religious artifacts that had adorned their homes, when Madonna became pregnant. Anthony was born on May 3, 1956. Madonna and Tony took to heart the Old Testament injunction to be fruitful and multiply – for most of their marriage Madonna was either pregnant or recovering from childbirth. Their second child, Martin, was born on August 9, 1957, while their third, Madonna Louise, arrived into the world on the morning of August 16, 1958. Her heavily pregnant mother had traveled to the home of her parents, Elsie and Willard, in Bay City for a rest, and had given birth at the local Mercy Hospital. The family nicknamed the dark-haired baby 'Little Nonni' to distinguish her from her mother, who from now on was referred to as 'Big Madonna.'

The baby Madonna may have been cooed over and cosseted as the first girl in the family, but her status did not last long. Another daughter, Paula, was born just a year later, followed by Christopher in 1960 and Melanie in 1962.

Yet Madonna stood out, her very name her badge of distinction. Unlike her siblings, who were given straightforward Anglo-Saxon Christian names, common and anonymous, Madonna's name automatically made her different, the choice of the Virgin Mary as a Christian name as audacious as it was devout. For many years her Christian name was a curse rather than a blessing, a cross she had to bear. Not only did it distinguish her from her siblings, it stood her apart from her schoolfriends while, later, when she ventured into the cool New York scene, her name automatically defined her as Catholic, ethnic and regional – a girl from an unsophisticated working- or lower-middle-class family. In short, a hick from the sticks. In a sense, the tension between the way she has both accepted and denied her family and her ethnic roots, and the enduring conflict between her stern upbringing and her creative inner self, are laid bare in that simple yet iconic seven-letter word: Madonna.

Added to that equation is her rather melodramatic appreciation of her life, both as it was and as it is, which often obscures rather than illuminates the existing narrative of her career. For although events may have been true to her, they did not always constitute *the* truth, only *her* truth. Thus in the melodrama of her life, because Elvis Presley died on her birthday (her nineteenth, August 16, 1977), she has since felt a deep spiritual connection to him and his work, coming to see his persecution for daring to swing his hips to his brand of rock and roll as being similar to criticism of her own endeavors to push back sexual boundaries.

By all accounts she was a bright, articulate and very expressive little girl, with a vivid imagination. She loved her mother to read her bedtime stories, her favorite about a garden populated with talking vegetables and friendly rabbits. Like many toddlers, though, she was afraid of the dark, and her earliest memories are of snuggling into bed with her parents, the feel of her mother's red silk nightgown invariably sending her off to sleep. 'I wanted to be with the A team,' she recalls. If her parents, in particular her mother, represented safety and security, her siblings were all too often a pain in the neck. Her elder brothers, Tony and Martin, relentlessly teased and tormented her, while the arrival of her younger sisters, Paula and Melanie, presented a threat of a different kind, focusing her mother's attention on their needs, rather than her own. 'She liked attention from the family and she usually got it,' recalls her grandmother, Elsie Fortin. 'I used to feel sorry for Paula.' Like a fledgling in an overcrowded nest, she knew that the emotional nourishment she craved would only be provided if she squawked the loudest and the longest. Thus, her later compulsion to shock, her itch to rebel, might be traced back to that childhood need to belong, her unquenchable thirst for love and admiration.

Naturally, the primary object of her love was her mother, whom she remembers with fondness and regret. In memory, Madonna sees an 'angelic, beautiful woman,' patient and long-suffering, who scrubbed and cleaned, prayed and nurtured. But Big Madonna had also been an accomplished dancer, and had had a passion for classical music so strong that the Fortin family often wonder if, had she lived, her eldest daughter's talents would have been channeled into the world of the classics rather than pop.

The other love of Madonna Senior's short life was her religion. A member of the Roman Catholic Altar Society, her faith was bone deep, reflecting not just her own deep sense of devotion but also that of the Fortin family, particularly her mother Elsie. During Lent she would kneel on uncooked rice and sleep on coat hangers as penance, and is even said to have covered the many religious statues in her home when a friend who was wearing front-zipped jeans came to visit. This faith helped her to endure her terminal illness with fortitude. While she was pregnant with Melanie in 1962, she was diagnosed as suffering from breast cancer. As her friends and family absorbed the awful news, they blamed it on the fact that during her days as an X-ray technician the protective lead-lined apron, now obligatory, was rarely used.

Crucially, treatment was delayed until after she had given birth to Melanie. By then doctors were fighting a losing battle. While Madonna Senior was in and out of the hospital undergoing painful and debilitating radiotherapy, the children, bewildered if unsuspecting, were frequently farmed out to relatives, Madonna, then four, often staying in Bay City with her maternal grandmother. During their regular early-morning visits to church, prayers were offered more fervently, the rosary whispered with real urgency and passion. Everyone was praying for a miracle.

Still nursing baby Melanie, Madonna Senior gamely attempted to run a home and minister to her children. All too often she slumped exhausted on a sofa in the sitting room as her children climbed all over her, wanting her to play or tearfully asking her to resolve disputes, or simply wanting a cuddle. Interpreting her mother's listlessness as rejection, little Madonna redoubled her efforts for attention, on one occasion drumming her fists into her mother's back in frustration when she was too tired to play with her. She vividly remembers the time her mother burst into tears and how she impulsively put her arms round her in a childlike gesture of comfort and support. Little Nonni recalls feeling stronger than her mother, that she was the one consoling her. 'I think that made me grow up fast,' she has said.

As Madonna Senior's condition deteriorated she spent more time in the hospital, her children seeing the forced cheerfulness and wan smiles, their father's quiet desperation – Madonna remembers him crying just once – and the relentless optimism of the adults around them. Yet they recall, too, how their mother was always laughing and joking with them, so that they looked forward to their hospital visits. Even when, in the final weeks, she was visibly wasting away because she could no longer keep down solid food, she remained cheerful, her faith and her inherited 'Fortintude' a comfort and source of strength in the face of the inevitable. On her last night, December 1, 1963, Madonna Senior, her six children gathered around her bed, brightly asked for a hamburger, such was her determination to keep up appearances. An hour after the children were led from her room, she was dead.

This comforting tableau of saint-like stoicism and carefree courage is now part of family folklore, the almost biblical imagery of her last supper – particularly her final request for that ubiquitous, all-American dish – helping to fix and burnish her memory. In a way this story, often told in the family, disguises as much as it reveals, the matter-of-fact, almost jolly, manner of her parting smothering the relentless tragedy of the death of a young woman, only thirty, saying her final goodbyes to six young children – one still just a baby, the eldest not yet eight – ironically at the start of the Christmas season, but also when the whole of America was in deep mourning for the death of President John F. Kennedy, assassinated nine days earlier in Dallas, Texas. The awful confluence of these tragedies, one national, the other family, was almost overwhelming for the Fortins and Ciccones. For all concerned it marked the passing of an era of innocence, the end of an American dream.

Yet in the immediate aftermath of Madonna Senior's death, so much was suppressed, so much left unsaid, so many untangled and unresolved emotions, of remorse, guilt, loss, anger and confusion, that in the atmosphere of resolute normality, it is little wonder that Madonna, then five, could not properly grasp the concept of her mother dying. It was only at her funeral at the Visitation Church in Bay City – the church where Madonna Senior had married eight years earlier – that her eldest daughter started truly to absorb the enormous and permanent change in her family life. The service of High Mass was deeply emotional, weeping and wailing a continual counterpoint to the hymns and prayers. It is not hard to see that, for little Madonna, a sensitive and imaginative child, this wave of suffocating emotion was both terrifying and traumatic.

She could see her mother, looking very beautiful and lying as if she were asleep in an open casket. Then she noticed that her mother's mouth, in her words, 'looked funny.' It took her some time to realize that it had been sewn up. In that awful moment she began to understand what she had lost for ever. That final image of her mother, at once peaceful yet grotesque, is one she carries with her to this day.

The Ciccone children reacted to their loss in different ways. Martin and Tony, the older brothers, expressed their anger by becoming rowdier than normal, throwing rocks around the place, lighting illicit fires or just making general nuisances of themselves in the neighborhood. By contrast, Madonna withdrew into herself, vomiting if she left her home for any length of time. Home was a sanctuary and a security blanket, a haven of safety and protection in a mixed-up world. Her sleep was often interrupted by nightmares and, as she shared a bed with her younger sister Paula, she regularly ended up sleeping in her father's bed, not only for comfort but also so that her younger sister could get some rest.

Instinctively loving and maternal, qualities often overlooked in any analysis of her personality, Madonna bustled round her younger brother and sisters, particularly baby Melanie, caring for them as she had seen her mother do. But they could never fill the gap left by her namesake's death. For a sensitive little girl who had already demonstrated her deep-seated need for love and affection, the loss of the one person who gave her patient, unconditional love changed for ever her relationship to the outside world, making her stronger and more self-reliant, yet with an insatiable need for love matched by fear of commitment. She had given her love once to someone she had completely trusted, and that person had gone from her life.

It would be many years before she could utterly pledge herself to another. Indeed, her quest for love without strings would define her behavior, in public and in private, and provide the momentum behind the relentless ambition and craving for attention that has propelled her to universal fame.

Years later, when she was in her early twenties and on the threshold of a music career, she was lying in bed in the New York home she shared with her then boyfriend, artist and musician Dan Gilroy. It was in the days when her personality was her performance and her performance was her personality. She was indulging in an early-morning reverie, talking into a tape recorder about a Korean woman she had befriended who had wanted to adopt her. That encounter clearly stirred the deep well of memory about her mother.

In a voice needy and plaintive, she said: 'I need a mother, I want a mother. I look for my mother all the time and she never shows up anywhere. I want a mother to hug.'

Clearly close to tears she repeats a slang phrase about being cheated: 'I got gypped, I got gypped, I got gypped . . .'

Chapter Three

'This Used to Be My Playground'

IN A WAY, it was all the fault – if fault is the right word – of the 1980s pop group, A Flock of Seagulls. Back when he was a music journalist in New York, Neil Tennant, now of the Pet Shop Boys, had an appointment to interview the one-hit wonders. They failed to show. Peeved, Tennant fell back on his contingency plan and called a young singer named Madonna, arranging to meet her for coffee in a downtown café. At that time she had a couple of singles released, but stardom was neither assured, nor swift in coming.

She arrived on time, eager to make an impression, knowing that good publicity would help the climb up the greasy pole to fame and fortune. Of course, striking publicity could only be achieved by ensuring she gave great copy, and that in turn depended on entertaining stories about her life – especially her sex life. If that meant a little embroidery and embellishment around the edges, so be it. After all, she was just another aspiring young singer, a co-conspirator in the unspoken pact between those who crave celebrity, and those who have the power to offer it, to give them the canvas upon which to paint their dreams. 'From the very start I was a bad girl,' she gushed. The tape recorder mechanically recorded her words, but not the ironic gestures and knowing winks that accompanied them.

'I hardly said a word,' remembers Tennant. 'I couldn't stop her talking.' Yet his second-choice interview made great copy, the result a major spread in *Star Hits* magazine in November 1983. It provided material which, together with other interviews Madonna gave at that time, has found its way into countless feature articles, films and biographies, so that now, like pebbles in a pocket, her anecdotes and vignettes from early interviews have grown smooth with overuse. When the efforts of her more excitable chroniclers, and especially those who have focused on the sexual and the sensational, are added to her own early propaganda, it is easy to see how the myth of Madonna was born: the ghetto childhood; the schoolgirl rebel; the flirty young Lolita who became a sexual athlete; the mistreated Cinderella, complete with Wicked Stepmother; the misunderstood artist.

Inevitably, all this makes for a confusing narrative. For it seems that at one moment a nun who taught the little girl is beating her over the head with a stapler, and at the next another teacher is writing on her report card: '12/1/63 Mother died. Needs a great deal of love and attention.' (Whether the kindergarten teacher in question wrote that assessment before she taped over Madonna's foul young mouth, or after she forcibly washed it out with soap and water, remains unclear.) Then we have the picture of the precocious five-year-old tease who taught a young boy how to bump and grind to a Rolling Stones record, set alongside another of the pubescent girl horrified at the mention of the word 'penis' when her stepmother attempted to teach her the facts of life.

For the biographer, it is difficult to find a path through the myths and half-truths and exaggerations, not all of them of Madonna's creation. Yet by reflecting further upon her early life and chiseling out a few of the less worn pebbles of fact from her past, a different picture emerges, a history that is altogether more plausible, and at once both more complex and more compelling. It is a picture that also helps an understanding of the central theme of this book, namely, that Madonna is a considerable artist who has used both her sexuality and her social and sexual codes as her weapons of choice, her method of connecting with her audience; in short, that she is a long way from the popular conception of her as a sexual Amazon who happens to be a singer and occasional actress.

Curiously, therefore, in any account of her youth, two competing and conflicting personal qualities are seen to dominate – her curiosity, and her conformity. As a child, she had a relentless and intelligent inquisitiveness about the world around her, as well as a self-absorbed fascination with her own physicality and, later, her nascent sexuality. But if the question 'Why?' was never far from her lips, neither was the question 'Why not?' – 'Why can't I wear pants to church, why can't I go out and play, and if God is good why did he take my mother?' At times, her insatiable curiosity could bring her pain. On one occasion, when she was riding in the car with her father, she refused to believe that the glowing, red-hot end of the cigarette lighter was hot. She put her finger on it to find out.

Of enduring fascination were the nuns, serene, powerful yet seemingly semi-divine, who taught her at the three schools – Saint Frederick's, Saint Andrew's, and the Sacred Heart Academy – she attended. Curious to discover if these mysterious creatures were truly human, she and a friend scaled the convent wall to see if they could find out what the sisters wore under their habits. They returned from their mission breathlessly discussing the extraordinary fact that beneath their wimples nuns had hair. Yet despite their apparent oddity, like many Catholic girls before her Madonna flirted with the notion of joining these ethereal beings – although probably not for long.

For all her later disenchantment with the outdated and essentially sexist practices of the Roman Catholic Church, the magical reality of the Catholic faith, its sonorous liturgy and baroque rituals, its teachings of fall and redemption, guilt and confession, and of the certainty of an afterlife, captivated and provoked a young imagination that was at times as melodramatic as it was morbid. 'I was very conscious of God watching everything I did,' she told *Time* magazine in 1985. 'Until I was eleven or twelve, I believed the Devil was in my basement and I would run up the stairway fast so he wouldn't grab my ankles.' If such a belief is little different from the 'bogeyman-under-the-stairs' terrors of less religious children, there is no doubt that Madonna's early upbringing in a deeply Catholic tradition profoundly affected her. Such was her fascination that at her Confirmation she chose the name Veronica to add to her own given names, because it was Saint Veronica who wiped the face of Jesus on the Cross and then carried the cloth with His blood and sweat on it.

Death and its gruesome yet fascinating consequences were never far from her thoughts. A favorite childhood rhyme, and one that she delighted in reciting to adult audiences, went as follows:

> Worms crawl in, worms crawl out
> The ant plays pinochle in your snout,
> Your eyes cave in, your teeth decay,
> Don't cry, don't cry, don't cry.

Children, and especially religious children, have always been both repelled and attracted by the mystery of death, as they are by anything that smacks of horror and decay. By the age of five, however, Madonna had already experienced it at first hand. Still emotionally raw and angry after her mother's death, she once told her father that if he died, she wanted to be buried with him, while on other occasions she daydreamed of life as an orphan, with both her parents killed in a car crash. These childish thoughts crowded into her nightmares, dreams of death and the process of dying that have haunted her into her adult life.

She admits that one of her recurrent nightmares is about the horror of being buried alive, of lying, trapped and helpless underground in a constricting coffin, unable to move as insects, rats and other creatures nibble her flesh. The enduring personal symbolism of this frequent night-time visitation is fueled not only by her fear of death, but also by an equally powerful dread of being constrained. This is not simply physical claustrophobia, but the sense that she is a genuine free spirit who has constantly chafed against anything that might bind her, ties that have included everything from her father's rules, the edicts of the Roman Catholic Church, or what she considered to be the constricting dynamics of her personal relations, whether sexual, social, professional or emotional.

Added to her thoughts and feelings about life, death and Catholicism, there is a sense that she was both fascinated and repelled by the untidiness – what she called the 'ickiness' – of life in general. One of her earliest memories is of an altercation with a little girl who gave her a dandelion. Madonna threw it away, explaining much later that she preferred things to be cultured and cultivated – in a word, controlled. Other handed down-versions of this story say that she attacked the girl, an extreme reaction which, if true, is the antithesis of any concept of 'control.'

Nowhere was the moist, strident messiness of life made more apparent than in sexual relations. As the whole notion of sex and the physical differences between men and women began to dawn upon the young Madonna's mind, she, like many of her girlfriends, found herself repelled rather than attracted. Given the teachings of the Church and the advice of her grandmother, Elsie Fortin, who warned of the dire consequences for girls who were not chaste, together with a confused understanding of the physical act, it is not surprising that the pubescent girl found the whole notion 'icky.' Glimpses of her brothers' naked bodies revolted her. 'I thought they were disgusting,' she recalled, and was 'horrified' when she learned about the, to her, awful reality of sex. She remembers, too, a biology lesson in which she and a fellow pupil, a boy her age, had to dissect a mouse. The sight of the corpse, reeking of formaldehyde preservative, proved too much for her and she left the classroom. When she returned her partner had dissected most of the mouse, but had left the animal's penis for her to deal with. She was appalled.

Far less threatening were the images of the men and women from the Bible. 'I think my original feelings of sexuality and eroticism originated in going to church,' she told the novelist Norman Mailer. If this was true, however, she clearly had a curious notion of eroticism and sexuality, for she admitted to feeling that there was an androgynous quality to Jesus and His disciples, with their long hair and flowing robes (and, presumably, despite their beards). To her mind they were the Barbie dolls of their time, asexual, unthreatening people who could have served as models from a jeans commercial.

If all this seems a far cry from the crotch-grabbing, man-eating persona Madonna was to invent for herself, it was nevertheless some distance from the conventional picture of her as a young girl, which portrays her as a sexual libertine-in-waiting. Yet the truth is that her physical self-awareness, even precocity, running around the schoolyard chasing boys of her age or younger, has all too often been confused with sexual promiscuity. In actuality, she was something of a paradox, her keen curiosity, fertile imagination and restless spirit balanced by the fact that, in childhood, she not only strove to conform, but actively enjoyed fitting in.

At all her schools, even at high school, she proved to be the quintessential all-American girl, effortlessly graduating from school-hall monitor and choirgirl to Camp Fire Girl and, later, teenage cheerleader, while at home she cheerfully moved on from Barbie dolls and bubblegum pop music to dressing up and experimenting with makeup. It was Madonna who told tales on her brothers and sisters or reported the misdeeds of her fellow students, who was first with her hand up in class, who regularly came home from school with good marks, thus earning a 50-cent reward from her father for every A grade she achieved. Indeed, her father's ambition that she study law captured rather shrewdly the conventional character she then presented. Bright, articulate, well organized and argumentative, Madonna would undoubtedly have made an excellent attorney.

If anything, and despite all the received wisdom about 'Madonna-the-bad-girl,' it was her siblings who were the rebels while she, in her own words, played 'Miss Goody-Two-Shoes.' As schoolboys, her elder brothers, Anthony and Martin, turned out to be real handfuls, not just for their harassed father, but for teachers and schoolmates alike. Lighting fires outside and other anti-social behavior was the norm. An innocent afternoon sketching the school buildings at Saint Andrew's school turned into a three-day suspension for fellow schoolboy Nick Twomey when Martin happened upon him. 'I was minding my own business when Marty came around me,' recalls Dr Twomey. 'He was the school goofball. He was always being a clown and getting into trouble. Anyone around him normally got into trouble too. I can't remember what happened, but the nun who was there took us to the Principal's office and we were kicked out of [temporarily suspended from] school.'

While still at school, both brothers started dabbling in drugs and taking part in clandestine drinking sessions, eventually becoming, in effect, fully paid-up members of the 'tune in, turn on, drop out' generation. The experience was not salutary. As a young adult, Anthony joined the Moonie cult, while Martin was to spend many months in private rehab clinics, often paid for by his younger sister. As for that sister herself, she stayed well clear of such diversions. As school counselor Nancy Ryan Mitchell remembers: 'I counseled Madonna's brothers and sisters much more than her.'

It is little wonder, then, that Madonna's memories of her brothers' behavior in adolescence are less than fond. They teased and tormented her mercilessly, while she loudly voiced her complaints about them to anyone who would listen; an American version of Violet Elizabeth in the *Just William* stories, who promised to 'thcweam and thcweam and thcweam' if she didn't get her own way. 'A bitch,' is how brother Martin described her in one interview. For her part, Madonna recalls how they spat in her mouth after she ratted on them; she also tells a rather implausible story of how one day they used clothespins to hang their outraged, squirming, 50-pound sister from a washing line by her panties.

Whatever the indignities she suffered at her brothers' hands, she gave as good as she got, the trio squabbling over everything from sharing the household chores to using the record player. An aficionada of mainstream pop, Madonna vividly remembers the day her brothers deliberately scratched her treasured Gary Puckett and the Union Gap single so that they could fill the house with the heavy psychedelic rock that they loved and she loathed.

In this scratchy, discordant household, Madonna's younger brother and sisters, Christopher, Paula and Melanie, fared as well as they could. Never as pretty, popular or clever as Madonna, Paula perhaps had the toughest time, always living in her older sister's shadow. She was the tomboy of the brood, and in consequence often sided with her elder brothers against her sharper and more articulate sister. Christopher, quiet, personable and artistic, was never a threat, while Melanie, who stood out physically because of a single blonde streak in her otherwise dark hair, was, as is common with the youngest in a family, the most indulged.

As is so often the case in large families, Tony Ciccone's six children were competing – for space, for time and, particularly the girls, for their father's attention. It was a competition Madonna needed to win, such was her longing for any crumbs of affection and approval. As she herself has said, 'I just tried to be the apple of my father's eye. I think that everyone else in my family was very aware of it. And I kind of stood out.' If winning approval meant helping with the daily chores – her father pinned a list to the fridge most weeks – or following him to Mass at six in the morning, before school, or helping to look after the younger children, then that was, for her, a price worth paying.

She brought other factors into play, too, apart from mere helpfulness or 'goodness.' Aware of her physicality from an early age, she used all her childish guile to woo and win her father, staging impromptu dance shows on the kitchen table, *à la* Shirley Temple, or making sure she won the race to sit on her father's lap, or to be the first to tell of the day's events at school. In a statement that seems to be halfway between an admission and a boast, she once said, 'I was my father's favorite. I knew how to wrap him around my finger, I knew there was another way to go besides saying, "No, I'm not going to do it," and I employed those techniques.' No doubt at times her insistence on being the center of attention was as perplexing for her harassed father as it was irritating to her brothers and sisters.

That her father, a quiet, even diffident, man who worked long hours in order to provide for his six motherless children, could not or would not satisfy Madonna's longing for his undivided attention was for many years a source of acrimony between them, an acrimony generated almost entirely by her. 'More than anything I want my father's approval whether I want to admit it or not,' she has said, at the same time acknowledging that her father was 'very affectionate' towards her. Yet her need for love and recognition appears to have been so deeply ingrained that it is debatable whether, if she had lived, even her mother could have quenched Madonna's seemingly insatiable thirst for affection, her fierce desire to be needed and noticed.

It would seem that she was born with this emotional hunger as an integral part of her personality, like her innate curiosity, which was then molded by her upbringing. 'She is,' as one of her close girlfriends pointed out, 'an alpha-A female. She has to be the center of attention no matter what.'

Like that other Hollywood celebrity, Barbra Streisand, whose chutzpah and determination enabled her to overcome the formidable obstacles in her path to fame, Madonna seems to be a star who was born, not made. In short, divas are different. Nor do the parallels between the two stars end there. Like Madonna, Streisand lost a parent when young and spent her early childhood years clinging to her mother for support and love. Then her world was turned upside-down when her mother met and married another man. Barbra tried to win her stepfather's approval, but he actively disliked her. In Madonna's case it was the slim, blonde, upright figure of Joan Gustafson who usurped the eight-year-old's place in her father's affections. Joan joined the Ciccone family in 1966 as the latest in a series of housekeepers employed by Tony Ciccone. Six months later they were married.

Ever since his wife's death three years earlier, Tony Ciccone had tried valiantly to juggle a demanding full-time job and life as a single parent of six children. Naturally other members of his family pitched in, the Ciccone children spending holidays with their grandparents in West Aliquippa or Bay City, or at the home of Tony's brother-in-law and friend, Dale Fortin, and his family. As his elder brother Guy Ciccone remembers, 'Silvio would bring the whole family to visit in the summers for vacation, or to weddings and family gatherings.' Madonna would help her grandfather, Gaetano, in his vegetable

[43]

garden, or show off her latest dance routine to the delight of the adults. 'Madonna was such a pretty little girl and she always loved dancing,' recalls her aunt, Betty Ciccone, adding, 'Silvio was a pretty good dancer too.'

Yet even as the Fortin family was coming to terms with Madonna Senior's premature death, tragedy struck once more. In 1966, Dale Fortin died of leukemia, leaving his wife Katherine to bring up seven children – three boys and four girls – on her own. 'I just had to cope,' she admits. 'A strong will and an iron hand was what it took. It wasn't easy, but in a way it was worse for Tony.'

Certainly Tony Ciccone followed the same course when disaster overtook him and his young family. A firm disciplinarian with a rigid sense of right and wrong, he did the best he could to bring his children up responsibly, but also within the tenets of his own moral code. His austere upbringing trans-lated into ensuring that his children worked and played hard. Television was rationed, as were candies, while household chores were apportioned on a daily basis. In this necessarily regimented world, it did not escape his notice that what his children needed was not the instability and uncertainty of life with hired help – that succession of housekeepers – but someone who would be a fixed point in their lives. For although no one could replace Madonna Senior, he believed that another woman around the house would provide the nurturing and guidance to which he felt his children, particularly the girls, would respond. Not to put too fine a point upon it, Tony Ciccone needed a wife, his own emotional needs balanced by the pragmatic realities of what was best for his family and for family life.

He could not have been more wrong – at least, as far as eight-year-old Madonna was concerned. Ferociously self-absorbed and self-centered as only the young can be, in her eyes the deep, unresolved anger she felt over her mother's death was now, at her father's marriage, compounded by what she regarded as his callous betrayal of the love and attention she had showered upon him. Not only had he deserted her for another woman, but her new stepmother had usurped Madonna's notional position as the 'little lady' of the household.

Whatever the reality, that was the truth as she saw it and she took action accordingly. Feeling, perhaps unconsciously, that if she couldn't win her father's attention by conforming then she would have to explore other avenues, she rapidly changed from childish coquette to 'difficult,' defiant daughter. As for her stepmother, Madonna viewed her from the first as the enemy, even refusing to honor her father's wish that she should call Joan 'Mom.' The simmering resentment she felt towards Tony's second wife has lasted to this day.

Within weeks of her marriage, Joan Ciccone became pregnant, giving birth to a daughter, Jennifer, in 1967, and the following year to a son, Mario. As though that were not enough, Tony Ciccone next decided that their house in Pontiac was way too small for a family that now numbered ten members. It was, he felt, time to make a break with the past, time to move from the down-at-heel, racially mixed neighborhood of Pontiac, where Madonna had happy memories of joining her black girlfriends in backyard dance sessions, to the nearby but infinitely more upscale – and exclusively white – suburb of Rochester. The family's new home at 2036 Oklahoma Street was typical of the modest affluence of a still-sleepy country town; a two-story clapboard and red-brick Colonial-style house where today Joan Ciccone runs a children's daycare center in a converted garage. Just down the road was Saint Andrew's, the Roman Catholic church that the family would now attend, with its own school to which the children would go, a brisk walk away for ten-year-old Madonna.

Her new classmates at Saint Andrew's were impressed by the bright and lively youngster, a darkly pretty girl who always seemed to have a way of standing out from the crowd. The Ciccones had arrived in Rochester at the same time as the Twomey family, and ten-year-old Nick, another new student at Saint Andrew's, immediately struck up a friendship with Madonna. He was the budding jock athlete to her flashy cheerleader, and they became child-hood sweethearts, chasing each other round the schoolyard and joshing each other in class. Like her, Nick was the middle child in a large family, and so realized instinctively what made Madonna tick. As he says: 'We were both narcissistic souls with an insatiable need to be noticed. When you are in a large family and life is busy and everyone is competing for attention you do what you have to to rise above the crowd. She is like everyone else, there is this huge gap in her soul to be loved and noticed.' Energetic and voluble, both were seen as leaders by their classmates, Nick by virtue of his athletic prowess, Madonna because of her manner in class. 'She was bright and always verbal,' remembers Nick, 'and when she had to give a report it was never just about the material – it was always about how she could say this in such a way to get her noticed or to get a laugh.'

Given her own extrovert nature, and her friendship with the equally outgoing Nick Twomey, it is perhaps surprising that one of Madonna's best friends at that time was Ruth Dupack (now Ruth Dupack Young), a shy, diffident youngster who was often so tongue-tied at school that the nuns at Saint Andrew's would sometimes call her parents to ask if there was a problem. Being almost a complete opposite in character, Ruth was no competition to Madonna, but rather the bashful foil to her extrovert personality. 'She was a happy girl,' recalls Ruth, 'never moody. She was pretty bold and confident about the things she said and did, more willing to take a chance at things.' The two girls enjoyed sleepovers at each other's houses, played Ruth's latest Tamla Motown records – Madonna preferred dance to music, Ruth remembers – gossiped, shopped and hung out like countless other teenage girls.

As she came to know the Ciccone family, Ruth realized that Madonna not only stood out from her classmates, but also from the rest of her family. Her outsize personality, her compulsive need to be noticed, were at variance to the characters of her father, stepmother and brothers and sisters. One aspect of that 'apartness' was only too glaringly obvious, however – Madonna's treatment of her stepmother.

Ruth, and others in her circle like Carol Belanger, were well aware of the animosity Madonna displayed towards Joan. 'I felt sorry for her stepmother,' Ruth confesses. 'It was tough for her. She always encouraged Madonna, she never complained about her. But you could see what was going on when you saw them together, fighting and bickering. Madonna would totally ride her, acting like a little kid. It was a big rebellion, a long running conflict.'

One particular battle was over makeup and what was or was not considered to be appropriate dress – not altogether surprisingly, since it is a battlefield familiar to most parents of girls. Joan did not want her oldest stepdaughter to use makeup, and, reacting to yet another act of defiance, ordered her to wear clothes that were suitable for school, rather than for a nightclub. So every day Madonna would leave for school dressed as her stepmother had decreed. As soon as she reached school, however, she would head for the bathroom, and there swap her 'sensible' clothes for a short skirt or skimpy top she had smuggled out of the house in a brown paper bag. Having changed, she would proceed to apply her warpaint. At the end of the school day she would change back again, wipe off the makeup and walk home.

The atmosphere in the Ciccone household came to be tainted all too often by Madonna's antipathy towards Joan. On another occasion, in 1972, she clashed with her stepmother when she returned home, feeling very grown up, after a summer break spent at her grandmother's home in Bay City. While there she had learned to smoke cigarettes, had worn tight jeans and makeup, and had watched her uncle Carl's amateur rock band, which used to rehearse in her grandmother's garage. Her changed appearance did not amuse Joan Ciccone, who was especially concerned that her father would be horrified if he saw his eldest daughter dressed like a 'floozy.' Rather than toe the line, however, Madonna and her friends deliberately dressed as 'floozies,' padding out their bras, wearing tight sweaters and daubing their faces with heavy makeup and lipstick.

With all the unfairness and self-indulgence of youth exacerbated by her highly developed sense of the melodramatic, Madonna came to view herself as the Cinderella of the Ciccones, forced to sweep and dust and care for her younger siblings while her older brothers ducked their responsibilities and her friends played in the sunshine. Years later, she was to claim, in an interview with Carrie Fisher for *Rolling Stone* magazine, that although her father never hit her, Joan Ciccone frequently slapped her around, on one occasion, when she was about twelve, giving her a bloody nose that forced her to miss church because the blood had stained her dress. To this and other complaints was added the fact that, allegedly, her stepmother would not allow her to wear tampons, viewing this form of sanitary protection as virtually equivalent to sexual intercourse, and so to be used only after marriage. If true, these are serious charges, but others seem to have been prompted simply by the usual gripes of adolescence. When Joan made identical dresses for the three elder girls using the same McCall's pattern and the same bolt of material she had bought at the local Kmart, Madonna resented the lack of individuality. Certainly Mrs Ciccone hotly disputes her stepdaughter's more serious claims, incredulous at the idea that she would hit her, or have been so blinkered about sanitary protection. This was, after all, the same woman who had tried to teach Madonna the facts of life one day as they stood by the kitchen sink, only to watch the girl run from the room in horror.

Conversely, what is not in doubt is that whenever her stepmother or father suggested anything, Madonna would complain or disobey almost as a matter of principle. It was an attitude that could lead to some preposterous situations. For instance, even though she had an obvious flair for performing, Madonna railed against taking piano lessons, years later telling Neil Tennant how she preferred to hide in a ditch near the teacher's home rather than attend the sessions. For a young woman who would, a few short years later, spend hour after painstaking hour learning to play the guitar and the drums, this was a remarkable example of cutting off your creative nose to spite your parental face.

Eventually she switched to dance classes, learning tap, jazz, ballroom dancing and baton twirling, thereby not only ensuring her place on the Adams High cheerleading squad, but also forming the basis of her future career. Virtually every Saturday she was at dance class, or taking part in local dance contests. Perhaps ironically, and whether Madonna would like to acknowledge it or not, her 'Wicked Stepmother' was with her every dance step of the way, encouraging her, praising her successes, and consoling her in her disappointments. Joan took her to lessons, and was in the audience when Madonna took part in competitions. 'For all the grief she put up with, Mrs

Ciccone was a real cheerleader for Madonna,' recalls Ruth Dupack Young. 'She was desperate to be a dancer and if she didn't win a competition she was very disappointed. Mrs Ciccone was always there to lift her spirits.' Nor could Ruth resist adding her own tribute to Joan: 'She is a good person who never let anyone forget Madonna's mother. When visitors came to the house she would show them pictures of Tony's first wife. She was very open about it.'

That, however, is not Madonna's recollection of her stepmother, whatever the difference between the truth and her own concept of reality. 'I never think of my stepmother as my mother. Just as a woman who raised me, a dominant female in my life,' she once said. 'I went through adolescence kind of ignoring her . . . I always consider myself an absolutely motherless child and I'm sure that has something to do with my openness.'

At times, this simmering kitchen-sink drama would spill over on to the public stage, as happened during one of Madonna's early dance routines. In 1970 she graduated from Saint Andrew's to West Junior High public school. For weeks Madonna, by then thirteen, and her fellow classmates had been practicing their routines for a talent contest in front of an audience of parents and faculty. While Ruth Dupack and another friend, Nancy Baron, choreo-graphed a gymnastics routine, Madonna rehearsed a solo dance number in which she came on stage dressed as a private eye. Wearing a long trenchcoat and a wide-brimmed hat she danced to the theme music from *Secret Agent*, a popular TV show. Her three-minute routine ended dramatically with the sound of gunshots ripping through the auditorium.

All went as planned during rehearsals, with Madonna's drama teacher suitably impressed by the inventive routine, unaware that the young dancer had a surprise in store. On the night of the performance Madonna's act went perfectly until the finale. Then, as the sound of gunfire echoed around the auditorium, she whipped off her trenchcoat, revealing that all she was wearing underneath was a black leotard. This impromptu 'flashing' display provoked gasps from the audience, and led to a furious Tony Ciccone grounding her for two weeks. Naturally she did not win any awards that night – the top prize went to Ruth Dupack and Nancy Baron for their gymnastics routine. But whatever the intention behind her small, defiant act, she did set tongues wagging. As parents drifted out of the hall there was an undeniable sense that Madonna was seen as a rather 'fast' and 'forward' teenager. 'People were saying: "My goodness, what behavior from a thirteen-year-old,"' Ruth admits.

If this incident seems a curious one, it has its roots not in the myths surrounding Madonna's supposed promiscuity, but in her childish craving for love and attention. Yet just as her skimpy school clothes were a sign of rebellion against her stepmother, so her behavior on the dance floor that night won notice from her father, however angry he may have been, attention that she felt she did not receive at home. This, far more than her burgeoning sexual awareness, was the overriding motive behind the last-minute alteration to her dance routine.

Unfortunately, her reputation as one of the 'hot babes' of West Junior High rather preceded her when, in 1972, she followed her brothers Tony and Martin to the coed Adams High School, Rochester, a sprawling complex a few miles north of the world-famous Meadowbrook outdoor music theater and the main campus of Oakland University. Close to several golf courses and shopping malls, it has the feel of a country club. This is not altogether surprising, since its student body is largely drawn from among the well-heeled sons and daughters of predominantly white middle-class families, in a catchment area where today the average home sells for a shade under $200,000. This is middle-class, middle-income, Middle America; and a far cry from the impression given by Madonna in some of her early interviews that her school was in the midst of an inner-city black ghetto. In fact, during her four years at Adams High, there was only one black student at the school. As to the 'ghetto,' among her fellow students were Cindy Kresge, one of the heirs to the Kmart billions, and the Caratos brothers, later to hit the headlines for their Mafia activities.

Although one of the youngest in her class, the fact that her brothers were already at the school ensured that Madonna was known to many of the older students. Sharp-witted, friendly and vivacious, she fitted in well. In her freshman year not only did she get through a series of auditions to make the junior cheerleading squad, but she was also awarded a plaque in a school ceremony for being one of the top ten academic achievers in her year. A member of the French Club and the school choir, she took a full part in school life, volunteering for the Help-a-Kid program and working as a lifeguard at the local swimming club. 'She was creative academically,' recalls Lucinda Axler, who was also on the cheerleading squad. 'A real cut up in class. She got into trouble for being out of line but she enjoyed life, she was a happy personality. Madonna always had chutzpah, courage and gumption.'

She drew the most attention, however, in her cheerleader outfit at football games. 'She was very good, very showy,' Lucinda adds. 'She knew how to draw attention to herself. She had a big mouth and had the moves too.' From the first, Madonna dared to be different, suggesting to her squad that they build a dance routine around a song by the rock band Uriah Heep, rather than the rather hokey tunes that were then in vogue. Their routine proved a great success: not only did the spectators go wild but, more important, the senior cheerleading squad was left feeling deeply envious.

Thus it came to be accepted by her contemporaries that Madonna had a certain edge, that she always tried a little harder to stand out. Another of her fellow cheerleaders, Carol Stier, remembers that when the two of them went shopping in the Rochester malls, Madonna always chose jeans and other clothes that were in some way unusual. Not conforming, it seems, was part and parcel of her personality. To Carol, it was clear that 'it was important for her to be in the public eye. She did a very good job of being the one who people would talk to and about.'

Nonetheless, on the surface she was a typical Midwest teenager, joining the other girls in the school bathrooms as they tried on each other's makeup, gossiping about boys, hanging out at Las Pumas, a doughnut-and-coffee shop, or the local McDonald's. She even won the annual hula-hoop contest. And, like the other cheerleaders, she was becoming more interested in those strange yet fascinating creatures known as boys. 'Her interests? Like the rest of us – boys,' remembers Lucinda Axler. As for boyfriends, 'She had her share. If Madonna wanted a guy she got their attention. She could capture their hearts.'

Her former school sweetheart Nick Twomey, whom she singled out as her top choice when she made a list of the boys she found most attractive, noticed the changes in Madonna when he arrived at Adams High after spending his early teens at a different school. 'I remember seeing her again and she was flirtatious off the charts,' he says. 'She did what she had to do to get recognized by the boys but I don't think she was running around sleeping with everybody. That's more myth.'

On one occasion she arranged to stay over at her friend Ruth Dupack's house, the two of them planning to spend the night in a tent in the backyard. It wasn't long before Madonna and Ruth sneaked off and walked a mile to a party at a boy's house. 'I was pretty nervous but it seemed to have been planned by her,' Ruth remembers. 'She and I once dated the same boy. But boyfriends never lasted long, she went from one to another.'

Her vitality and physical awareness, her need to attract attention and her lengthening list of admirers soon inspired rumors about her sexual behavior. 'Madonna always had a reputation of being one of those girls, you know, kinda fast,' recalls Lia Gaggino, the class valedictorian and now a pediatrician. Her reputation as a 'nympho' was one Madonna was well aware of at the time, and resents to this day. 'I was necking with boys like everybody else,' she says. 'So I didn't understand where it all came from. I would hear words like "slut" that I hear now.' Once she was confronted outside school by a girl student who, after a few harsh words, slapped her full in the face. The jealous teenager, doubtless mindful of the other girl's reputation, however ill founded, had thought Madonna was making moves on her boyfriend.

In fact her first serious sexual experience was as conventional as it was prosaic: cheerleader makes out with football jock in the back of his car (a blue 1966 Cadillac, for the curious). After dating for six months, Madonna, then fifteen, and her boyfriend, school sports hero Russell Long, went all the way at his parents' house. 'I was so nervous I couldn't get her bra strap undone,' recalls the gallant Mr Long, now a trucker for UPS. They continued dating for several months afterwards, Madonna sometimes worrying her boyfriend by wondering aloud whether she should tell her father just what she had been getting up to.

Although still obsessed with winning her father's favor, Madonna had changed. No longer was she the little girl eager to please, but a questioning, irreverent teenager. Tony Ciccone's stern authority no longer commanded her as once it had. Neither, for that matter did the Catholic Church. It was a period of vast social upheaval, much of it fueled by the actions and opinions of the young. Beneath the surface normality of high-school life in Midwest America in the early 1970s, there were tensions that reflected the temper of the times, and the mood of a troubled land in which, for many, long hair represented rebellion and a rejection of the old order. As President Nixon fought for his political life during the Watergate hearings, young men, soldiers not much older than the teenagers at Adams High, could be seen on the evening TV news fighting forlornly in Vietnam, in a hopeless war now entering its death throes. Closer to home, books and articles by feminists like Germaine Greer and Gloria Steinem were winning the hearts and minds of a generation of women. The resonance of all this resistance, protest, sometimes outright rebellion, was felt even in the heartlands of America. 'I remember when Nixon pulled the troops out of Vietnam [in 1973], all the male students breathed a huge sigh of relief,' Nick Twomey admits. 'The fear of going there was almost tangible.'

Like many other teenagers, Madonna was embarking on her own journey of discovery. For her, however, it was a quest for self-knowledge, for although the churning issues of the day were at the edge of her consciousness, central to her emotional being was still her fractious relationship with her father, and her unresolved feelings about her mother's death. Below her personal radar, but moving inexorably into range, was that great imponderable, destiny.

Early in the morning of Easter Sunday 1970, a long-haired student named John Michael Tebelak was stopped by a uniformed policeman in the nave of Saint Paul's Cathedral in Pittsburgh and frisked for drugs. He was already in a pensive mood following the service he had just attended, and which he described as 'devoid of feeling'; in the sermon, Tebelak felt, the speaker had been trying figuratively to roll away the rock that sealed Christ's tomb, rather than celebrate His rebirth. The hostility of the policeman and the dismal religious experience proved life changing. When he returned to Carnegie Mellon College, John Michael, a fine-arts student, asked if he could write a musical based on the Gospel according to Saint Matthew as part of his graduate thesis.

Drawing on his experiences that fateful Easter Sunday, he produced the outline for one of the most successful stage musicals of all time. *Godspell* gave a contemporary twist to a traditional theme, the last seven days of Christ. In performance, Jesus sported clownish makeup and wore a Superman costume with a large 'S' on the front, while His disciples were dressed as hippies and flower children. Although more conventional Christians were dismayed, and fundamentalist Christians outraged, by what they considered to be this outrageous treatment of the Gospels, the show, an imaginative rather than an irreverent interpretation, seemed to capture the changing mood of the times. It played to packed houses around the world, running for more than 2,700 performances on and off Broadway.

When the Adams High Thespian Society, which Madonna had helped to found, decided to put on a version of the show, Madonna was deemed perfect for the role of Sonia. The show's lyricist, Stephen Schwartz, describes her character as 'sassy and slightly cynical, the most urban of the group. Also the sexy one, but her sexiness contains a large element of put-on, in the manner of Mae West.' Madonna had already played a creditable Morticia in the school's production of *The Addams Family* and had taken leading roles in *My Fair Lady* and *Cinderella*. The part of Sonia was tailor-made for her talents. So when, a few weeks later, the school announced a talent show, Madonna decided to perform a solo song-and-dance routine to the *Godspell* song 'Turn Back, O Man.' For weeks she was Sonia, endlessly practicing her moves and rehearsing the words of the song. Her hard work paid off, for when she was announced before an audience of fellow students and staff gathered in the school gymnasium, she had the words, notes and steps down perfectly. Dressed in dark satin pants and a grey satin blouse, her performance, polished, confident and sexy, mesmerized students and teachers alike. As she finished her act, the hall erupted into a cacophony of whistling, catcalls and whooping, the audience rising as one in a spontaneous standing ovation.

'I will never forget it,' recalls Carol Stier. 'We [Madonna's friends] were both shocked and impressed because we were not aware that she had this talent. Teenagers are pretty hard to impress and they would much rather make fun of a peer than see them succeed. So to get that kind of reaction shows just what a standout performance it was.' Others were equally impressed. According to Nick Twomey, 'It was a breakout event for Madonna. She pretty much seduced the entire gymnasium, myself and the teachers included. It wasn't wildly erotic, but Madonna was Madonna even back then, and she knew how to work the crowd.'

As she took her bows, Madonna was in tears, the nervous tension of the performance mingling with the thrill of being the undeniable center of attention. Once the applause and congratulations had faded she felt somehow changed. She found it difficult to put that feeling into words, but later reflected that it was akin to 'coming home.'

The all-American girl was about to follow her destiny, and her dream.

Chapter Four

Destined to Be a Dancer

CHRISTOPHER FLYNN made a very unlikely Professor Higgins. A master of caustic sarcasm, and capable of being brutal to the point of sadism, he was in every respect a caricature of the frustrated former ballet dancer. The man who had once danced with the Joffrey Ballet and harbored dreams of stardom now found himself, in his early forties, teaching evening class to a bunch of gawky, giggling teenage girls in a dusty second-floor studio in an obscure Midwest town.

What this flamboyant homosexual, who at times seemed to take an almost perverse delight in hurting and humiliating his young charges, thought when a rather meek, gamine fifteen-year-old walked into his class at 404 Main Street in Rochester, clutching a two-foot-high, curly-blonde-haired china doll, is anyone's guess. Certainly not that she would soon become his protégée, his Eliza Doolittle, nor that, one day, he would weep bitterly when she left him.

The very fact that Madonna looked so fey and lost may have stilled Flynn's initial impulse – reflex, even – to indulge in sarcasm. Nervously, she explained that she wanted to study ballet with him, like her schoolfriend and fellow cheerleader Mary-Ellen Beloat. A simple enough request, but it had taken all her courage to walk through the studio door. Not only had the ballet teacher's reputation gone before him, but Madonna was taking a huge personal risk. While she had studied tap and jazz dancing and taken part in local dance contests, this was a true challenge. Ballet training demands a remorseless physical discipline that can, and does, daunt even the most talented and determined. For Madonna there was one overriding concern – would her talent and physical ability and talent match her self-belief and ambition? In taking that chance, she had to steel herself to face her deepest fear, the fear of failure.

Over the next few months she characteristically buckled down to the stern routine, dancing for two hours each night. Sometimes she would end a session with her feet bleeding. 'Classes could be quite brutal,' recalls Mary-Ellen. 'If you did something wrong, Christopher would hit you with the stick he used to point at things.' During one ballet exercise, in which the girls swung their legs to the side, he would pinch the tender flesh of their inner thighs to force them to stretch higher and wider. A favorite form of torture, often used on Madonna, was to place a sharpened pencil vertically between a dancer's throat and her chin to make sure she kept her head straight while dancing.

His chief weapon remained his tongue, however. To his sarcasm was added the unlovely, sexually colored imagery he employed to illustrate particular points. 'Imagine as you lower yourself in a plié that there is a radio antenna beneath you and it must slide straight inside you,' was advice he often repeated. A deeply disappointed, even frustrated, man, he would regularly reduce his students to tears with his tirades and withering invective. 'He used to shout at us that dancing always had to come first, before anything else,' Mary-Ellen adds. If Madonna and her colleagues left a session with nothing worse than bruises and blood blisters then they considered themselves fortunate.

Yet, fierce as he could be, Flynn was always entertaining, his enthusiasm for dance inspiring those who were willing to place their talent in his care, and their trust in his skills. Certainly Madonna, the girl who railed at her father and stepmother at the slightest provocation, proved an eager disciple. She willingly accepted his harshest admonitions, and masochistically came back for more. Starved – at least as she saw it – of her father's love and attention, she looked for scraps of compliments and praise wherever she could. Flynn the tormentor could also be a flatterer, his approval all the sweeter because his standards were so exacting, and his soul so stern. She remembers to this day the moment when Flynn looked at her after a class and told her that she was beautiful, with a face like that of an ancient Roman statue. For a girl who described herself as looking like a 'dog,' and gave herself the nickname 'Mudd,' it was a compliment to treasure. 'No one had ever said that to me before,' she remarked years later. 'He told me I was special, and he taught me to appreciate beauty – not beauty in the conventional sense, but really about beauty of the spirit.'

In the cause of instilling that sense of beauty, he took his eager disciple on a kind of miniature, contemporary American version of the Grand Tour, the two of them going to Detroit to visit museums, art galleries and concerts. They discussed poetry, books and art, Christopher happy to pass on his knowledge and insights, Madonna an eager and inquisitive pupil. As his dance classes explored the physical limits of her coltish body, so their daytime excursions – Detroit is only a few miles to the south of Rochester – proved, for her, an exhilarating voyage of artistic discovery, pushing back the boundaries of her intellect and sensibilities. At that time her taste was that of a sensitive, rather intense teenager: the Romantic poets, the Pre-Raphaelite painters, the novels of Steinbeck and Scott Fitzgerald, tragic poets like Sylvia Plath, the films of James Dean.

Under Flynn's guidance, however, her horizons broadened. Just as the Modernist movement placed the artist outside or on the periphery of society – the artist as anti-hero – so Madonna, like thousands of angst-ridden teenagers before her, found in the Modernists' work a lush expression of her thoughts and impulses. Her introduction to the Humanist tradition, the celebration of the individual within society, and of humankind as responsible intellectual beings, neatly dovetailed with her exasperation with the Catholic Church, which teaches the submission of Man to the will of the Almighty, as well as with her increasing involvement in the world of dance, a discipline which revels in the physical self.

Without doubt, this personal quest for knowledge and understanding, familiar to intellectuals and artists through the ages, significantly altered her relationship with others. In the same way that she had come to see herself as an outsider within her family, so, as she went into her senior year at Adams High school, she viewed herself as remote and aloof from the concerns and priorities of her fellow pupils. Christopher Flynn had provided the key that had unlocked the door into a world of art and artistic endeavor. This is not a fanciful notion, for Madonna herself is on record as saying: 'He was my mentor, my father, my imaginative lover, my brother, everything. He understood me.' For her friends, however, the changes in her behavior were as striking as they were unnerving. The key, and the door it opened, were not, it seems, for sharing. Carol Stier remembers her shock on first encountering the 'new' Madonna. 'I remember walking into English class on the first day of term and seeing this person and thinking, "We've got a new kid in class." She had a bandanna with bold print wrapped around her short hair and was wearing blue jean overalls and ankle-high combat boots. She had no make up on but was still pretty. Then I realized it was Madonna. I was shocked. It was a big change. She no longer bothered talking to us, not interested in being friends any more. During class she was quiet and studious. The wisecracks were out.'

As it happened, Madonna was not the only one among her circle to go through a personal metamorphosis. After a period in which he dabbled with drugs, Nick Twomey, her one-time sweetheart, had found religion. His conversion was so profound that he zealously turned every conversation, whether with members of the faculty or fellow students, to the subject of Christianity. Now an evangelical pastor in nearby Traverse City, Twomey recalls the changes in the girl he had once chased around the playground. 'I went through this dramatic spiritual conversion and as my life zigged hers zagged, so that she became almost like a gypsy. She broke away from the group of kids we hung out with and when we met I was trying to ram Jesus down her throat. She was never rude or offensive, but I remember her asking me to dial down the intensity, to chill out.'

The change in Madonna, however, was not merely intellectual or spiritual. As part of her new Bohemian look, she no longer shaved her legs or her armpits, or bothered to pluck her eyebrows. 'My younger sister Morisa was really scared of her because Madonna took her for swimming lessons and didn't shave under her armpits,' recalls Lia Gaggino. 'She wasn't afraid to be different, and at that age it's hard to be different without worrying what other people think of you.'

In the first semester of her senior year, which proved to be her last at Adams High, she no longer tried to be the center of attention, content to spend time on her own. The girl who once lined up with her friends at McDonald's and shared her makeup in the bathroom was now a vegetarian who lived a simple, even ascetic life. Her friend Ruth Dupack thought, 'It was a major flip-flop. People were thinking: "What is with it with her?" In the end I didn't understand Madonna but I was happy for her.' In a telling aside, however, Ruth adds, 'I found it easier to talk to her stepmother than her.'

Faced with this reconstructed, aloof, austere Madonna, the gossips had a field day, and rumors were soon flying round the school that she was having an affair with her dance teacher. Whether or not she and Flynn enjoyed a brief flirtation, what was certain was that she spent almost every spare moment she could with him. For his part, he introduced her to the gay clubs of downtown Detroit, a world away from the coffee shops and school dances a girl of her age was used to. Here disco ruled supreme, the atmosphere – an equal mixture of energy and *joie de vivre* – pungently exciting. As one of the few girls among hundreds of sweating, gyrating gay men, Madonna felt free of all the sexual baggage normally associated with dancing. This was dancing for the sheer love of movement, rather than a clumsy courtship ritual. Years later, Christopher Flynn was to tell the writer Chris Andersen: 'She loved it and God, was she hot. She just cleared the floor and we just cut loose and everybody loved her. It's not that she was showing off, she just thoroughly enjoyed dancing and it just sprang out of her.'

In spite of the drug-taking and the outrageous sexual behavior, to Madonna the men who peopled the gay clubs were unthreatening, entertaining and full of life. More than that, however, she considered them to be just like her, outsiders, sneered at by uptight, strait-laced, white Middle America. For her, of course there was also the little matter of her rebellion against her father. Before she began going with Flynn, the last time she had been in Detroit was on a trip to see David Bowie in concert at Cobo Hall. On her return Tony Ciccone had been furious, and had grounded her. To him, therefore, her apparent infatuation with a gay man who was literally as old as her father was now a further cause for concern, especially as she had encouraged her younger brother Christopher to join her in the regular dance classes in downtown Rochester. Indeed, 'cause for concern' is an understatement; in Madonna's own words, her father was 'weirded out' by her friendship with a gay man.

It was at Christopher Flynn's urgings that, in 1976, the seventeen-year-old Madonna decided to leave school a semester early and try for a place in the dance program at the University of Michigan. That Flynn had won a teaching post there was a source of mutual encouragement and, for Flynn, not a little self-interest. In spite of the age gap he found his young pupil spirited, eager and quick to learn, and he enjoyed her company as well as her adulation. For all his sardonic cynicism, he was becoming quite attached to Ms Ciccone. With his enthusiastic support, she applied for and gained a scholarship, both an indication of her talent and potential, and a source of great satisfaction. Her belief in herself had been triumphantly vindicated.

Yet despite her artistic and intellectual pretensions, and for all Flynn's teachings, at heart she remained unsophisticated and quite naïve. To look at photographs of her at that time is to be reminded that, at seventeen, she was not the young woman whose knowing and aggressive sexuality would define a generation, but a youthful ingénue whose carefully constructed carapace of self-conscious indifference to the world around her belied a deep sense of insecurity and uncertainty.

Nowhere was this more apparent than in her dealings with her friends and contemporaries. In showing her private feelings, her façade of cynical worldliness and indifference easily gave way to sentiments as gauche as they were generous-hearted. In one note in the 1974 Adams High yearbook, a juvenile Madonna wrote to Mary-Ellen Beloat: 'You are the craziest person I know. I love you.' A couple of years later, when she graduated in 1976, she expressed herself in a similar vein to her favorite teacher, Marilyn Fallows. 'Mrs Fallows,' she gushed, 'I can't begin to tell you how I feel about you, and how I will always treasure your words of encouragement. Sometimes I think you might explode with so much energy inside of you. I think you are crazy and I am really in love with your craziness, and of course, you.'

Nevertheless, for all her sentimental musings, after Madonna left Adams High School she never once went back.

According to romantic legend, in the early days of the American colony a young Frenchwoman named Ann d'Arbeur led a group of settlers lost in the wilderness surrounding the Huron River to a place of safety where they could rest and recuperate. The hamlet they established there, Ann Arbor, a settlement of some 640 acres forested with burr oaks, was named after her in appreciation of her courage, leadership and navigational skills.

So much for legend. More prosaically, the village was actually founded in 1824 by John Allen of Virginia and Elisha Rumsey of New York, and named after Allen's wife, Ann. She was the sole inspiration for the name, preferring 'Annarbour' (*arbor* is the Latin for tree) to her husband's choice of Allensville or Annapolis.

With the opening of the University of Michigan in Ann Arbor in 1841, the town, which had started life with a population of fifty, established itself as the education capital of the Midwest. White, Anglo-Saxon and Protestant, its citizens adopted a high moral tone, in 1916 voting for Prohibition before the rest of America (it became law in 1919), reserving their strongest criticism for saloons which, before the nationwide ban on alcohol was enacted, pandered to students. What the founding fathers would have made of modern-day Ann Arbor, with its Queer Aquatic Club 'dedicated to gay, lesbian and bisexual swimmers,' or the downtown Aut Bar, which boasts a 'leather night' on the last Friday in every month, or the activities of the local Grizzly Peak Brewing Company, or Vivienne, resident 'female mystic imbued with the DNA of past clairvoyants,' is not hard to guess.

Certainly, when Madonna arrived in the fall of 1976 she found Ann Arbor, with its well-established arts festival and gay and underground scenes, an eye-opening change from the suburban life she had led in Rochester. For all Flynn's guidance in art and literature, and for all their forays into the world of gay clubs, she remained a high-school student beneath the veneer of sophistication. It was, however, the support and encouragement of teachers from her former high school that had given her the chance to move on. Marilyn Fallows wrote to the Music Department of the University of Michigan in April 1976, stating that she found Madonna to be 'an intelligent, sensitive, and creative young woman,' while her counselor, Nancy Ryan Mitchell, was equally effusive, telling the university authorities that the young dancer was 'extremely talented, motivated, experienced, open to improvement' and possessed of a 'sparkling personality.' Naturally Christopher Flynn, now Professor of Dance on the university faculty, also helped smooth the path to a full scholarship.

Yet, whatever Flynn's part in the award, the scholarship was still a remarkable achievement for a teenager who had only taken up ballet seriously some three years earlier. Moreover, while her father may have harbored the hope that his eldest daughter would go into a more practical career like the law, there was no doubting the fact that he was proud of her success. Proud and excited, he made one stipulation before she set off for Ann Arbor – that she room in an all-girl dormitory.

When she arrived at the university, Madonna picked up where she had left off in Rochester, spending much of her time with Flynn, attending his classes, and going out dancing with him in the local gay clubs. It was apparent to other students that she was devoted to her mentor, slavishly following the wishes of this flamboyant Svengali, however perverse. Some of those wishes made sense, helping the young dancers to a greater understanding of their art, or otherwise improving their skills. Others were less healthy. One of the latter would bring Madonna – and others, no doubt – to the edge of illness. At the start of every class he would force students to weigh in. If the scale went over 110 to 115 pounds he would humiliate the errant performer, ordering them to get a grip on their eating. Madonna took him at his word, living off a diet of popcorn and ice-cream sundaes, and punishing her slender body with endless sit-ups that left her flesh dark with bruises. Her friend and fellow student Linda Alaniz remembers that: 'She had a really unhealthy diet and I'm sure at that time she was borderline anorexic. But she desperately wanted to please Christopher.'

Like the other students, Madonna had a punishing schedule of two ninety-minute technique classes a day, with a further two hours of rehearsal for college performances at the Power Center for the Performing Arts. Even in that hothouse atmosphere she stood out, not just for her abilities as a dancer, but also because of the intelligent commitment she brought to her art. She had, it seems, given herself over to dance, body and soul, and her classmates found her enthusiasm infectious, as when she arrived one day raving about her African dance class and the Mujaji, a rain dance she had learned.

Professor Gay Delanghe, the head of the university Dance Department, remembers a 'colt-like' teenager who quickly developed a 'fine dance facility'. 'She had the dedication, commitment and energy to do so,' she says. 'She had both the body and the chops to be noticed by faculty, guest choreographers and her fellow students. She possessed the brain power to learn movement and make it look like something. Many are called but not all can do it. She can.'

At the same time, that hunger for attention that had characterized her school career was soon all too apparent to fellow students, as Linda Alaniz remembers. 'She would come into ballet class chewing gum and with a cut-up leotard held together with safety pins. It was a punk look but really it was childish, a little girl desperate for attention.' It seemed to be a case of 'any-thing to be noticed.' On one occasion, when the class were holding in their stomachs and keeping their heads still for a deep plié, Madonna let out a huge belch. Such adolescent attention-seeking took other, less obvious, forms, however. Another friend, Whitley Setrakian, who became her room-mate in her second year, felt that behind the wisecracking exterior was a rather lost soul. 'She was the most openly affectionate girl I had ever met. She was forever putting her arms around me. But you could sense it was a little bit of an act. She was needy and there was something a little fragile and sad about her.'

Like Mary-Ellen Beloat and Marilyn Fallows before her, Whitley was to experience at first hand that neediness, wrapped in endearing if earnest sentimentality. She returned from Christmas vacation to find a six-page letter from Madonna waiting for her. 'I've realized how much I've grown to depend on you as a listener, advice giver and taker and general all around most wonderful, intimate friend in the whole world,' she wrote.

Photographs of her at the time give a sense of the two sides to Madonna, one the serious-minded ballet student, the other the attention-seeking, exhibitionist teenager. Linda Alaniz, who was taking a photography minor as well as majoring in dance, asked Madonna to pose for her for a series of studies in her loft apartment during Halloween. Her black-and-white photographs show a poised and composed young woman, high-minded, sophisticated and elegant. She seems very feminine, the quintessential swan-like ballerina pursuing her art with single-minded purpose and dedication.

In other contemporary photographs, however, taken by hairdresser and one-time boyfriend Mark Dolengowski, the wisecracking, attention-grabbing party girl enters the picture. She mugs for the camera, blowing gum bubbles, pulling faces, striking street-punk poses, a far cry from the lithe, serious dancer of Linda's artistic studies. Yet both sessions reflect fragments of Madonna's personality, as confusing as it may be to reconcile the sassy, panty-parading show-off with the poised ballet dancer.

Indeed, the way she started dating Mark was vintage Madonna. He was working as a hairdresser on campus, she was one of his clients. One day during her first months at college, she passed by his salon, stuck her tongue out at him – and then, when he came over to talk to her, invited him to join her at Dooley's, a college bar where she occasionally worked. He dutifully bought her a drink, and from then on they began dating. Mark took her dancing or out to dinner – he always paid, because she was permanently short of money – and before long they embarked upon a short-lived love affair. If anything, the end of the brief fling strengthened their friendship, the two of them staying in touch when they both eventually moved to New York. 'She was very dedicated and disciplined with her dancing. Very focused,' recalls Mark, who joined Christopher Flynn's dance classes for a time. 'Madonna was good fun when she let herself have fun.'

To her, fun was dancing, either in class or in clubs. She regularly went out with Linda, Whitley and another friend, Janice Galloway, and danced the night away. It was during one of these forays that Madonna met a young man who was to have a profound influence on her future. She spotted Stephen Bray in the Blue Frogge bar, and for the first time in her life asked a man to buy her a drink. Soulful, quietly spoken and gentle, the black waiter embodied many of the same qualities of the men who would come to matter in her life. She discovered that he was a drummer in a local band, and for the next few months she and, as often as not, Linda, Whitley and Janice, would go along to dance at their gigs.

For the most part, when Madonna and her girlfriends went out on the town their primary aim was to enjoy themselves dancing, not to pick up any of the girl-hungry young men who frequented the clubs. Madonna and Linda laughed off accusations from would-be suitors that they were lesbians because they danced with each other, and spurned the advances of local guys. For that reason they often frequented the gay clubs, reveling in the energy, abandon and freedom of that scene, aware that they could enjoy the music and the dance for their own sake. 'We had a blast,' Linda says, although their presence on the gay scene inevitably increased the gossip about their 'lesbianism.'

It was at this time, however, that Linda first noticed a quality about her friend that became more evident the closer the young dancer came to the seductive glow of fame. In the choreography of her life, Madonna's sense of fun, even her outrageous behavior, came strictly second to her driving ambition. As far as she was concerned, her dance career was her passport to stardom. As Linda puts it, 'We would get home late but she was incredibly disciplined. She would always be ready for the dance class at eight in the morning. She never missed one.'

Clearly, Madonna sensed that she was destined for bigger things – and, as far as she was concerned, the sooner the better. Moreover, if dance was her passport to fame, then New York was the utopia in which she would realize her dreams. It was not long before she started railing against the slow pace of life in Ann Arbor, seeing her future further east. In a letter to a friend she wrote: 'I just gotta get to New York. I also realize that the chances of me making it dancing are extremely slight and I gotta prove something to myself.'

Like her Cinderella childhood, the story of her arrival in New York has become part of the Madonna myth. According to her version of events, in the summer of 1978 she bought a one-way air ticket to New York, arriving with just $35 in her pocket and a burning desire to find fame and fortune. Hailing a cab, she confidently told the startled driver, 'Take me to the center of everything.' He promptly dropped her off in Times Square where, dressed in a heavy winter coat on a warm summer's day, she dragged her suitcase around looking for a place to stay. A kindly stranger, said to be an out-of-work balletdancer, took pity on her, and she slept on his couch for a couple of weeks until she found her own place.

Sadly, as with the legend behind the naming of Ann Arbor, the truth is less romantic. In fact, her first trip to New York had been more than a year earlier, in February 1977, courtesy of her boyfriend Mark Dolengowski. She had applied for a scholarship to dance with the Alvin Ailey American Dance Theatre at their six-week summer workshop in New York. An audition was arranged and Mark, borrowing her father's car, gallantly drove more than 600 miles through the night from Ann Arbor to Manhattan so that Madonna could keep her appointment. She duly performed for the audition panel and, after grabbing a quick bite to eat, the young couple headed back to Ann Arbor. In all they were in New York for less than twenty-four hours, leaving on the Friday and arriving back at college that Sunday so that Madonna would not miss her Monday-morning class. 'I remember it was a sixteen-hour round trip,' says Mark, 'and I did all the driving.'

The trip proved to have been well worth the effort. She won her scholarship, and at the end of that term, spent an exhausting but fulfilling summer in New York, staying with friends on the Upper East Side. On a couple of occasions Mark visited her, concerned about her safety. It was the summer of the 'Son of Sam' killings, when the whole of New York was living in fear of a serial killer; he was later arrested and identified as David Berkowitz. 'Everyone was freaked out and I was worried about her,' he recalls. 'We went to a concert in Central Park but she was often too tired to go dancing. Her classes were really hard work.'

To Madonna, nineteen that August, passionate about, and wholly dedicated to, her dancing, the experience was almost as intimidating as it was exhilarating. For the first time in her life she had mixed with young dancers who were as voluble, aggressive and ambitious as she was. 'I thought I was in a production of *Fame*,' she once said in an interview for *Rolling Stone* magazine (although *Fame* did not in fact appear until 1980). 'Everybody wanted to be a star.' Nevertheless, her appetite whetted by the experience, she returned to college for her sophomore year even more focused, if that were possible, on her dream of becoming a professional dancer.

That dream reached a turning point when the noted ballet choreographer Pearl Lang – a former lead soloist with Martha Graham's modern dance troupe, founder of the Pearl Lang Company and co-founder with Alvin Ailey of the American Dance Center in New York – visited Ann Arbor as artist-in-residence. While there, she created a work for the students based on music by the Venetian composer Antonio Vivaldi. Madonna was one of the dancers who performed the new work at the Power Arts Center, impressing Lang with her talent and sensibilities, and her dance professor, Gay Delanghe, with both her increased assurance and the way in which she had developed artistically. Clearly Madonna, who was inspired and impressed by Lang's work, was growing in stature and poise. While by no means the finished article, it was obvious that she was a credit to her college, and more than justified her award of a scholarship.

As it turned out, however, her mentor, Christopher Flynn, had other ideas for his charge than completing a dance major at a Midwestern university. Even though she was not yet halfway through her four-year course, Flynn told her to listen to her heart and seek her fortune in New York. 'There can be something thrilling about academic dance,' he would later remark. 'But it has its limits. Madonna was just so much bigger than that – I could see it even if she couldn't. There were just so many more things for her to explore and they were all in New York. Stop wasting your time in the sticks. Take your little behind to New York. Go! Finally she did.'

In spite of her earlier impatience with college life, Madonna hesitated, knowing that she would automatically lose her scholarship as well as forgo any chance of a college degree. She knew, too, that abandoning her course would be viewed with disfavor at home, where her father, reasonably enough, stood by the pragmatic view that she should first earn her diploma before heading for the bright lights, where the potential risks were at least as great as the rewards.

Tony Ciccone was not alone in that opinion. Madonna's college professors all expressed their concern, arguing that her artistic development would best be served by staying at college. With strongly implied criticism of Flynn, Professor Delanghe remembers that 'We all gave her the usual "NYC will still be there waiting for you when you have more maturity and more to offer artistically" but some are driven to leave despite adult recommendations. I always got the impression that she didn't have much direction or support at home. Madonna had a parent in Flynn and he told her to follow her heart.' To which she added, 'She was young, naïve and without good advice, would be my view of it.'

While it is true that Flynn may have been trying to fufill his own thwarted dance ambitions through his protégée, it is to his lasting credit that he appreciated the essential restlessness of her spirit, her unwillingness to be pinned

Previous page: Madonna Louise Ciccone dressed for her First Communion

Left: Silvio Patrick Ciccone, pictured here in his graduation photograph, June 1955. Just over three weeks later he was married. Madonna's relationship with her father has been a complicated one; while wanting his approval, her unconventional behavior has often upset staunchly conservative 'Tony' Ciccone

Below: 'Little Nonni' (*left*) is held by her adored mother, Madonna Louise, née Fortin, who died of breast cancer when her eldest daughter was only five

Facing page, above: Madonna, aged nine, the year she appeared 'practically naked' in a talent-show performance, and aged twelve

Facing page, below: Madonna (*center*) as a high-school cheerleader in 1973 – her second year at Adams High in Rochester, Michigan

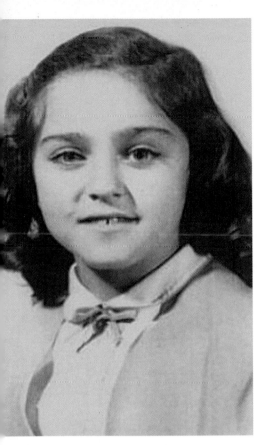

Left: Madonna always took the lead in school theatricals, which drew her the applause she craved, including a standing ovation for her role in *Godspell*

Below: As a gangster's moll at a costume party at her high school in Rochester, Michigan. Contrary to her claims that she grew up in a black neighborhood, there was only one black pupil at the school

Right: Madonna in 1976, posing for fellow University of Michigan student Linda Alaniz. Dressed here in conventional dancewear, she would attend her classes in ripped-up leotards held together with safety pins. Her slim physique was due to a diet of popcorn and ice-cream sundaes

The eighteen-year-old Madonna poses for Peter Kentes, a graduate student in dance at the University of Michigan. Her pencil-thin physique and erratic eating habits at this time caused alarm among her friends

Two more of Linda Alaniz's photographs of Madonna during her time as a dance student at the University of Michigan

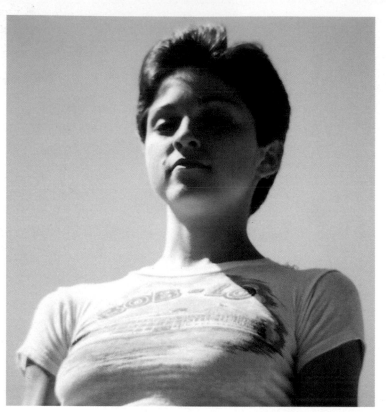

Previous page, left, and facing page: Madonna has always enjoyed showing off — especially her underwear. Here she poses for her then boyfriend, Mark Dolengowski

Below: Madonna in 1978 with her dance coach, friend and mentor Christopher Flynn, the man who would first push her on to the path to stardom. Here, having convinced her that she should leave college and pursue her dreams in New York, Flynn drives Madonna to the airport

Previous spread: In New York Madonna auditioned for, and was accepted by, the highly respected Pearl Lang Dance Company. As well as pushing herself to the limit in the punishing classes, Madonna ran three miles every day

Left: Madonna in May 1979, posing before a medieval cross in the Cloisters, a branch of New York's Metropolitan Museum of Art. The photograph shows that her use of religious iconography began long before 'Like A Prayer'

Right: Madonna in the summer of 1979, on the roof of the converted synagogue where she lived with her boyfriend, musician Dan Gilroy

Below: Realizing that she was but one among many talented dancers in New York, Madonna turned her back on the world of professional dance and redirected her energies into a music career, guided by Dan Gilroy. The photo shows her first band, The Breakfast Club: Angie Smit, Ed Gilroy, Dan Gilroy and Madonna

After Angie Smit left The Breakfast Club, Madonna appointed herself the band's lead singer. However, her need to be the focus of the group led in part to the breakdown of her relationship with Dan Gilroy

Above, and right: Madonna and the Gilroy brothers, dressed all in white in the New Romantic style, play a gig at Bo's Space in downtown New York

down by anyone or anything, as well as the special talent that was beginning to glow inside her. Indeed, it was her free-spirited nature that made her so ideally suited to the physical expressiveness, continual movement and acute sensitivity of her chosen discipline. In the end, and even though she appreciated the risks, Madonna, then nineteen, was so much in thrall to Flynn – and still distanced from her father – that any doubts she may have had were cast aside. Beyond those considerations, however, her experience the previous summer had whetted her appetite for the Big Apple and a chance to fulfill her own ambitions there.

With the decision taken, and conscious that she would lose the scholarship money she depended on to live, Madonna started working nights and weekends, doing shifts at a Baskin-Robbins ice-cream parlor and waitressing regularly at Dooley's bar. As well as bar work, she, Whitley and Linda earned an occasional $10 an hour posing as nude models for local art courses, their toned bodies and well-defined musculature ensuring that they were much in demand for life classes.

Somehow, she began slowly to acquire the money she would need for her dramatic change of direction. On one occasion a college teacher asked students if they wanted to go to church to dance in a performance of the Stations of the Cross. Everyone declined until the lecturer mentioned that they would be paid $50 each. At once Madonna, Linda and Whitley volunteered. As a result, Linda and Whitley were to be privy to one of their friend's earliest singing performances. When they arrived at the church, Madonna stood behind the pulpit and began to belt out a raucous version of the Little Richard hit, 'Good Golly Miss Molly.' 'The teacher yelled at her to stop, saying that it was sacrilegious,' recalls Linda. 'It was priceless. But that was the only time I heard her sing.'

Madonna carefully saved the $50 from that performance, as well as her bar tips, hiding the money, appropriately enough, inside a coffee-table book of Martha Swope's photographs of the New York City Ballet. According to Linda, 'She had hundreds of twenty-dollar bills squirreled away. I saw the size of her stash. It was way more than the thirty-five dollars she talked about, I can assure you of that. Even Madonna wasn't ballsy enough to arrive in New York with just thirty-five dollars.'

In spite of the opposition to her decision to quit the University of Michigan prematurely, Madonna was supremely optimistic when, in July 1977, at the end of her second year, she smilingly waved goodbye to her college friends and was driven from the campus to the airport by a beaming Christopher Flynn. As far as Flynn was concerned, their parting was full of sweet sorrow. Even though he had been instrumental in encouraging her to leave, he went into a deep depression, almost a period of mourning, after she had gone. 'He loved her, he really did,' Linda Alaniz believes. 'He was so sad when she left.'

Dance teacher to the core, however, he did remind her to attend the annual American Festival of Dance, held at Duke University in Durham, North Carolina in July 1978, once she had got settled in New York. Madonna did as Flynn had advised, teaming up again with other University of Michigan dance students who had made the long bus journey south to take part in what proved to be a cultural orgy of experimentation and exploration. 'A stream of images inspired by Surrealism,' ran one *New York Times* headline, describing a work by a Chinese choreographer.

Madonna was in her element at the festival, her enthusiasm matched only by her desire to excel. She was only one of hundreds of eager dancers from all over the country who had applied for a scholarship to pay for the six-week dance program, but her talent shone through at the auditions. Pearl Lang, who was choreographing one of the workshops at the festival, announced her name as one of the winners. When she walked to the table to collect her prize, she innocently told the choreographer that her dream was to work with the great Pearl Lang. 'Her eyes popped out of her head when I told her that I was Pearl Lang,' Ms Lang remembered, before dryly adding that she had worked with Madonna only a few months before at the University of Michigan.

Yet although her attempt at ingratiation had been nothing if not transparent, Madonna was genuinely excited, mesmerized even, by Lang's work. As a student, Madonna gravitated towards modern dance, inspired by this sophisticated, rather cerebral form of high art, a world away from her future pop persona or, for that matter, from what one might call the *Swan Lake* school of classical ballet. She described Lang's approach as 'painful, dark and guilt-ridden. Very Catholic,' its very difficulty forming a part of the appeal for a young woman immersed in the creative process that formal dance training inspired in her. As a former pupil, and later a disciple, of the arch-priestess of modern dance, Martha Graham, Lang represented, for Madonna, a link with the highest reaches of that art.

So it came about that, only a few days into the course, she approached the choreographer and asked if there was any chance of a place in Lang's company in New York. The older woman was ambivalent. While she was impressed by her 'talent and determination,' she wondered whether the girl knew anyone in the city, and how she would live. 'Don't worry, I'll manage,' came the confident reply. In the end Pearl Lang relented, and offered her a provisional place with the company, starting in November that year.

When, late in the summer of 1978, Madonna arrived in New York for good – the time of the $35-in-her-pocket legend – she was half in love with the romantic idea of the misunderstood artist starving in a garret, but wholly in thrall to her ambition to become a professional dancer. She realized it was going to be tough. 'I knew I was going to suffer, I knew it was going to be hard,' she told the writer Ingrid Sischy. 'But I was not going back and that's how it was, period.' Even when, shortly after she had arrived, her father made an unexpected visit to her apartment in the run-down Lower East Side to try to make her see sense and come home to Michigan, back to comfort and security, she refused to abandon her dream. Her memory of that encounter is that he was appalled by the squalor in which she was now living, the cockroaches in her bedroom, and the smell of stale beer in the communal hallway where homeless drunks bedded down. He left empty-handed, understandably horrified. This may be, however, yet another story that has burnished the Madonna myth, the old tale of the misunderstood runaway defiantly suffering for her art and her vision.

In fact, others who knew her at that time remember that she initially roomed with a college friend at Columbia University before moving to an apartment in Hell's Kitchen, on the west side of New York. Yet, whatever the truth of her own version of events, what is clear is that within a matter of months the dream Madonna had cherished had turned to dust, leaving her just another starry-eyed hopeful broken on the wheel of aspiration. The journey to New York was a personal odyssey that had begun with such shining hope, but which ended in rejection, disillusion and even horror.

In the first few months, though, it seemed that her gamble to leave Ann Arbor had paid off handsomely. After joining Pearl Lang's company, she was cast as a dancer in a piece entitled *I Never Saw Another Butterfly*, a work about the Holocaust. Lang felt that Madonna, thin, dark and hungry-looking, perfectly fitted the role of a Jewish ghetto child. Even so, she ordered her pupil to lose a further 10 pounds, prompting a return to her now famous diet of popcorn and the occasional butterscotch sundae. However, the image that stayed most strongly in the choreographer's mind was a pose Madonna struck while dancing in a modern ballet entitled *La Rosa en Flores*. 'Madonna did it beautifully,' Lang remembered, praising the dancer's sensitive interpretation of her choreography.

There were, too, other qualities that marked Madonna out as special in her teacher's eyes. 'I was fond of her for her arrogance, her hunger and her spunk,' Lang continued. 'Nothing fazed her. She was going to do something and nothing was going to get in her way.' Even the fact that she turned up to rehearsals in her by then trademark ripped leotard and safety pins did nothing to alter Lang's opinion: 'When she started to work she was quite wonderful.'

Knowing that Madonna was looking for a job to fund her studies, Lang even found her a part-time job as a hatcheck girl at the Russian Tea Room, near Carnegie Hall. She held the $4.50-an-hour job for a couple of months before manager Gregory Camillucci fired her. She worked longer at the Russian Tea Room than she managed in most of her jobs, however. She was fired from Dunkin' Donuts after a single day, allegedly for squirting filling over a customer, while menial jobs at Burger King and other fast-food restaurants lasted little longer. 'It was simply that she couldn't stand them,' recalls Mark Dolengowski, who moved to New York a few months after Madonna.

She quickly fell back on the work which had paid so well in Ann Arbor – nude modeling. This time the going rate at the local art school, the Art Students' League, was $7, although during the winter of 1978 she supplemented her income with nude-modeling sessions with two 'art' photographers, Bill Stone and Martin S. Schreiber. Although some of these photographs were to come back to haunt her, both men remember her as professional, at ease with her body but quiet to the point of being taciturn.

It was just another job as far as she was concerned, a way of getting by. So when Schreiber offered to take her on a date, her thoughts were of a free meal rather than romance. In fact, she was becoming quite adept at freeloading, using her charm and growing street wisdom to get what she wanted. Her old college friend Linda Alaniz remembers with a wry smile how, when she visited her in New York, Madonna persuaded her to pay for dinner at an expensive restaurant, even though neither had that sort of money to spare. Knowing her friend's wheedling ways and modest diet, Linda takes with a pinch of salt her story, frequently repeated in books and articles, that she had picked food out of garbage cans in order to survive in the city.

To her sorrow, Linda Alaniz was equally dismissive when Madonna confided to her that, in the fall of 1978, she had been sexually assaulted at knifepoint on the rooftop of a tenement building. Tragically, this time the story was true, as Linda later realized, the experience inevitably leaving a deep psychological scar on its victim. At the time, Madonna was living a precarious existence, still trying to find her feet in the city, still learning to be streetwise. Trouble came out of the blue one day when she was outside a run-down tenement building. As she herself recounted the story, a well-built black man approached her in the street. Trustingly, she let him come close, noticing too late that he was holding a knife. Pressing the blade to her throat, he spun her round and forced her into the entrance of the tenement. Then, with the knife held to her back, he made her walk up the stairs to the rooftop. As they slowly climbed the steps – the tenement did not have an elevator – Madonna was paralyzed with fear, terrified that she was going to die. Thoughts raced through her head: was he going to cut her throat? Mutilate her? Throw her off the roof? Her abductor gave not the slightest indication of his intentions, and because he did not speak, she was unable to guess even what sort of man he was, or his mood. Dragging her feet up the steps, one after the other, she decided that she would do anything he asked in order to survive.

When they reached the rooftop, the attacker forced Madonna at knife-point to perform oral sex on him. Almost paralyzed with fear, she obeyed, not knowing whether she was going to live or die. When it was over, and still without a word, her assailant left as abruptly as he had appeared, leaving her alone in a state of utter shock. She sat there for a long time, convulsed with tears, her emotions churning with fear, relief and horrified humiliation in equal measure, and too terrified to retrace her steps in case the sinister knife-man was waiting for her in the stairwell. When she finally plucked up the courage to make her way nervously back down to the street, the whole awful experience seemed to have almost a surreal quality to it, even as vile and grotesque as it had been. Shattered, she made her way home, there to begin the long process of trying to come to terms with her ordeal.

For a long time she tried to shrug the whole incident off. When she told a few friends, as she did Linda Alaniz, it was as though she were recounting one of her crazy anecdotes, no doubt her own way of coping with the trauma. Later she consulted and confided in a therapist, before very publicly telling the world about her ordeal. 'I have been raped and it's not an experience I would ever glamorize,' she said in an interview, adding that the trauma had made her a stronger person, even though it had put her off oral sex for good. Years later, during the filming of *Dangerous Game* in the early 1990s, she recounted the ordeal in character for the cameras almost exactly as it had happened, although she added that the attacker had cried afterwards. The film's director, Abel Ferrara, has observed that the irony about her screen admission and description of the assault was that no one believed that it was true. 'It did happen, but then nobody believes it because she made it unbelievable. It was a very heavy sequence. I didn't know she was going to tell that story', he added.

Like so many victims of sex attacks, at the time she felt violated, embarrassed and ashamed, which undoubtedly increased her sense of isolation and loneliness – years later she would recall the day she sat weeping by the fountain at Lincoln Center. She would often confide her sadness and pain to a journal she kept, writing an entry every day without fail. It is a lifelong habit, and one that has frequently been the source of the raw emotional material for many of her lyrics. That, however, was on the days when she felt sorry for herself.

True to her own character, she only allowed herself a limited time for self-pity. If nothing else, Madonna is a fighter, picking herself up after every knockdown, squaring up to the world again more determined than ever. She used all her considerable willpower to push the incident to the back of her mind, trying to get on with her life, her steely inner resolution, her 'Fortintude,' refusing to buckle under the strain. Within her immediate circle, she was still the one telling the off-color stories, the craziest dancer, the girl with the look-at-me style.

'Go Madonna, go!' were the first words Norris Burroughs heard when he arrived at a party in Pearl Lang's Central Park apartment just before Christmas 1978. There she was, dressed in leopard-skin tights, twirling and spinning at the vibrant center of a circle of dancers. 'It was like a ritual', he recalls, 'as though she were dancing in a ring of fire.' He immediately joined the group, but quickly realized that his standard disco moves couldn't compete with the movements of the student dancers who surrounded him. But he made an impression of sorts on Madonna – even though he quickly saw that he faced stiff competition. The following day his friend Michael Kessler, who had first introduced him to Madonna, called to invite him over. As he was telling Norris that Madonna was with him, she grabbed the phone and shouted, 'Get your gorgeous Brando body over here!'

They started dating, and before long she was spending two or three nights a week at his apartment. Their romance only lasted a matter of months, but even so Norris, an artist and son of the radio actor Eric Burroughs, gained a vivid insight into the direction of Madonna's life, and the drive behind it. 'The moment you laid eyes on her you knew that she was a person of destiny, a force of nature, an elemental being. When you are with someone like that you are immensely privileged and hang on for the ride. I felt like I had fallen down the rabbit hole and didn't know where the adventure was leading.'

She maintained a determinedly Bohemian lifestyle, a young artist hungrily devouring Hemingway, absorbing Picasso, and savoring Browning – food for the soul, not the body. Nor did the daily cares of makeup, hairdressers or hot showers concern her. Style was what she woke up in. She wore Norris's cast-offs, an old pair of jeans she tied with string to make them fit or a moth-eaten sweater. Here was someone who traveled light, unimpressed by the pretentious and self-conscious – an anti-material girl. To her lover of the moment, 'Madonna struck me as a free spirit who was unwilling to be encumbered or tied down or pigeon-holed. I never tried to put a chain around her neck and that's one of the reasons why our relationship lasted as long as it did. Everything I recall about her physically or sexually is misty and romantic. She brought out the tender and sensuous.'

Norris gathered early on, during their long rambling walks through Manhattan, visiting churches and art galleries, that she had one vision, to be a principal dancer with either the Alvin Ailey or the Pearl Lang company. Touched by that ambition, and the determination that lay behind it, one of the first presents he gave her was a biography of Nureyev. 'I got a sense that she was going places but didn't yet know how,' Norris remembers. Curiously, though, in view of her later career, he also reflects that while she liked singing around the apartment or on their walks – Donna Summer's 'Hot Stuff,' Nancy Sinatra's 'These Boots Are Made for Walking,' and songs by Blondie and Chrissie Hynde were favorites – there was never any feeling that she wanted to be a musician. Dance was her art and her ambition.

Yet just a few months after articulating her dream of becoming a principal dancer, Madonna walked away from dance for good. The reasons are many and various; and, as so often with Madonna's history, it is not always easy to distinguish fact from legend. Clearly, though, something was wrong. The young dancer started complaining that Pearl Lang's style was too old-fashioned, that she worked her dancers too hard, that there were too few opportunities. There was also the painful realization that there were many other dancers with similar, if not greater, talents than her own. The subtext is plain. Madonna craved acclaim, applause, even adulation, her individualism jarring upon other members of the troupe. Only now had it begun to dawn on her that it would take another three to five years of remorseless grind before she could even think of joining a major touring company. Then, if she did so, she would face fierce competition from dozens of other equally motivated and talented young dancers. The glittering prize of stage stardom, let alone that of being appointed principal dancer, seemed even more distant than at Ann Arbor, where at least she had appeared in two dance concerts a year.

She took out her frustrations in a series of confrontations with Pearl Lang, on one occasion banging her head against the studio wall in anger when she couldn't perform a difficult dance step to the veteran choreographer's liking. It heralded the parting of the ways, the recognition that Madonna's individualism would never fit with the somewhat collegiate world of a dance troupe. Pearl Lang remembers the day she quit. 'One day she said: "You know this dancing is difficult," and I said: "I know it's difficult," and she said: "I have pains in my back." I replied: "Everybody has pains in their back. It comes with the territory."

'Then she said: "I think I'm going to be a rock star." She left and I never saw her again.'

[71]

At that stage in her life, Madonna had never sung a song or played a chord on a public stage, other than at school. It was a convenient fiction for both sides, a way of avoiding the cruel reality that in the world of dance, as her dance professor at the University of Michigan remarked, many are called but very few are chosen. For months afterwards the pain of the parting was almost tangible. Indeed, for a long while she talked about getting into this or that troupe, the reality becoming ever more distant. But she remained very much the party animal, loving to dance, out clubbing every night. Tellingly, though, the one thing she hated, passionately, was when a young girl in a nightclub would watch her move to the music and then come over and ask, perfectly innocently, 'Are you a professional dancer?' Madonna's face would become a frozen mask, her manner icy cold as she briefly answered in the negative. The reason is not difficult to find, for the question forced her to confront her failure, to reflect for a few cruel moments upon what might have been.

A few minutes later, though, and she would be on the dance floor again, swirling, whirling and spinning to the song that was to become her personal anthem, Gloria Gaynor's 'I Will Survive.'

Chapter Five

The 'Lost' First Songs

T HE SEARCH FOR LOST RECORDINGS of a pop star's early songs is not, perhaps, an activity likely to excite most archeologists. Nonetheless, in terms of the archeology of pop the site yields treasures as priceless as anything lifted from the Valley of the Kings. True, the 'dig' takes place in the basement of a converted synagogue in Queens, New York, rather than among the royal tombs of ancient Egypt, and the guide, Ed Gilroy, wears a white baseball cap rather than the sun helmet or panama hat favored by the stereotypical archeologist of popular legend, but even so the thrill of discovery is palpable.

There is even a green parrot – imaginatively named 'Birdie' – squawking in the background as Gilroy makes his way down the spiral staircase into the gloom of the building's extensive basement. He swings his flashlight around until its beam picks out a nondescript white plastic bag nestling among several paintings his artist brother Dan had left stacked against a wall – landscapes, flower studies, and figures in a glade, one of them a youthful Madonna running through the long grass. Ed Gilroy rifles through the plastic bag until, with a smile of satisfaction, he pulls out a spool-to-spool four-track tape with an almost indecipherable label stuck to its center. Closer scrutiny of the hieroglyphics scrawled on the label in black ink yields the curious words: 'Bkfst Club Set – Work Percuss 2 End'.

He carefully places the spool on a dusty thirty-year-old tape recorder, threads its free end on to the machine's reel, and then shines his flashlight on the counter to line up the tape correctly. Satisfied, he presses the 'Play' button and, almost unbelievably, the ancient spools begin to turn. Instantly we travel back in time, to the summer of 1979, the days of punk rock and New Wave. Through the headphones can be heard the muddy but driving sound of the drums and two guitars, pounding out a rock beat. The voice belting out the lyrics is young, energetic, rather nasal, yet altogether unmistakable. This is Madonna, recording the first song she ever wrote.

The song, which runs for about three minutes, has simple pop lyrics, describing, appropriately enough, her belief that that she was born to dance and how she enjoys moving her body to the sound of the music inside her. As it reaches a crescendo her voice becomes slightly hoarse, straining for the higher notes, especially when she yells her words in the final chorus. Yet that very rawness gives the song a sharper edge and a greater sense of excitement. As Ed, who played lead guitar on the track, observes, 'The quality of her voice is so pure. It just comes out, totally uninhibited. Nowadays studios would hack out the struggle in her voice but that's too bad. It's almost like a window into her soul.'

As he reflects on those early days he is sitting on a worn cherrywood chair on castors that Madonna had used when she first auditioned the song before him to see if he thought it was good enough to include in the repertoire of their band, The Breakfast Club. Behind him is the same Carlo Robelli acoustic guitar on which she had learnt her first chords, the instrument she had used to pick out the melody as she had put together the words to her first song.

Ed Gilroy's nod of approval for that first song meant an enormous amount to the would-be singer. For months Madonna had been floundering impatiently, almost obsessively seeking a new purpose and direction for her life. And it was in the unlikely setting of a converted synagogue that she found for a while a home and a haven, an opportunity to express herself, a chance to regroup and rethink after the collapse of her dance career and the frustrations of the past year.

It might all have been so different. A chance meeting with her former boy-friend Norris Burroughs in April 1979 changed her destiny for ever. While they had drifted apart as lovers, they remained friends and, after exchanging their news, he invited her to a May Day party at a friend's downtown loft. Knowing her eagerness to make a name for herself, he promised that there would be lots of 'scene makers' at the party. She duly arrived, her hair up and dressed in two tee-shirts and a ballet tutu. 'Very New York,' observed Curtis Zale, an artist who spent some time chatting with his friend Dan Gilroy that night. 'She was being fun and coy and loud, like the twenty-year-old kid she was. I wasn't interested, but Dan was.'

Madonna and Dan Gilroy met up a few days later and took the bus uptown to the Cloisters, a branch of the Metropolitan Museum of Art housed in a series of buildings, modeled on five medieval French cloisters, in Fort Tryon Park, overlooking the Hudson River. During their day together she happily mugged for the camera, joining on to the end of a line of visiting nuns, posing by a fountain, and kneeling as if in prayer before a medieval altar cross. As they walked and talked Gilroy learned that she was about to embark on a new career in France. Indeed, a part of the reason for their visit to the Cloisters was to give Madonna, ever the professional, a feel for the country by immersing herself in the French paintings and artifacts on show, many brought over by Philip Lehman and his son Robert, who bequeathed the collection to the Metropolitan Museum in 1969.

A few weeks earlier, she had been auditioned by two somewhat larger-than-life Belgian TV producers, Jean van Lieu and Jean-Claude Pellerin, who were managing the European disco star Patrick Hernandez. His single, 'Born To Be Alive,' which had grossed $25 million, had made him an international star, and his two managers were looking for dancers to strut their stuff while he went through his routine. Since he did not have a strong voice there was talk of grooming a couple of dancers to double as backup singers in performances and to work with him on his second single, 'Disco Queen.' Madonna had been singled out from 1,500 other hopefuls as a possible candidate. Defiantly, she insisted that she would only be a dancer, initially refusing to sing at the final audition. In the end she gave a very grudging rendition of 'Happy Birthday.'

The plan formulated by van Lieu and Pellerin was to develop, in Paris, a Las Vegas-style cabaret act around Hernandez, using jugglers, fire-eaters and comedians, including a talking dildo and a black dancer dressed only in a skimpy thong being dragged around the stage on a chain. Indeed, Dan Gilroy and Curtis Zale even suggested a stage name for Madonna, 'Mademoiselle Bijoux,' a sobriquet she took to using on postcards and letters home. A world away from Pearl Lang's work, *The Patrick Hernandez Revue*, as it was billed, was hardly high art. Much of the concept was based on *Voideille*, a New York underground show in which Dan Gilroy and his brother Ed had featured. In it they had performed a musical-comedy act called 'Bill and Gil' and had, at one time, talked of auditioning for a place in the Hernandez cabaret routine.

While nothing ever materialized for the Gilroys, Madonna, after her audition, had become part of the Hernandez troupe and in late May 1979 had moved out of the apartment she then shared with the writer and dancer Susan Cohen on Bleecker Street in Greenwich Village, to the Gramercy Park Hotel, prior to flying to Paris. Even though her Belgian patrons' largesse was becoming legendary in underground New York, she herself was still chronically short of money. Before she left, in June, she borrowed $15 from Dan Gilroy to tide her over, carefully writing out a check in return. That, Dan thought, was that – he would not be seeing her again for a good while. 'I imagined that she wanted to come back to New York a huge success,' he remembers.

In the event, matters did not turn out as he had predicted, or as Madonna had hoped. Driven, disciplined and businesslike, she was very quickly to learn that not everyone shared her commitment. While she wanted to live her life on 'fast forward,' she soon discovered that her Belgian patrons had pushed the 'pause' button on their creative endeavors. She would spend hours on her dance routines, practicing her moves, eager and ready for action. By contrast, her genial hosts enjoyed long and lavish lunches, spent hours glad-handing Parisian socialites, and took their young New York friend to fashionable nightclubs like Régine and VIP.

The effect on Madonna was one of culture shock. While she was interested in advancing her career, her producers, as far as she was concerned, were keener on increasing their waistlines. 'She called up a few times,' recalls Dan, 'complaining that all they did was sit around and eat. She kept feeling like, "Let's go do it, let's get something going." It just wasn't happening.' The fact that she was living in the smart Parisian apartment of Jean-Claude Pellerin and his wife Daniele, had a new wardrobe and food and drink on tap, all without paying a cent herself, meant nothing to her. This girl wanted to see her name in lights, to be treated as an artiste, not as arm candy.

Even when the Hernandez troupe began rehearsals, Madonna felt distanced, even disconnected, from the creative process. She had become a cipher, a pretty puppet on a string, waiting for her cues and her moves. Moreover, although she had the gamine hairstyle and soulful eyes, her producers soon realized that she was not going to be the new Edith Piaf. Nor did she want to be. Madonna still saw herself as a dancer, not a singer. When she witnessed at first hand the adulation enjoyed by Hernandez, however, her earlier opposition began to crumble. For his part, the singer now says that Madonna was inspired to try singing because of the success he enjoyed.

Nonetheless, as the weeks passed it became clear to Madonna that the whole concept was artistically too middle-of-the-road and 'hokey' for her tastes. There were, too, other impulses at work. The two Belgian producers, like others before and after, discovered an essential Madonna characteristic, that she has a different sense of time from the rest of the world. For her, every moment is precious, every hour to be used productively. There is a kind of obsessiveness to this, as though she feels she is being chased through life by Time's wingèd chariot. Whether this trait was inherited from her father's insistence on using every minute constructively, or from her acute awareness that her mother had died in her early thirties, Madonna has an almost frenzied impatience, never knowingly or willingly wasting any time. It is a feature that occurs again and again throughout her career, and does much to explain why she abandoned dance.

When, after a matter of only weeks, it became clear to Madonna that the van Lieu/Pellerin production was not moving quickly enough for her, she decided to leave, telling Hernandez before she flew home in July, 'Success is yours today, but it will be mine tomorrow.' She returned to New York full of colorful stories: how she and Hernandez had had a romantic fling; how she had roared round the Parisian boulevards on the backs of motorcycles driven by Vietnamese punks; how two suitors had fought with knives over her; how she had flown to Tunisia with the singing star for a photocall, and how a simple cold had turned into life-threatening pneumonia. Other accounts allege that she amassed a portfolio of lovers during her brief French sojourn.

Yet as she approached her twenty-first birthday, the uncomfortable truth was that she was a penniless dropout who seemed to be going nowhere. Far-fetched anecdotes, no matter how many, and however amusing, could not camouflage the fact that she had left college without graduating, had fallen out with Pearl Lang and ditched her chosen career, and had now run away from Paris. These bald facts did not tell the whole story, however. Madonna was searching for an artistic identity, a sense of self, and sometimes even a new name. At the same time, as her remark to Patrick Hernandez indicated, she had an unquenchable sense of her own destiny. Thus, despite the Paris fiasco, it was not long before the bubble of her creativity and ambition began inexorably to float to the surface once again.

For a time she lodged with a philosophy student in Manhattan, but began seeing Dan Gilroy more regularly, and before long had moved in to the synagogue in Queens he shared with his younger brother, Ed. 'It was a com-fortable place for her,' Dan explains. 'Here was this girl without work, bum-ming around, not knowing where to go. Here was a place with enough space to do her dancing. There was a washing machine and a dryer. Plus it was in an Italian neighborhood. What more could she want?' he adds, with a smile.

Of course, the fact that, once more, Madonna enjoyed what she has described as some of the best times of her life, was due in no small part to the creative, amusing and generous-spirited personalities of the Gilroy brothers. Born in New York, the sons of a former air force and civil pilot, Dan and Ed discovered music early on. Their first duet, played on their mother's pots and pans, was an inspired ditty that ran:

> Biccy, biccy, biccy, bongo,
> That means 'I love you' in the Congo.

Over the years they had formed a variety of bands with friends, enrolling schoolfriends Gary Burke and Mike Monahan, as well as other friends like Madonna's former lover Norris Burroughs. When Madonna came on the scene, the brothers, as 'Bill and Gill', were playing everything from small downtown clubs to Boy Scout troops, and even Bellevue mental hospital. When they weren't making music, Dan, who had taught painting, sculpture and photography, was a partner in a fashionable Manhattan fabric outlet called Gossamer Wing, while Ed worked full-time counseling families of which a member was in the final stages of terminal illness.

For Madonna, the year she stayed with Dan and Ed Gilroy proved to be a turning point, both creatively and personally. She arrived with desire but no direction, with ambition but little ability, other than as a dancer. By the time she left, she was ready to take on the world. Like Christopher Flynn, Dan Gilroy, twelve years her senior, took on the mantle of her muse and mentor. Just as Flynn had expanded her horizons as a dancer, so Dan opened her eyes to the possibilities of music.

One day he took up his trusty Carlo Robelli acoustic guitar and showed her how to play the simplest chord, an open E. Almost at once she discovered that she was able to run her fingers up and down the frets and sing along to the music she made. 'It was a real eye-opener for her,' Dan recalls. 'She was always impressed by people who write songs and then she realized, "Wow, it's not hard." I remember one night she played her first little thing on the guitar and from then on she just wrote lots of songs.'

Nevertheless, because she was a trained dancer and already had a superb sense of rhythm, Dan believed that it would be best for her to start her musical career on the drums. He showed her the basic techniques and after that she was away, practicing for hour after hour on the drum kit in the basement where she and Dan slept. As Ed Gilroy remarks, 'Dan is like a muse, he brings it out of you. He's a very nurturing, creative guy. When he showed her the drums you could see the light go on in her. She was thinking, "I can't believe all this sound's coming out of me." Then someone joins you with a guitar and all of a sudden, Wow, man, you can create music and song. You've got an instant band.'

The transition from dance to music was not an overnight conversion, however. Madonna still went to dance class in Manhattan, she and Dan religiously running three miles around Flushing Meadows Park every morning before she continued in the studio with endless dance and stretching exercises. Yet something was changing. Under Dan's tutelage, she was beginning to see another world of possibilities and opportunities, an easier way of gaining the applause and, ultimately, adulation she craved without the endless grind of dance rehearsal.

On one occasion they went to see a band called Get Wet run by a young man called Zecca and fronted by the improbably named Cherie Beachfront, a kind of sexy forerunner to Cyndi Lauper. As the singer strutted round the stage in her bustier and crinoline, Madonna watched her severely, arms folded across her chest in mute disapproval. Cherie's voice was passable, her dance steps rudimentary, while the band was just about in tune. Yet for a while they were the talk of the local underground, predicted to be the next big thing. As she stood watching the band, Madonna's thoughts were plain for all to see – 'I can do that.'

A few months later, Zecca was walking through the East Village when he was startled out of his morning reverie by Madonna. Wagging a finger in his face, she yelled, 'I'm going to be somebody and you're going to be nobody.' Then she stalked off leaving Zecca standing in the street, flabbergasted. Her prediction came true; the band's only album bombed, Cherie Beachfront stopped making waves, went into therapy and then married her therapist. As a singer, she was last heard of playing gigs in Boston.

Besides the changes in the direction of Madonna's life, there was, too, the influence of her striking friend Angie Smit, a beautiful Dutch girl whom she had met at her dance class in Manhattan. Before long Madonna discovered that Angie played bass guitar and brought her back to the synagogue to join Ed and Dan in jamming sessions. The quartet coalesced, Angie's presence and relative inexperience as a player giving Madonna more confidence to perform before two far more experienced musicians. So it came about that, in the late summer of 1979, The Breakfast Club was born, so named because they would often rehearse through the night and then go out for breakfast at Army's, a local Italian diner.

The birth of the band, combined with Dan's nurturing nature and the safety and freedom of her synagogue home, proved fertile soil for Madonna's creative nature, which blossomed under these benign influences. They also gave her the security to reach back into herself, to explore and chart territory that was, in emotional terms, both difficult and painful for her. Those charts survive in her early songs.

On the surface she was loud, brash, gutsy and in-your-face. Full of wise-cracks and off-color jokes, she seemed to be one of the guys. Favorite phrases at the time were 'You wish' and 'Special titty.' On one occasion Dan, Madonna, Ed and his Indian girlfriend, Sudha (now his wife), set out on a double date. During the drive into town, Ed reached over to fetch something from the glove compartment. 'What are you looking for, condoms?' Madonna quipped. The brash comment caused an embarrassed intake of breath among the other occupants of the car, the Gilroys acutely aware that Sudha came from a different continent and a different culture, where women did not behave in such a forward manner.

As Dan Gilroy observes of Madonna at this time, 'She took on a tough persona, kind of a wiseguy, not someone who is delicate. But there was another side, very fragile, which she kept pretty much under wraps.' He remembers one night when he awoke to the sound of her sobbing beside him in bed. 'She started crying, a racking, guttural crying, so deep that I couldn't even say, "What's the matter?" She was so involved in the physical experience of crying and it went on for two minutes or more. Nothing was said, there seemed no point. I mean this was way bigger than "I've lost my paycheck." It was, like, elemental.'

Tears were not for tough characters like Madonna, and she was careful to shed them in private. 'When you cry, do you taste your tears?' she once asked Dan. 'I don't want to cry when everyone's looking at me. I can only cry alone because my face gets ugly when I cry. It gets all scringy like a newborn baby's face.' Her deep-seated longing for her mother, her distance from her father, her melodramatic sense of her loneliness and angst, all these fueled her fundamental insecurity, while at the same time feeding the creative processes lying dormant within her.

The lyrics she wrote at that time – raw, uncompromising and self-revelatory – give an insight into a personality much more vulnerable and uncertain than the aggressively exuberant young woman she liked to play for the world. For her, clearly, writing songs mirrored her performance of them; as she herself once said, 'I think when you are singing a song, you are making yourself very vulnerable. It's almost like crying in front of people.' And that, of course, was something she never did.

She began that process of self-revelation almost as soon as she had learned to tap out a rhythm on the drums. Dan gave her a masterclass in writing lyrics, using the sentiments from a letter she had sent him from Paris as the basis for one song, which became a staple of their punk repertoire. Like her performance, years earlier, of the *Godspell* song, song-writing proved another wondrous discovery for Madonna, bringing with it the realization that the everyday events of her life, the thoughts and feelings and memories that she recorded religiously in her diary each night, could form the basis for her lyrics. Struck with the wonder of it, a clutch of songs flowed from her pen and guitar. 'I don't know where they came from, it was like magic,' she once observed. 'I'd write a song every day. I said: "Wow, I must be meant to do this." I played the first things that came out of me.'

Her first effort was swiftly followed by an angry rock song which expressed her sense of alienation from the world. Then came another up-tempo piece with lyrics that dealt with the eternal themes of a love gone wrong and the pain of parting. She co-wrote another song with Dan about a failed romance, this time featuring a strong woman who tries to convince her former lover to pull himself together, reassuring him that she is still his friend and that if he could only be open to her friendship, he would be less unhappy at the parting.

The three-verse song was the first she had written to a track, rather than thought up as she strummed the guitar. It was also the first time she had recorded a song with the backing track playing in her headphones. After she had listened to it being played back she told Ed, 'It sounded good, didn't it? Your voice sounds better in here than real life.'

With their author in the throes of classic juvenile angst, it is not surprising that others of her songs were sad, reflective mid-tempo ballads telling of her loneliness and sense of isolation. In one she speaks rather than sings the song, which, yet again, is about the pain of parting, the references to her mother apparent in her final verse. While an organ plays plaintively in the background, Madonna recalls the empty spaces where her mother used to be, her beauty, and the pain of bereavement and loss.

In another lament, the lyrics are introspective, her apparent insignificance and low sense of self-esteem painfully evident as she sings of feeling displaced and incomplete, always moving on, always alone.

The mournful, self-pitying tone runs through all the verses, Madonna describing herself as being as insignificant as a speck of dust in the breeze or a smear on a glass pane. The chorus maintains the melancholic mood, repeating the lonely refrain that even her tears leave her, and expressing her longing to be rescued from her unhappiness.

Ed Gilroy remembers those early songs: 'She is talking about loss, low self-esteem, things that had been inside her for who knows how long. She had stability here, security here, a positive environment to reach back into those times and try and express herself. Nowadays when you see her she is guarded, there's a lot of holding back. Back then there was no holding back. It was completely out there.'

While these gloomy, introspective lyrics reflected a genuine aspect of her personality, albeit one she kept well concealed, on the surface Madonna was never a melancholy person. If anything, these early songs were a kind of catharsis, therapy that enabled her to address and confront her past before moving on to a more dynamic future. In public she was positive, lively and gregarious, with a generous streak often overlooked by earlier biographers or commentators eager to argue that she used everyone, and particularly those she met during her New York days, as stepping stones to stardom. Dan Gilroy gives the lie to this picture of Madonna as a selfish and callous, even ruthless, manipulator: 'I love people who are passionate about their stuff. She was excited and intense about working and preparing for whatever – yoga, running, music, dance. She would get on her drums and practice like crazy.' When she and Ed performed their first ever duet to his song 'Cold Wind,' she was as enthusiastic about supporting him as he and Dan were about helping her. Ed seconds his brother's view of a warm and open-hearted friend, remarking, 'I liked her generosity in lending herself to what we had here. She was very co-operative and worked so hard on my song. She gave me all her time and effort.'

After weeks of practicing, Dan decided that the moment was right to give his girlfriend a taste of live performance – on the street. Deciding to dress entirely in white for impact, they then hunted around the house for enough change to pay for the subway into Manhattan. With Dan wearing a battery-powered pig-nose amplifier strapped to his chest and Madonna carrying an electric guitar, they stood outside the Gulf and Western building and played their songs to a modest lunchtime audience of office workers. Inevitably, it was not long before the sound of Madonna running through the guitar scales attracted the attention of the police and they were promptly shooed away, still playing as they sauntered off, like wandering minstrels.

Madonna's next gig was rather less frivolous, although still scarcely the big time. Their band, The Breakfast Club, was invited to play a number on Unique New York, a trendy cable-TV station. They would not be on camera, but it was a chance for a live performance, and for their music to be heard more widely. Before they arrived at the Manhattan studio Dan and Madonna had been food shopping, and she walked in with a giant leek under her arm. So while Dan, Ed and Angie played guitars, Madonna accompanied them on the leek, using it as a percussive instrument. When she wasn't strumming the leek, she shook an old electric toaster as a makeshift tambourine.

For Madonna, and for the band, the wheel was beginning to turn. True, its movement seemed almost imperceptible as they moved on to the mundane and, for struggling bands, traditional world of small clubs. Madonna's first ever live gig took place at the now long defunct UK Club, a downtown music venue known as much for its hard drinking as its collection of British memorabilia. They practiced day and night until their nine-song set was perfect. The line-up of the band at this time featured Madonna on drums, Angie on bass guitar, Ed and Dan on vocals and lead guitars. When she wasn't rehearsing or practicing, Madonna spent hours on the phone trying to get something – anything – going for The Breakfast Club. For the UK Club gig she invited agents, record producers and others connected with the music business – none came – as well as friends to help swell the audience. 'It was like a coming-out party,' recalls Ed. Madonna wore a flared cocktail dress she had bought in a thrift store, while Angie stole their after-hours show with her sultry dark-haired beauty and a flimsy black see-through top – and no bra. For most of the set Madonna played drums, only taking the vocal lead for one number, the song she had written under Dan's tutelage. With Mark

Dolengowski, Curtis Zale and so many other friends in the crowd they were assured of a great reception, and at the end both girls remained on stage, soaking up the applause. Meanwhile Dan and Ed, veterans of these one-night gigs, waited for them backstage so that they could come back on to perform an encore. Madonna and Angie, however, spent so long out front that when they eventually came backstage the crowd had drifted to the bar and the moment was lost. It was a sign of their lack of experience, perhaps, but as they loaded their gear into the hired van it was obvious that both girls were enraptured. One successful gig was never going to be enough. Now they wanted more.

Among their next gigs was one at Country Bluegrass Blues or CBGBs, a legendary, if grungy, Lower East Side club that has become a fixture of New York's underground scene, home to bands like Talking Heads, Blondie and The Ramones. While it is a somewhat rough-and-ready dive, the walls plastered with hundreds of posters of previous bands who have performed there down the years, music-industry scouts often hang out there, something the Gilroys were well aware of. When they went on to play, Dan noticed that 'Bleecker' Bob, a leading record-store owner known to have good music-business connections, was in the audience. The Breakfast Club went through the set with all its members playing to impress him. At one stage Madonna left the drums and took the mike to sing a couple of sugary songs written by Dan, and was thrilled when she won an enthusiastic reception from the audience. Then, during a lull between numbers, she let out a huge belch, much to Bleecker Bob's irritation, who told her afterwards that she was 'an amateur.' Dan Gilroy, however, saw that gesture in another light, remarking that 'it was an early indication that she wanted to be the center of attention, no matter what. She had always loved to get noticed, loved to get a reaction, but now this was in a band context.'

With a couple of gigs and a handful of lyrics and songs under her belt, Madonna's musical confidence began to bubble. So too did her impatience. The energy and enthusiasm she had once devoted to dance she now poured into her budding musical career. Every day she was on the phone, contacting clubs, agents, anyone of influence or importance in the music industry, trying to organize gigs, and endlessly searching for that elusive Holy Grail to which all ambitious bands aspire – a record deal. When she wasn't running up Dan's phone bill, she was practicing on the drums. By now Ed's girlfriend Sudha had moved into the converted synagogue and they built what they called the 'Madonna wall' to mask the sound of her drumming, allowing Sudha to study for her nursing exams in relative peace.

Even when she was working at one of the series of jobs she had at this time, music was never far from Madonna's mind. For a time she colored silks at Gossamer Wing, the fabric company in which Dan was a partner. While everyone else enjoyed a smoke or a sandwich during their lunch break, Madonna would sneak into an empty back room and practice her guitar for an hour. That same enthusiasm and will to succeed were evident during rehearsals. 'We took it very, very seriously,' Ed Gilroy remembers. 'Of course there was joking and ranking out, but it was very professional.'

As a result, with the band improving all the time, it was inevitable that her disappointment would be all the keener after the apparent failure of one of their early gigs, held at a sports bar owned by former New York Yankee baseball player Phil Linz. When the quartet went through their routine, which was by now well-rehearsed, polished and tight, the reaction of the audience was one of profound indifference. There was no cheering or clapping, or even whistling and booing as the set ended, just the buzz of a preppy bar crowd more used to watching the game and drinking a beer with their buddies. The Gilroy brothers, who had played all kinds of oddball gigs and curious venues, simply shrugged off the crowd's respectful silence. For Madonna, however, just a few performances into her career, the lack of reaction struck a raw nerve. 'It meant a LOT to her,' Dan remarks, stressing the noun. 'This gig precipitated the break-up of the band in that configuration as much as anything.'

For the truth was that there were other tensions in the band which ran deeper than a miserable reaction to a single performance. While Angie and Madonna were still friends, it was becoming clear that the Dutch dancer was struggling to keep up with the other band members. More of a performer than a musician, she was not as committed as Madonna and the Gilroys, often arriving at rehearsals under-prepared. A parting of the ways was becoming inevitable.

On the surface, however, everything seemed fine, with Ed, Sudha, Dan, Madonna, Angie and her Dutch boyfriend Henry celebrating Thanksgiving together with a very genial dinner in a restaurant at the World Trade Center in November 1979. Indeed, in October, only a few weeks earlier, Angie had played Madonna's 'sex slave' in a low-budget underground film called *A Certain Sacrifice*, a movie that would return to haunt Madonna.

Her journey into film had begun just after she moved in with Dan in July 1979 and was casting around for work. An ad in *Back Stage* magazine, placed by former director Stephen Jon Lewicki, caught her eye. Lewicki was looking for 'a dark, fiery young woman, dominant, with lots of energy, who can dance and is willing to work for no pay.' She sent him a wry two-page résumé and a handful of photographs, including some of the shots taken by Dan Gilroy during their first trip to the Cloisters. Impressed by her open, articulate and amusing letter, Lewicki arranged to meet her in Washington Square Park. His initial instincts were confirmed and he decided to cast her in the role of Bruna, a vengeful dominatrix. The hour-long, erotic art film, made for $20,000 – although it has to be said that it seems much less – features copious nudity as well as violence, including a gruesome rape scene in which Bruna is violated in the bathroom of a sleazy diner in downtown New York. With stilted, cliché-ridden dialogue and overwrought acting, the only feature missing, according to Dan Gilroy, who watched the filming, was 'a laugh track.' (It was, however, a step up from her first ever movie role, when an egg had been 'fried' on her belly button for a school film.) Perhaps mercifully, part way through the filming of *A Certain Sacrifice* Lewicki's cash ran out and the cast dispersed, leaving Madonna more time for her music.

Now, just as Madonna and the band were getting into the groove, Angie Smit, beset by personal problems, seemed to be finding it difficult to commit herself to the band's rehearsal schedule. So when, early in the New Year, former band stalwart Gary 'the Bear' Burke returned from Atlanta looking for a place in another group, it was not long before it was decided that Angie should go. 'It was a tough call,' admits Dan. With Gary joining as bass guitarist and an old schoolfriend of the Gilroys, Mike Monahan, taking over on drums, Madonna was 'promoted' to the front of the stage, now learning the Farfisa keyboard with the help of Dan and a teach-yourself book.

The change in the dynamics of the band soon became apparent. Just a few short months previously, Madonna had auditioned her songs before Ed and Dan Gilroy. Now Ed was singing his material before his brother and Madonna. 'I would play a song and they would look at each other and go: "Naaah." It was like being found guilty in front of the Politburo,' Ed recalls.

The issue was as old as rock and roll itself – control. Now the questions were not about where they would play, or what songs would make up their set, but about who was going to front the band, and whose material was going to be used. The addition of Gary and Mike had given the band a much tighter sound, with Dan, Ed, and Madonna each singing three songs in any nine-song set. Yet even so, Madonna pressed continually to place more of her own material. The discussions would continue long after rehearsals were over, and Madonna and Dan often talked of changing the configuration of the act during their early-morning jogs.

There were, too, other changes in evidence. With Angie gone, Madonna was now the band's only woman member. Content to play the sexy tomboy, she was still not above using her feminine wiles in her attempts to exert influence. On one occasion she purposely spilled water on her blouse so that it became semi-transparent. Mike and Gary were transfixed. 'So suddenly

Madonna's left breast was controlling the rehearsal,' notes Dan dryly. 'Effectively, that meant Madonna was in charge.'

Nonetheless, even amid this creative tension, the band was moving forward. They were now playing regular gigs at CBGBs and other downtown clubs, and had garnered a smattering of favorable reviews in local listings sheets. As a result a band meeting was called, at which it was decided that the new Breakfast Club would record a demo tape to send out to local clubs as a kind of calling card. During a break in the recording session for that tape, Madonna and Gary Burke sat in the alleyway by the side of the synagogue and discussed the future. To Burke, her ambition was plain to see. 'Oh, I so want to be famous, I want to be famous,' she repeated, hugging her knees with the strength of her need. She wanted to equal or outstrip her musical heroines, as Gary Burke recalls: 'She loved it when people compared her to Debbie Harry from Blondie, although the woman she absolutely worshipped was Chrissie Hynde of The Pretenders. She thought she was so cool.'

After a sell-out gig at Bo's Space in the spring of 1980 her dreams seemed to be coming a little closer to reality. With Madonna dancing around the stage and the group dressed in white outfits, The Breakfast Club seemed to have all the makings of a New Wave band that had arrived. For Madonna, though, there was an additional fillip. After the gig, a scout from Co Co Records took her aside and suggested that she would do better fronting a band on her own. He was not alone in that view. Both Gary and Mike were as keen as she to sign with a record company, and felt that their only chance was if Madonna led the band. Their judgment was, however, also influenced by the fact that they were utterly infatuated with her, as both men have admitted.

When, in the summer of that year, the band went on a weekend break to a country retreat, owned by Mike Monahan's family, at Candlewood Lake in Connecticut, it marked a turning point. The excursion started badly, their car breaking down on the drive from New York. While the car was fixed, Madonna made the best of a bad job, playing a guitar and singing at the top of her voice, much to the amusement of passing motorists. Then she stood by the side of the highway, holding up a sign that read 'Wrench.' A couple stopped to help, having mistaken the word on her notice for 'Wench.' It was, perhaps, a small, symbolic indicator of the track her future career would follow.

When they finally reached the house, they cooled off with a swim in the lake before Madonna cooked them all 's'mores,' a glutinous mixture of graham crackers, marshmallows and chocolate, which they ate by the campfire while Gary serenaded them on the guitar. Beneath the surface calm, however, the tensions were discernible, with whispered conversations and huddled meetings between band members, a tangled skein of the professional and the emotional.

Back in New York, rehearsals became more businesslike rather than fun, more of a job than rock and roll. Then, at a 'testy' band meeting, Mike, Gary and Madonna argued that (as rumor had it) with Blondie's star on the wane, a group fronted by a good-looking woman would have more chance of securing a record deal. They added that Madonna should sing most of the songs, effectively sidelining the Gilroy brothers. It was not a route either Dan or Ed wished to take. As far as they were concerned they wanted to continue to write and perform their own work. When a half-and-half compromise was rejected, the band was thrown into turmoil. One thing was clear, however, a breakup was inevitable. For Madonna there was an additional, emotional complication, since intertwined with her own ambitions was her relationship with Dan. Yet even in this she was lucky, for while they were lovers and friends, they had realized from the start that theirs could never be a long-term relationship. So as she and Dan cooled off after their daily run one morning, she explained to him that she had to go, to follow her heart and her ambition. Dan remembers the moment with his customary generosity. 'It was sad, sweet and rather poignant. She did it rather well and I have always appreciated that. There had always been the sense that she was passing through. Now she was moving on.'

As a breakup, both professional and emotional, it was as civilized as these things can be. The quintet remained good friends, the new band even practicing in the synagogue from time to time. Madonna took her suitcase to a pleasant and leafy neighborhood called Douglaston on the North Shore, where Mike Monahan was renting a room from his friend Larry Christiansen. For a time she and Mike were lovers, Madonna never long without a male protector and admirer in her life. Besides rehearsing at the synagogue, the new three-piece combo, who called themselves 'Madonna and the Sky,' found rehearsal space in Queens and Chelsea, although for the most part they used Larry's garage in Douglaston. Here Madonna recorded three songs, using a $300 Rickenbacker guitar given to her by her adoring new boyfriend.

The safe neighborhood was also a quiet neighborhood, and it was not long before complaints from local residents forced the garage-based band to look for new quarters. They settled on a tenth-floor rehearsal space in the Music Building, a noisy, seedy hell hole on West 39th Street, used by several dozen bands for rehearsals and recording. The place was as dangerous as it was dirty; drug addicts lurked in the entrance hall, and the hallways smelled of urine. 'It was awful, loud and disgusting,' according to Dan Gilroy. 'The kind of place you only went to rehearse and got out as quickly as you could.'

They shared the space with a Long Island band called Buddy Love, which was managed by a young man known only as Mark. He had seen Madonna and the Sky play at their one and only gig at the Eighties club, and now offered to look after their interests as well. It was not a happy collaboration. Mark and Gary both had designs on Madonna, while Mike, her current boyfriend, was finding it increasingly difficult to juggle a full-time job as an insurance agent for Equitable Life with nighttime duties as the band's drummer. He would leave the air-conditioned comfort of his midtown office and rush down to the insalubrious neighborhood and grungy ambience of the Music Building, where Madonna and Gary were waiting for him. After a quick change, he would wearily begin rehearsals, knowing that Madonna would be on his back if his drumming did not come up to her expectations. After a few weeks it became clear that he had had enough of Madonna's constant criticism, the endless commuting, and the seedy atmosphere of the Music Building. One evening he arrived at the studio and announced, 'Sorry guys, I can't do this any more.' Then he walked out.

Down but not out, the two remaining band members advertised for a drummer. In the meantime, Madonna used the synagogue to phone Steve Bray, her old boyfriend in Michigan, to ask if he would like to join the band. He had been at the back of her mind ever since it had become clear that Mike Monahan was thinking of leaving, and she was delighted when he accepted, arriving in New York in early November 1980. She promptly took him off to a Talking Heads concert in Central Park before he had even unpacked his bags.

Fired by ambition, Madonna was determined to make a success of the new band. And it was at another Talking Heads concert, this time at Radio City, that the faithful Gary Burke witnessed and, for the first time, really understood her desperate desire for fame. He had bought two tickets for the gig in the forlorn hope that he could somehow kindle a romance. Soon after the concert began, she left her seat and went to stand in front of the stage, watching enthralled as David Byrne and company went through their paces. Afterwards they met up with Steve Bray, she and their new drummer dancing down Broadway and serenading onlookers with the chant, 'We want to be in the clique, we want to be in the clique.' As Gary now reflects, 'It was clear that fame was more important to her than the music. She had a real hunger for success, and she wanted that success *yesterday.*'

In Bray she found a colleague who was as relentless in the pursuit of perfection and, ultimately, glory as she was. 'His drumming gave a huge lift to the energy of the band,' Dan Gilroy recalls. 'He was a real drill sergeant during rehearsals, as soon as the song ended he would want to do another take and start the count down.' Bray soon realized, however, that Madonna's skills as lead guitarist were limited and they advertised for a new player. Madonna traveled to Brooklyn to audition an Italian named Vinny, who lasted for a few weeks before Bray, who didn't like his playing, fired him.

Bray, a born-again Christian, could be every bit as tough and stubborn as Madonna. When Mark eventually got them a gig, the drummer put his foot down at the idea of using the name Madonna and the Sky, deeming it to be sacrilegious (ironically, this was precisely the reason why Mike Monahan had liked the name in the first place). Madonna caved in, the manager coming up with the name The Millionaires, which later transmuted to Emmy, Dan's nickname for Madonna.

The fortunes of The Millionaires ebbed and flowed swiftly and dramatically. No sooner had they recruited a drummer and a new lead guitar than they lost their manager. Somehow Madonna was maneuvered out of her Music Building lease, leaving the band Buddy Love in sole possession. When they were evicted, Gary, who blamed the machinations of their manager – and Love – for the loss of their rehearsal space, angrily confronted Mark in the street outside the Music Building, watched by an embarrassed Madonna. His outburst ensured the departure of their manager.

The comings and goings continued apace. Resourceful as ever, Madonna persuaded Brian Syms, a young musician from Virginia who rented a studio on the fifth floor of the Music Building, to give them rehearsal space. As a quid pro quo Syms took over from Vinny as Emmy's lead guitarist. In the meantime, they borrowed a studio in Room 1002, home to Regina and the Red Hots, an up-and-coming band that had played with the Irish group U2. On November 30, 1980, Emmy recorded a four-song demo tape to send out to clubs and record companies. This time they were going for a Chrissie Hynde rather than a Blondie kind of feel to their music. At last they got a break, hired to appear at the Botany Talk House a couple of weeks before Christmas. They had a group photograph taken, put up billboards and seeded the festive audience with friends and admirers. The gig went well, and Madonna left to spend Christmas with her family back in Rochester in good spirits.

Her mood did not last long. For her, that midwinter proved to be especially bleak. Perhaps it resulted from the fact that she had spent a couple of weeks back home without having to worry about keeping warm or where the next meal was coming from. Perhaps it was because she was now living in an insanitary and dangerous loft space just round the corner from the Music Building and was forced to wash in public bathrooms. Or perhaps it came about because of yet another setback for Emmy, a band held together by hope and dreams and not much else. But whatever the reason, even her iron resolve and physical toughness failed her.

One morning in January Gary Burke came round to her dismal West 37th Street loft to find Madonna lying, fully clothed, on the floor, curled up in a fetal position and sobbing uncontrollably. It was the middle of a vicious cold snap in New York, and with the thermometer well below freezing the heating and water in her building had finally given up the unequal struggle. She had no money, no job, no prospects and, to crown it all, was coming down with the flu. 'Madonna was a whisker away from throwing in the towel,' recalls Gary. 'She was going to go home, back to Detroit. For a girl with such burning ambition it shows you how low she had got.'

As her tears continued to flow, the Bear knelt down, gave her a hug and told her that everything would work out just fine. He knew, however, as she did, that the town she had dreamed of taking had finally tamed her.

Chapter Six
Madonna, Max's, Midnight

S HE WAS THE SEXY QUEEN of underground New York, gyrating on stage in ripped stockings, her slinky bodystocking held together with safety pins, her makeup and lipstick as loud as her words and movements were lewd.

This was not Madonna. Her name – at least for stage purposes – was Cherry Vanilla. A former publicist for David Bowie, she was one of the first of a new wave of women performers to win fame for being themselves, rather than for being some rock star's girlfriend. By the time Madonna arrived in New York, Cherry Vanilla had been joined by singers Patti Smith and Debbie Harry, the latter once a waitress at Max's Kansas City, the downtown venue where, for a time, Cherry reigned supreme. Part of her appeal, and her success, lay in her desire to shock; a worshiper at the altar of sex and sexual freedom. She had published *Pop Tart*, a controversial book of black-and-white photographs of herself in a variety of revealingly exotic outfits and compromising poses.

As the 1970s drew to a close, the hip New York underground scene was in a state of creative flux. It was an exciting, vibrant time when the social, cultural and ethnic boundaries that had formerly defined high art and music, gay and black, poetry and rock, graffiti and punk, Latino and white, were beginning to be broken down. The buzz phrase 'death to disco' became a shorthand for the artistic backlash against 'stale' stadium rock, 'staid' radio playlists and 'blinkered' uptown art houses. And it was in clubs like Max's, CBGBs, and the Roxy that the leading lights who would provoke, excite and, ultimately, define a generation came to mix and mingle. Ever responsive to trends, New York's underground became a melting pot for the wealthy, the wild, the witty, the beautiful and the plain weird.

In this heady milieu, painters and sculptors, the Andy Warhol crowd among them, rubbed shoulders with drag queens or punk stars like Malcolm MacLaren, or with The Ramones and The New York Dolls, while Truman Capote might be found swapping anecdotes with Freddie Mercury of Queen, or David Byrne of Talking Heads. 'It was a very special time that has not been duplicated since,' recalls Vito Bruno, manager of the Roxy. 'We were all very much anti-Studio 54. They were elitist, while we believed that it was what's in your bones rather than what's on your bones that gave you entry; kids with sparkle, rubbing shoulders with Warhol and Mick Jagger.'

Looking back, Jimi LaLumia, a one-time Max's headliner and habitué, describes the scene as 'a psychotic cabaret.' 'You always had the sense in the air that things were going to happen,' he remarks. 'You would have a young Debbie Harry asking you for a light, Johnny Thunders at the bar and Cherry Vanilla teetering by on gigantic spike heels. If Paul McCartney was in town, a visit to the club was almost obligatory.'

At the time, Madonna was just another youthful face in the crowd, soaking up the ambience and watching the whirl go round. 'I'm sure this chick from the Midwest was absolutely bedazzled and wanted to be part of the scene,' recalls LaLumia. 'At that time she was just wanting to squeeze in. If we'd only known how she would end up, we would have been nicer to her.'

She was not to remain a nameless face in the crowd for long. In March 1981, Max's Kansas City was the scene of one of the first gigs performed by Madonna and her band, Emmy. Ironically enough, it was also their last. After weeks of arm-twisting and pleading, bass guitarist Gary Burke had managed to secure the band a spot at the club and this had led to a second booking. During that gig there was only one person in the crowded club whom Madonna wanted to impress – a crop-haired, lesbian, fellow Italian-American, named Camille Barbone. Born on the same day as the singer, August 16, albeit eight years earlier, and brought up in the same neighborhood of Corona, Queens, where Madonna had lived with the Gilroy brothers, Camille had one burning ambition in life. Unlike Madonna, however, she didn't want mass adulation. She simply wanted to manage the biggest rock star on the planet. As she watched Madonna perform that night, Camille knew that she had discovered her dream ticket. Her verdict was simple and uncompromising: great face, dramatic dancer, lousy band.

The two women had first met a few weeks earlier in the elevator of the Music Building. Madonna knew that Camille and her business partner, Adam Alter, ran Gotham Records, the only recording studio in the Music Building, and that, if she attracted their notice, it might lead to opportunities for her and Emmy. The way she grabbed their attention was nothing if not gauche, but it was also intriguing: she flattered the bearded Alter by saying he looked like John Lennon, and later confronted Camille in the elevator and posed a series of *non sequiturs*. 'Do you get it yet?' was one question she threw at a bemused Barbone, before stalking off. It was a classic Madonna tactic, employing that rare ability to intrigue, shock and captivate, and with a touch of the apparently wide-eyed wonder she had deployed before Pearl Lang at the dance festival.

By then, Madonna was living off her wits – and bags of paprika popcorn. In January 1981, when the heating in her West 37th Street loft had failed during the cold snap and Gary Burke had found her lying curled up on the floor, she had considered leaving New York and going home. Instead, sick and suffering, she had picked up the phone and called Dan Gilroy, plaintively asking if she could return to the synagogue for a while, to recuperate. She and Dan had remained friends after their breakup the previous summer, and he was happy to help her out. Indeed, a few weeks later, she sent him a home-made Valentine's card, calling him the 'big noodle head of my dreams.'

She was nothing if not resilient, however. After only a few days, she forsook the warmth and security of the synagogue and headed back downtown, desperate to keep Emmy together. 'I could feel the band breaking at the seams,' Gary Burke remembers. So, too, could Madonna. With her loft room virtually uninhabitable, she moved in with Gary, Steve Bray and Brian Syms, sharing a cramped, one-room apartment near the Music Building. Although it was far from ideal, after Gary secured the Max's gig, the four of them at least knew they had a goal to work toward. In their hearts they all also understood that the performance at Max's would make or break the band. They rehearsed constantly, Madonna sometimes sleeping over in the studio space. It was a hand-to-mouth existence, one step removed from Skid Row. She earned a little money by life-modeling, mainly for the painter Anthony Panzera in his SoHo studio, and she had now become adept at scrounging meals from friends and acquaintances. From time to time, Dan's friend Curtis Zale would come by with a couple of bags of cast-off clothes for her, along with his mother's discarded makeup.

It seemed that, as with her earlier decisions to leave college, to give up dance, to return from Paris, and then to leave Dan, Madonna had chosen risk over safety, suffering over comfort, apparently bent on enduring her own artistic Calvary. The most pointed example of this tendency toward martyrdom was when her father, then earning a substantial salary in the defense industry, visited her in New York in the fall of 1978 and offered her financial help, which she rejected. 'It was as if she was giving him and her family permission to write her off,' observes Camille Barbone. 'She was very much into the drama and romance of going without for the sake of her art.'

So when Madonna cornered Barbone in the elevator of the Music Building, it was not only a last, desperate throw of the dice for her and Emmy, but also yet another indicator of her absolute determination to be recognized. Camille agreed to see Madonna in concert at Max's Kansas City and went to watch the band rehearse a couple of times in the Music Building. Unfortunately, she missed the first gig at Max's because of a migraine. The outraged singer stormed into Camille's studio and verbally attacked her, complaining that she was just like other potential backers who had let her down. It was a performance as aggressive – and risky – as it was desperate. Madonna was rapidly running out of options in her self-imposed quest for stardom.

Fortunately, the management at Max's had been sufficiently impressed by Emmy to invite them back for a repeat performance a few days later. The club, which had its own independent record label, had its own ideas for the band. So when Camille turned up to watch the gig, Madonna pulled out all the stops, dancing on tables and cavorting with patrons as she went through the five-song set. She had even been to see her old boyfriend, Mark Dolengowski, and had him cut her auburn hair and give her a more 'punk' style like that of her heroine, Chrissie Hynde.

After her set, Camille brought Madonna a cup of tea with honey to soothe her throat, raw from the performance, and asked her if she wanted a manager. The tousle-haired girl, still sweaty after performing, threw her arms around the older woman and shouted: 'Yeah.' Minutes later, the manager of Max's came to congratulate her and promptly offered the band a coveted record deal. In twenty-four hours they had changed from nobodies to rising stars. Yet even as Madonna caught her breath, she began to realize that she faced a dilemma.

Barbone made it clear immediately that she was only interested in Madonna as a singer with a backup band and not Emmy. As well as offering to mastermind her career, Madonna's potential new manager, aware of the squalid conditions in which she was living, promised to fund an apartment of her own, give her a salary of $100 a week and find her part-time work. Madonna had to make a decision: to strike out on her own, or to stick with the band that she had helped to found, and which had just been offered a record deal. In a matter of days, and without telling the other band members of her decision, she chose to go with Camille, signing a contract with Gotham Records on March 17, 1981 – Saint Patrick's Day. Afterwards they celebrated with pints of green Guinness.

As she toasted her new artiste, Camille believed she was on the way to making her dream of managing the biggest star in the world a reality. It was a dream that rapidly turned into a living nightmare, a year-long emotional rollercoaster ride of drink, fights and, ultimately, a nervous breakdown. Her first mistake was to try to tame Madonna. Her second was to fall in love with her.

In Camille's view Madonna was a rough-cut artistic diamond who needed careful polishing in order to shine. Her stage act was all wrong, disguising her greatest asset – herself. In performance she had an adequate, although not a great voice, and hid herself behind a guitar she could hardly play. For her part, Camille instinctively understood what Madonna, and the world, would later come to appreciate: that the key to the singer's power and appeal was in the whole package – dance, movement, song and music. In short, Madonna's latent energy and charisma had to be released.

Camille's first order of business, within days of Madonna signing the contracts, was to fire Madonna's backup band, a brisk procedure that left Steve Bray, Gary Burke and Brian Syms feeling rather sore and used. A few days after the breakup of Emmy, Gary confronted Madonna in the Music Building and yelled at her, accusing her of 'betrayal.' Later they made up, Madonna often visiting her three former partners in the apartment she had once shared with them to ask for musical advice and tuition.

At first, Madonna was very much in awe of the older, more experienced Camille and initially deferred to her judgment, even though she was keen to continue her unusual collaboration with Bray. Camille delved into her contact book and brought in an array of top-class musicians to audition for a new band. It was a process that took months. Session players like Jeff Gottlieb, John Kaye, David Frank and Jack Soni, musicians who had played with artists of the caliber of Dire Straits and David Bowie, jammed with the young Madonna. Moreover, just as she was flattered and impressed by this level of musical interest, they, in turn, recognized her potential.

As well as taking charge of Madonna's musical career, Camille set about re-ordering her day-to-day existence. Besides paying her $100 a week and finding her a job as a house cleaner, she gave her unlimited access to her studio, where Madonna endlessly wrote lyrics and practiced her music.

Madonna's new management also helped find her a place to live, a shabby, one-room apartment on West 30th. This arrangement did not last long, however, for she was forced to move a few weeks later, after a break-in. It appeared that she had been stalked, the intruder climbing in through a window and stealing only a packet of nude photographs from one of her numerous photographic sessions. While Madonna, cavalier about her own safety despite her earlier experience, was happy to stay on in her room on 30th Street, Camille and Adam Alter thought otherwise and installed her in an uptown apartment off Riverside Drive.

As the months passed, it was clear that Camille had become much more than a business manager. She was Madonna's mother, her best friend, and her guide, the heroine who had come to her rescue at a time of need. Upon Camille, eight years her senior, Madonna exerted a continual fascination and a seductive charm. Camille found herself falling in love with her – an affair which, although never consummated, profoundly altered the dynamics of their professional relationship. While Alter provided the funding, he admits that he too was drawn into the intensity of this new 'family.'

'There was this raw sexuality about her,' Camille recalls. 'The attraction was there, I mean TOTALLY. But you don't go there with someone like Madonna because she controls people through her sexuality. It was taboo. It isn't true that we were lovers, but was I in love with her? Yeah! It was a crazy kind of thing, protection, maternal, playing with each other in a very flirtatious way. Was she in love with me? In her own way, I think so. She loves strong women and I was her hero. She loves handsome, powerful, mothering women. Always did.'

For a long time they were an inseparable double act, going to the movies together, scouring the thrift stores, going out to clubs and restaurants and attending business meetings where they would work the room and, as Camille puts it, 'kick ass.' They went out to Fire Island that summer, Camille taking her lover, Madonna bringing her on-off boyfriend of the moment, artist Ken Compton. Like a doting parent, Camille constantly indulged her younger friend, bringing food for her to the studio, lending her money, organizing her contraception, taking her for surgery to have impacted wisdom teeth removed, and bandaging her up when she cut her finger during her work cleaning houses.

Aware of Camille's feelings toward her, Madonna constantly teased and tormented her would-be lover, at the end of one concert stripping off and then asking Camille to towel her down; on another occasion deliberately making out with a girlfriend, Janice Galloway, her old friend from Ann Arbor days, in the back seat as Camille drove them in her car.

Yet although the sexual tension placed Madonna in a position of power and heightened the intensity of their relationship, Camille could smell the fear at the heart of the young girl's being. Her hunger for fame and love was matched only by her low self-esteem, her self-abasement leading to a chronic unwillingness to accept just how special and different she was. Camille came to realize that the more outrageous Madonna's behavior, the greater her terror of failure.

So, for example, when she went out for dinner in a Japanese restaurant with music scouts from the prestigious William Morris agency, she deliberately let out a huge belch during the main course. (It has to be said that belching does seem to have been a favorite attention-seeking ploy of hers.) The scouts dismissed it as obnoxious behavior, but Camille saw it as a nervous reaction from a young woman fearful of rejection. On another occasion, Madonna walked into Camille's office while she was on the telephone and proceeded to shave her armpits in front of her. She told Camille that she had to shave at that very moment and as the only mirror in the place was in Camille's office, she had had to come in to use it. When Camille asked her to leave, she smirked and flounced out. 'At that moment it was meant to shock,' recalls Camille. 'In reality she was afraid that the [telephone] conversation might be about her and whether or not she was going to make it.'

Her belligerence and rudeness colored her working relationship with her acting coach, Mira Rostova, a Russian émigrée, to whom she was sent by Camille. It was a short-lived education. Madame Rostova, who had worked with Montgomery Clift and other Hollywood greats, considered the time she spent with Madonna thoroughly disagreeable, remarking, 'She was vulgar and very unladylike. Her acting was not particularly interesting.' As with her clashes over her dancing with Pearl Lang, Madonna's attitude was an affirmation of her fear of failure, with her always preferring to explain away any difficulties in terms of personal differences, rather than admitting to any professional inadequacy of her own.

Just how desperate she was for the limelight became apparent to director Ed Steinberg when, in 1981, he was shooting a music video called *Konk*, in which Madonna and her friend Martin Burgoyne appeared with dozens of other dancers. As he panned the camera around the dance floor, Steinberg realized to his amusement that Madonna was doing all she could to get into every single shot. He calmly explained to the fame-hungry youngster that he wanted to include more than one dancer.

Camille understood Madonna's fears and in general tolerated her behavior, partly because she was perfectly well aware that too strong an objection would most likely drive the singer to greater excesses. She drew the line, though, when Madonna sprayed her beloved pet poodles, Norman and Mona, orange and pink respectively, and then stenciled the words 'Sex' and 'Fuck' on their colored coats. Camille also remembers a photo shoot for designer Norma Kamali, at which Madonna wore rosary beads and a cross that hung down to hover over her waistline. 'See, Camille,' she yelled. 'Even God wants to get into my pants.' This bratty behavior manifested itself again and again, typified perhaps by an incident when they were waiting in line outside the trendy Underground Club. Impatient as ever, Madonna shouted at the doorman, 'Remember me? – We made out the other night.' Camille took her home, scolding her like an errant schoolgirl and pointing out that she had neither reason nor need to behave in such a fashion.

For behind the brash image lay a sensitive, intelligent, yet uncertain young woman; a starkly honest girl who wrote a stream of raw, self-exposing lyrics in a composition book with black-and-white marbled covers, songs about being hungry, penniless, hurt, abandoned and unloved; a young woman who loved to read poetry, and who was fascinated by the activities of the Bloomsbury Group, a loose assemblage of British artists and writers influential during the 1920s and 1930s; a contemplative soul who enjoyed the peace of downtown churches, and loved to wander around the Museum of Modern Art and other galleries to gain a greater understanding of the creative process. As Camille observes, 'This was not some trashy kid who needed to stick her tongue down a doorman's throat at Studio 54.' She also noted, however, that Madonna did need time and encouragement if she was to absorb the message that she was no longer just an aspiring run-of-the-mill pop singer, but a star in the making. An evening at the Ritz Club watching Tina Turner strut her stuff across the stage, utterly in command of herself and the audience, gave Madonna an insight into how it could be for her one day. Even so, Camille adds, 'It took many hours of stroking and building up her ego for her to believe it and own that idea.'

Madonna still had a long journey ahead of her, although by the spring of that year, she was making progress. By now, several session musicians had been signed, although Madonna, perhaps typically, complicated things by having a brief affair with the new drummer, Bob Riley. Since Barbone did not approve of love affairs between band members, Riley was unceremoniously fired. As it happened, that suited Madonna, who had been lobbying for her own candidate for drummer, her old college boyfriend Steve Bray, who was still working in the Music Building.

With Bray on drums, Jon Gordon on lead guitar, John Kaye on bass guitar, John Bonamassa on keyboard and Madonna on vocals, the revamped group made its debut at Max's Kansas City, followed by gigs at Cartoon Alley, Chase Park and other downtown clubs. Given these modest successes, and even though she was still serving her musical apprenticeship, Madonna was by now taking herself very seriously indeed. On one occasion she shared the billing with an eight-piece combo fronted by Michael Musto, now a *Village Voice* columnist. Even though The Must were the first act on that night, Madonna spent so long on elaborate sound checks that Musto's band, left without time for practice, had to go on unrehearsed. Nor would she agree to share the dressing room set aside by the management for both performers. As far as she was concerned, only one person had top billing – Madonna. Musto never so much as saw his face in the dressing-room mirror.

Yet even though she was guaranteed regular gigs – and a steady income – Madonna constantly itched to move faster, even beginning to wonder whether she should have signed the record deal offered by Max's Kansas City.

If the wait seemed a long one, it proved to have been worth it, for the longed-for breakthrough came in June 1981 with the signing of a deal with John Roberts and Susan Planer of Media Sound to record a demo tape in their 57th Street studio. This was a real coup: Planer and Roberts were renowned in the music industry, one of their most famous feats being the part they had played in organizing the legendary Woodstock festival. Their recording studio, an old church that had once been home to the Hungarian classical composer Béla Bartók, had been used by innumerable artists, from Frank Sinatra to The Beatles.

Madonna was thrilled with the deal, and honored to be working where musical greats had gone before. The week that she, Camille and the band spent in the church in August 1981 was probably the most creative and happy of their relationship; the experience tamed her impatience, and in breaks from recording she would sit quietly reading or reciting poetry to her friends.

With Jon Gordon and Alec Head producing, and Steve Bray on drums, Madonna laid down four tracks. Typically, the lyrics dealt with her life, particularly her love life. She had written one of them for her lover at that time, Ken Compton, although he drove her crazy by employing her own tactic of playing hard to get. Her relationship with Camille featured in another, in which Madonna lamented her hunger and poverty. She had also written a sheaf of other songs, in one of which she described herself as a bad angel. Few of these songs featured on the demo tape, however; indeed, it took all their time to lay down the first four tracks.

Under Bray's influence, Madonna was beginning to follow the R and B and disco route, moving away from the punk style of the Gilroy boys. Yet she was learning all the time, absorbing styles and constantly making changes on her own. The notion that Camille Barbone tried to make her sing mainstream rock like Pat Benatar, rather than gritty punk, is wide of the mark – Madonna was, and is, her own woman, and however much her style may be a fusion of other influences, it was not dictated to her, by Camille or anyone else. At the end of an exhilarating week the whole group took off for Fire Island to celebrate the joint birthdays of Camille and Madonna, lazing in the sun and tucking into lobster and salad on the beach.

For a few weeks, their salad days continued. Madonna now had a modest but loyal following in New York, and evidence of her steady progression mounted when she and her band were hired to open for another group, Over Easy, at US Blues, a biker club on Long Island. The band's leader, Bill Lomuscio, was a close friend of Camille. Before Madonna was hired, Camille gave him a friendly warning, telling him that the new singer was so good that her appearance would spell the end of his time as a headliner at the club. Sure enough, Madonna wowed the hard-to-please audience and Over Easy were left in her shade. The feisty young singer was now on the way up, earning $800 a gig.

Lomuscio bore no hard feelings; in fact, he took over from Adam Alter as joint manager with Camille and raised $10,000 to propel Madonna's launch into the big time. The plan was to showcase her demo tape to record-company executives, in the hope of securing an album deal and finally clawing back some of the investment in Madonna. As part of this strategy, Barbone set about trying to create a buzz around her protégée. She gave $20 to a trio of breakdancers she spotted in Times Square to spin and groove while Madonna performed at a nearby club, and before each gig she paid teenage girls to dress in Madonna's charity-shop-chic style. At the same time, she invited music agents to come and watch her girl in action.

Ironically, the goal Camille had been working toward all her life proved in the end to be her downfall. The early signs came in September 1981, when Madonna was asked to renew her management contract. She prevaricated, complaining that her career was not moving fast enough. However, after she was told that a projected showcase gig at the fashionable Underground Club, planned for November, could only go ahead if she was under contract, she finally signed an extension to her contract.

At this time Madonna's relationship with Camille, always stormy, was beginning to spiral out of control. Both extremely strong-willed, their disagreements became fiercer and more acrimonious, band members often walking out of the room during their catfights. Looking back, Camille admits that she tried to force her stubborn client in directions she did not want to go. Worse still, in trying to cope with the pressures, both emotional and professional, of dealing with a woman she loved, who was on the verge of success, Camille began to drink heavily. Evenings were the worst. During one particularly vicious row, Camille broke her hand when she smashed it into a wall in fury and frustration. After this display of temper, Madonna snarled: 'You've fallen off your pedestal now,' and stalked off into the night. As Camille candidly admits, 'I'm a nasty drunk and most of the fights and insanity would ensue then. I have to admit that she could no longer rely on me.' The woman Madonna had once idolized could no longer command her respect.

To make matters worse, as Camille's drinking grew heavier, the buzz around Madonna was getting louder. Club managers, college promoters, record scouts were all beating a path to her door. Concerned that Camille was missing opportunities, Madonna started seeing music-industry executives behind her back, further damaging the already frayed relations between them. 'I was under siege and didn't know how to handle it,' admits Camille. 'I tried to hold her tighter, which was a big mistake.'

A showdown meeting between Madonna and co-manager Bill Lomuscio ended with the nascent star tearfully promising to abide by their contract and to stop pursuing her solo agenda. Inevitably, however, the truce did not last long. Madonna could not resist using her sensuality, street savvy and musical experience to seduce any number of record-company executives into thinking that she was theirs for the taking. They treated her to dinner or concert tickets, while she kept them intrigued and excited, teasing them with the prospect of delivering more.

Much now depended on the crucial gig at the Underground Club in November. Invitations were sent to dozens of movers and shakers in the music business, Madonna appeared in a fashion spread in the influential *Village Voice*, and the club was decked out with exotic flowers for the performance. As a result, she found Curtis Zale's well-meant but ill-timed donation, just before the gig, of another couple of bags of old clothes for her, not at all in keeping with the rather more hip image she was now trying to convey.

It was well into the early hours of the morning by the time Madonna performed and the only music executive who had stayed long enough to watch her set was Paul Atkinson of Columbia Records. He had listened to her demo tape and was considering whether to offer her a deal, and if so, a single or album deal. After the gig he was still undecided and, like several other executives from rival companies, decided to hold fire until he had seen and heard more material.

The band, meanwhile, went from strength to strength. On New Year's Eve they won their biggest break to date when they opened for David Johnason of The New York Dolls at a club called My Father's Place. On stage, Madonna's act was seductive and sensual, leading her younger sister Paula, who was watching from the wings, to berate Camille Barbone for sexually exploiting her. Fresh from Madonna's old college, the University of Michigan, Paula had clearly never heard that sex and drugs made rock and roll. The audience, however, liked what they saw. Madonna pranced off the stage, all smiles, ready for her next big date – the New Year's Eve party hosted by a recently launched television company that broadcast only pop programs and music. The fledgling company was called MTV. She arrived in a limo and David Johnason, who recognized her star potential, escorted her all evening, introducing her to many of the big names on the music scene.

Elsewhere, however, matters were coming to a head. The fact that her showcase performance at the Underground Club had not immediately yielded results was, in Madonna's eyes, a further sign of the weakness of her management team. How much longer must she wait? By now she was being actively, if secretly, courted by agents like Rob Prince of the powerful William Morris agency. He suggested that she should privately discuss her future with music attorney Jay Kramer, who then represented Billy Joel, among other big names. As a result, in February 1982 Camille and Bill found themselves invited to a meeting with the high-powered attorney, ostensibly to discuss Madonna's future. The night before, Madonna had called her manager and said, 'You're a bitch, I'm a bitch. We work well together and we can still work together.' Little did Camille realize that Madonna was offering her a job, albeit as her publicity manager. Even less did she realize that the brief call was to be their last conversation.

The legal meeting lasted precisely five minutes. While Madonna sat silently on a sofa, Kramer told Camille and her partner that the singer no longer required their services. When Camille protested that Madonna had a legally binding contract, he told her that they were terminating it. Stunned, Bill and Camille walked out, resolved to take legal action against their mutinous client. This led to an endless series of legal wrangles, drawn out over the years, that has left Madonna's songs from this period, the so-called 'Gotham Tapes', in limbo with regard to copyright and ownership issues. A decade later, Barbone secured a modest settlement from her former client.

For Camille, the emotional fallout was, if anything, even more catastrophic, akin to experiencing a sudden death or a brutal divorce. 'It was like the breakup of a love affair,' recalls Camille. 'We were a team, a marriage that in better circumstances would have thrived.' She suffered a nervous breakdown, withdrew from the music industry, went to cooking school, and then spent a year working in a nursing home because 'I needed people to say "thank you."' Camille, who is now a non-drinker, found that she couldn't turn on the radio without hearing Madonna's voice, open a newspaper without reading a story about her, or walk down the street without seeing her picture on a billboard. 'I just about went out of my mind,' she admits. 'I felt like I was the only person on the planet feeling these things. It was scary.'

At the time of the split, however, it seemed that Madonna was the biggest loser. Prince did not end up managing her after all, so she was almost back to square one, with no manager, no income, no record deal and now no band. In addition, she faced the prospect of a lawsuit for walking out on her contract with Barbone and Lomuscio. However damaging or exhausting the personal conflict with Camille, she was risking much and gaining little. Her natural – indeed, ingrained – impatience to move on, doubtless contributed to her decision to drop her managers, coupled with the fact that she had begun to suspect Barbone no longer had the money to back up all the promises she had made. Even so, she had once again traded security for uncertainty, with only the vaguest prospect of success to buoy her.

That said, the Madonna of 1982 was a very different proposition from the rather jumpy, uncertain young woman who had first arrived in Camille Barbone's office. Sassy and savvy, Madonna had proved, in Camille's phrase, 'a quick study,' not only learning the ins and outs of the music business, but also filling up her little black book with useful contacts. In addition, she felt deeply that other creative artists and performers of her generation, many of them friends, had been moving forward in their careers while she had been marking time. By now she was well established as a member of New York's in-crowd of young artists, singers and performers who all seemed to be going places. The clubs were both their meeting place and their collective office, where they went to dance, have fun and to network. Just as CBGBs and Max's had spawned stars of the seventies and early eighties like Blondie, Talking Heads and Television, now the new places to be seen at were Danceteria, the Roxy and the Mudd Club. The British singer Sade worked behind the bar of the Danceteria, while the graffiti artist Keith Haring, whose paintings would sell in the future for hundreds of thousands of dollars, was a coatcheck boy there, sleeping on subway trains by day and working in the club at night. On any one night the place would be filled with emerging artists and musicians; the Beastie Boys, LL Cool J, Grandmaster Flash, and makeup artist Debi Mazar (now a Hollywood actress), could be found dancing, drinking and trying to get noticed. Congregating over at the Mudd Club were black graffiti artists like Michael Stewart, Lenny McGurr (aka Futura 2000), Jean-Michel Basquiat, whose tag or signature 'Samo', shorthand for 'same old bullshit', would one day see his art worth millions, and rap artist Fred Brathwaite (aka Fab Five Freddie).

On the surface, Madonna was simply one attractive face among a remarkable crowd, but she did have her own 'crew' of friends. At first glance, it was a pretty motley crew, running around town in their rags and tatters. Yet club owner Erika Belle, smart-mouthed New Yorker Debi Mazar, dancers Martin Burgoyne and Bagens Rilez, fashion retailer Maripol, poet and impresario Haoui Montaug, even her old college friend Janice Galloway – all displayed a kind of insouciant artistic integrity that set them apart from the crowd.

By the 1980s, these bright young things, defined as much by their creativity as their ambition, had become colorful, stylish reinventions of their earlier, younger selves. Their talk was always of the future, of dreams and deals, schemes and ruses. The past was another country, a world only ever discussed in amused, exaggerated anecdotes, usually dismissive. It would probably never have occurred to Erika Belle or Madonna to swap notes about their fathers, both successful, highly paid scientists; indeed, Madonna's only apparent reference to her past at this time was when she chastised a friend for wearing the same eyeshadow as her stepmother. Their chatter was only of themselves, the next gallery opening, the newest club – and the next big idea.

As exhibitionist and self-absorbed as they may have been, Madonna and her brat pack nevertheless made an impression on downtown New York, turning every head when they walked into a club. 'Madonna and her friends were the kind of kids you wanted in your venue,' recalls Roxy manager Vito Bruno. 'She was a stand-out, trendy and eye-catching. They got into the VIP rooms before they were VIPs.'

They dominated the dance floor – Debi Mazar was an early exponent of break dancing – but they were also at the cutting edge of style, with attitude to spare. The flair Madonna's displayed for fashion, and for that matter in terms of her music, lay in her ability to pick and mix from her friends, from the streets and the clubs, and from these and other influences make her own statement. In dress, her style was a blend of leggings from her dance days, cute cast-offs from Curtis Zale, thrift-store chic and clothes hand made by Erika Belle, topped off with crucifixes and rubber bracelets (actually electric-typewriter drivebands, supplied by her friend, the French socialite Maripol, who had her own store). She also mixed and merged New York street culture and fashion, especially that sported by chic Latina girls, with the hip New Romantic look, transforming it into her own fashion statement. It was a style that would, within two years, clutter the wardrobes of teenage girls around the world.

Most important, though, was Madonna's attitude. She could be sexy and wild, but she always remained in control. At that time the most outrageous dance on the scene was called the Webo, corrupted Spanish for 'ball-shaker', an explicitly sexual routine in which a girl would be 'dogged' by several male dancers wildly grinding their pelvises against her. It was sexy but it was also sexist, the girls obvious victims of male desire. Madonna and her crew turned the tables, earning the nickname the 'Webo Girls' from those who watched them perform. For they deliberately 'dogged' the guys, dry-humping them on the dance floor, laughing and joking as they did so. As Fab Five Freddie, who had been on the receiving end of Madonna's fake sexual attentions while dancing, observes, 'You could say she was a tramp but that was missing the point. She was never some ding-y white chick who slept around with the guys, she was smarter than that. All the way through her career she has been very sexy but take a closer look and she is always in control. Like Sharon Stone in *Basic Instinct*, she flashes you her pussy, but she's in charge. A strong woman with a sense of humor.'

Her attitude said it all: attractive but in command, a modern-day Calamity Jane who, instead of a pistol, packed a can of spray paint with which she scrawled her tag, 'Boy Toy', on the walls of downtown New York. Her tag, which eventually became the name of her company, perfectly illustrated her self-conscious approach to sexuality, tongue-in-cheek, arch and knowing, but utterly removed from the sexual plaything of many men's dreams. 'Early on she knew what she wanted, she was incredibly focused but could play the little innocent girl,' recalls a senior music producer.

That focus was fixed firmly on becoming famous, and not for one moment did Madonna ever deviate from that goal. So much of her life was a matter of calculation that she even calibrated her spontaneity. She would be outrageous and wild, but never in such a way as to interfere with her primary ambition. 'When she told me that one day she would be the most famous person in the world, I totally believed her,' recalls Erika Belle. 'She had a highly attuned self-protection mechanism that many of us at that time didn't have. Her risk-taking would be choreographed. She would never be so out of control that it would, for example, stop her writing lyrics in the morning.'

At a time when many of her contemporaries were in thrall to drugs or drink – or both – Madonna kept a clear head and a clean body, allowing herself only the occasional puff on a joint or a vodka tonic. 'She never suspended reality for one second,' recalls Steve Torton, who shared an apartment and worked with the artist Jean-Michel Basquiat, later, briefly, one of her lovers. One night Steve Rubell, owner of the Palladium Club, waved his arms and offered Madonna her heart's desire: coke, booze, girls, boys, anything. It was two in the morning. She yawned and replied, 'A nice big salad, please.'

Hungry only for success, Madonna was, as one friend noted, 'pure unrefined ambition,' and would seize every opportunity that came her way. She used the club scene in the way a successful businessman uses his country club, to network and broker deals. 'Restlessly ambitious to the point of exhaustion,' as one contemporary described her, it was therefore entirely appropriate that she should take her next step on the ladder of success in her 'office' – the nightclub scene.

In February 1982, after the breakup with Barbone, Madonna effortlessly eased back into the popcorn-and-phone routine, making endless calls while she munched. At first she appealed to the charity of her old college buddies. She moved in with Janice Galloway, before teaming up with Steve Bray to continue their musical collaboration. They worked well together, Bray's approach complementing Madonna's drive and earnest ambition. While she wrote the lyrics, he would help her out with melodies, chords and musical progressions. After several weeks' work, Madonna and Bray felt that they had enough material to ask a couple of the musicians who had worked with her over the previous eighteen months to help them record a demo tape. They took over a studio and recorded a four-track demo for her to tout around town, for with Camille Barbone out of the picture, Madonna had to do her own legwork. These four tracks, 'Burning Up,' 'Everybody,' 'Ain't No Big Deal' and one other, were the songs that finally got her noticed.

What better place to begin than Danceteria, the club in which she spent most of her waking hours? The hottest DJ in the four-story club was Mark Kamins, who also worked as an A-and-R (artists and repertoire) scout for Chris Blackwell's Island Records. As legend and 'made-for-TV' bio films describe it, Madonna virtually seduced Kamins into playing her demo tape, flirting madly with him as she tore up the dance floor. In reality, Kamins, who was handed numerous demo tapes every week, was passed a copy by her, listened to her songs on his headphones, and decided to give her sound a spin. The crowd liked it, and he liked her. 'She was cute and we went out for a while,' he recalls. 'I can't say I saw a star but she had something special.' For a time she shared his bed, or what passed for a bed – a collection of egg crates in the middle of a spartan room on East 73rd Street. Not that she was a fixture – Madonna was always on the move, dashing from one place to the next on her bicycle, always with people to see, places to go. 'I believe she suffered from ADD [attention deficit disorder]; she was never still,' Kamins continues. 'Like she was wired all the time even though she never took drugs. A lot of artists have that.'

She was always juggling, whether it was her career, her jobs or her men. For a time she was dividing her time between Mark Kamins, Steve Bray and Ken Compton; indeed, in a fit of jealousy, Kamins banned Compton from the Danceteria nightclub. It always bugged him when she came to the club, borrowed some money and then promptly hightailed it to another venue where, he suspected, she was seeing someone else. As he observes, 'She's an incredible juggler of people. With regards to her sexuality she is more like a guy keeping several different girls on the go at one time.'

In truth, Madonna and Kamins were drawn together as much by their mutual ambition as by sexual attraction. Knowing that she was without a manager, he promptly signed her to his own fledgling music company and made an appointment with his boss, the legendary Chris Blackwell, who was making a flying visit to New York. He met Madonna, listened to her tape and then, after she had left, told Kamins that he didn't sign the girlfriends of his A-and-R scouts. As would later emerge, the real reason was rather more earthy; 'She smelled too bad,' the offbeat record mogul told Kamins some time later.

Undeterred, Kamins called Seymour Stein, president of Sire Records, an arm of the giant Warner Brothers music corporation, whom he knew after working with Stein on projects with the Tom Tom Club and Talking Heads. Stein expressed muted interest after listening to the demo tape but referred him to his thrusting young A-and-R agent, Michael Rosenblatt, to deal with the details. After listening to the four tracks, Rosenblatt chose two to record, 'Ain't No Big Deal' and 'Everybody'. As far as he was concerned, 'Ain't No Big Deal' was the A-side. 'She had a great tape but what's more she had that intangible certain something,' Rosenblatt remembers.

While Madonna's eventual success, bolstered by hindsight, has made Stein and Rosenblatt seem like musical oracles, the reality was rather different. Madonna's romantic version of the story has it that Stein was so keen to meet her that he signed the deal from his hospital bed while recovering from a heart operation. 'I could tell right then that she had the drive to match her talent,' he has said. In fact, according to Kamins, Stein didn't meet Madonna until after the success of her first single, 'Everybody' – although admittedly the meeting did take place in the hospital where he was recuperating.

In fact, there was no need for such a meeting – the deal was between Kamins, who had her under contract, and Stein's company, Sire Records. Nor were the terms especially generous. They offered $15,000 for a two-single deal, out of which Kamins and Madonna would have to pay all recording costs. 'It was supposed to inspire you to save money,' recalls Mark, dryly.

Madonna, however, was thrilled. In acknowledgment of that first singles deal, she sat down and wrote a song on a yellow legal notepad, dedicating it to her latest mentor, Kamins. The song, 'Lucky Star,' was to be one of her most enduring hits of the 1980s. At long last it seemed that her dreams were about to come true, and the young singer celebrated with a visit to the East Village hair salon where her old boyfriend, Mark Dolengowski, worked.

There, Madonna excitedly told the woman shampooing her hair, 'Martha, I'm going to be a star.'

Chapter Seven
DeMann and De Woman

BEARDED AND LONG-HAIRED, Arthur Baker cut an unimpressive figure as he shambled through the lobby of a downtown New York hotel on a summer's day in 1982. Yet once inside he was greeted like a long-lost brother by many of the participants of the New Music seminar that his friend and record distributor Tom Silverman had organized. For to them the Boston-born Arthur was 'The Man', responsible not only for that season's seminal record, 'Planet Rock' by Afrika Bambaataa, but also for bringing the new sounds of rap and hip-hop to a wider audience. He spotted Mark Kamins, one of New York's hottest DJs at that time, and walked over to talk to him. By Kamins's side was a dark-haired Italian girl dressed, with artful carelessness, in jeans, tee-shirt and an oversize shirt, whom he introduced to Baker as Madonna. 'What kind of whacked-out family names a kid "Madonna"?' thought Baker, as the DJ explained that she was his latest find, that they had just concluded a singles deal with Sire Records, and that he was producing the song.

After this Madonna offered Baker a battered Sony portable tape recorder and asked him to listen to the songs, 'Ain't No Big Deal' and 'Everybody.' Good-naturedly, he did so, offering his verdict that her sound was just like that of Patrice Rushen, then riding high in the charts with 'Forget Me Not.' 'Oh thank you,' cooed Madonna, 'I love Patrice Rushen.' Baker, who would go to work with U2, Bob Dylan, Pulp and Bruce Springsteen, wished her luck and moved away, reflecting to himself that she was just like a million other girls he had met in his music career.

He was more than a little surprised, therefore, to receive a phone call the next day from a rather anxious Mark Kamins. 'What does a producer do?' the DJ asked plaintively. Baker gave him an instant tutorial and recommended a couple of musicians, including keyboard player Fred Zarr, whom he thought Kamins should enlist. In double quick time, Zarr found himself at Blank Tape studios in New York, working through the night with Madonna. 'She only had a singles deal, and if that had failed no one would have heard of her, but I remember telling friends afterwards that I was working with someone who had magical star quality,' recalls Zarr, who was to work with Madonna on other occasions in the future.

She was a star with an eye on the budget, however. Conscious that she was paying for recording time, she even persuaded Zarr and the recording engineer to eat their sandwiches while the tape was being rewound to save precious minutes. 'Time is money and the money is mine,' intoned Madonna, carrying the precept into practice when they had finished by begging a ride home from Zarr, as she didn't have the money for the cab fare.

During the recording session, a rather apprehensive Mark Kamins looked on from the other side of the glass, as he listened to his girlfriend belt out her two songs. As a DJ, he was confident about the kind of feel he wanted for the record. As a producer, however, he didn't really know how to achieve it. Madonna became increasingly frustrated as he struggled to give her direction, especially as she no longer had Steve Bray to rely on.

That she did not was partly her doing, although not altogether her fault. She and the drummer had had a major falling out after he had argued that since he had recorded the demo, he should be the one to produce the single. While Madonna has often been blamed, if not demonized, for leaving him in the lurch, in truth she had little room for maneuver. As far as Kamins was concerned, his role as producer was non-negotiable. He had taken all the risks, brokered the deal, quit his job at Island Records, and signed the artist. The result, however, was that Madonna and Steve Bray split.

Worse still, their first experience of working together did not end happily for her and Kamins. As Mark says, 'Things fell apart between us after that because I did not give her enough direction in the studio and the A-side did not come out as successfully as everyone had wanted.' In fact, when Michael Rosenblatt of Sire Records listened to the scheduled A-side, 'Ain't No Big Deal,' he was so unimpressed that he decided to put the B-side, 'Everybody,' on both sides of the 12-inch dance disk.

The record company was not especially eager to promote the artist, either. For a start, Warner only spent money on publicity for artists with an album release. Madonna did not even register on their PR radar. In an attempt to make the best of what they considered to be a bad job, Sire Records, which did not specialize in dance music, decided that the soulful dance sound of 'Everybody' was tailor-made for a black audience. So Madonna, with her newly bleached blonde hair, was in effect, marketed as a black artist. It was done by sleight of hand. For the cover of the single, which was issued in October 1982, Sire executives had given the go-ahead to a hip-hop collage image of downtown New York, rather than a portrait shot of Madonna, allowing the sound to convey the impression that she was black. 'I was shocked,' recalls Mark Kamins. So too was Madonna's old friend from college days, photographer Linda Alaniz, who had been asked by the singer to take a photograph of her for the cover.

The idea seems extraordinary now, if not preposterous; indeed, as Arthur Baker observes of the song, 'When you listen to it now it's a laugh that people thought she was black.' Marketing Madonna's single as black dance music was a hard-headed business decision however, one that reflected the reality of the times. In 1980s America, popular music was still delineated by category, defined by radio-station playlists and a couple of TV shows, and within each category competition for air time was savage. The time when club DJs and MTV and other television music shows could make or break a single was still to come.

Although Sire's marketing strategy came as a bitter blow to her, for once Madonna bit her tongue on her objections and toed the company line. Michael Rosenblatt was aware of the tensions, but commented sternly, 'She will do anything to be a star, and that's exactly what I look for in a star: total co-operation. I need the artist to be there to do whatever I need.'

In the froth of corporate self-congratulation and the soft-focus haze of hindsight that followed her rise to stardom, it is easy to forget that in the beginning, Madonna had been dealt a far from winning hand: a cut-price single deal, a record no one was enthusiastic about, no personal publicity and, as a final insult, the active promotion of the artist also known as black Madonna. Her recording career could hardly have got off to a worse start. 'Sire just weren't sure about her. She could have been a one-hit wonder – or a no-hit wonder,' one music producer comments.

Undaunted, Madonna called on the one person she could always rely on – herself. Just as she had pestered her former manager, Camille Barbone, so she hustled and hassled in the way she had learned in the last four years of living in New York. She did everything she could to get a buzz going. At night she toured the clubs with her 'crew,' handing out her record and encouraging DJs to play the song. During the day she would stand on street corners giving out leaflets advertising her single.

In much the same way that she had seemed reluctant to trust her career to Camille Barbone without taking a hand herself, Madonna was anxious to ensure that no opportunity, however small, would slip through the corporate fingers of Sire Records. She attached herself to one of Sire's dance record promoters, Bobby Shaw, accompanying him from time to time on his 'milkrun' rounds of radio stations and club DJs. Her visibility rather undermined Sire's strategy of marketing the Madonna of the single as a black singer or group, but her presence undoubtedly helped to bring the record to wider notice.

It was during one milkrun that she was introduced to John 'Jellybean' Benitez, the DJ at the Funhouse, who listened to 'Everybody' and promised to 'rock the house.' The first meeting, in October or November 1982 – sources disagree – was to change both their lives, for she and Benitez would eventually become musical collaborators, as well as lovers. For a time, though, they were, in Benitez's words, 'playing little cat-and-mouse games,' neither prepared to commit to a relationship.

Relationships, as far as Madonna was concerned, could wait. Lovers could come and go, but for her there was only one game in town – making her record a success. It was a measure not only of her ambition, but also of her absolute commitment, that she was the only one of Sire's artists who joined Shaw and a number of club DJs in his eighth-floor office on 54th Street, every Friday afternoon. Here they discussed the business, gossiped and sampled the latest releases. Her presence guaranteed her an opportunity to influence the DJs' playlists and, as importantly, did much to ensure that no one would badmouth her single while she was around. Nevertheless, on occasion the record-industry rookie could go a little too far, as Bobby Shaw recalls: 'One time I was playing something and she said, "Please take this off." I looked at her and said, "This isn't your party."' For the most part, however, he thought she was 'vivacious' and 'wanted to learn,' even if her enthusiasm and desire for success sometimes outran her good sense.

For her part, Madonna was eager to teach senior Sire Record bosses, particularly Seymour Stein and Michael Rosenblatt, that, given the chance, she could graduate in the music business. While her cause was certainly not hurt when Rosenblatt began dating (and eventually married) her one-time roommate Janice Galloway, Madonna was anxious to showcase her talents independently. As luck would have it, she had the perfect opportunity when one of her New York friends, the poet and impresario Haoui Montaug organized one of his by then notorious *No Entiendes* ('You Don't Understand') cabarets, to be performed at Danceteria. Among the cast of jugglers, fire-eaters and other esoteric acts was Madonna. Conscious that here was the perfect opportunity to influence her promoters, she invited Stein, Rosenblatt and other Warner executives, including the head of dance music, Craig Kostich, to come along.

With her usual attention to detail, and in what was to become her professional trademark, Madonna left absolutely nothing to chance. She hired a dance studio on the Upper West Side for rehearsals and persuaded three of her crew, dancer Erika Belle, British-born artist Martin Burgoyne and Bagens ('Bags') Rilez, to be her backup dancers for the show. Knowing that most of Montaug's cabaret acts were under-rehearsed, Madonna was insistent that their choreography should be professional and polished. The four of them practiced endlessly, Madonna always the first to arrive, the last to leave.

On the night of the performance, Montaug, dressed in top hat and tails, introduced Madonna and her single, 'Everybody.' As the 300-strong audience boogied along and Stein and company watched from the wings, the singer and her dancers went through the three-minute song-and-dance routine they had worked out, described afterwards as a 'disco act backed by avant-garde dancers.' This performance is often taken as the seminal moment in Madonna's career, the point at which the seers at Sire realized the singer's visual impact, and decided to promote her through the new medium of video. As with so much that has been written or said about Madonna, however, the reality was a little different. The truth was that the record executives' reaction was, at best, rather muted. Nevertheless, Rosenblatt contacted Ed Steinberg, who ran the Rock America video company, and asked if he had a few hours spare to make a no-frills company video of Madonna on stage at her next performance at Danceteria. The idea was to play the video to the rest of their promotional staff across the States, to give them an idea of their new artist's music and performance. At a time when artists like Duran Duran and Michael Jackson thought nothing of spending a six-figure sum on TV videos, Rosenblatt offered Steinberg $1,000 for the strictly in-house production. They agreed on $1,500 – although the video producer jokes that he is still waiting for the other $500. While Sire was hardly pulling out all the stops for its new star, in fairness, MTV, then the only media company devoted to pop, was still in its infancy and never played dance videos.

Instead of shooting Madonna at a live gig, Steinberg suggested that they film her on location at Paradise Garage, a downtown gay disco he could use for free. It was a cut-price production; Madonna's friend Debi Mazar did the makeup and then joined the crowd of dancers on the club floor, while Erika Belle and Bags Rilez were her backup dancers. Since Martin Burgoyne was not a professional dancer he was dropped from the troupe, although later he acted as Madonna's tour manager for a time. She also brought a group of friends to make up the disco crowd, including the black graffiti artist Michael Stewart, who would die after being beaten by police a few months later.

As so many others have been, Steinberg was immediately impressed by Madonna's professionalism and willingness, the singer never once complaining as he asked her to perform the song over and over again and again, until he was satisfied with the shot. 'Before the shoot I had heard that she was a nightmare and very difficult,' he remembers. 'At that stage in her career she was relying on people who didn't really know what they were doing, so it is easy to see why she got impatient,' he adds, in barely concealed criticism of those around her at that time.

Sire Records got their in-house video, but Steinberg, impressed by the singer and her song, took matters further, sending copies of the tape out to those nightclubs all over America which used dance videos in their entertainment. It was a clever move that helped Madonna's single, already storming up the dance charts, to grow from being a hit in New York, where it was played by black stations like WKTU, to gain a nationwide following.

All the energy and hard work now began to pay dividends. In November 1982 'Everybody' hit the dance chart, and made it to the top slot weeks later. True, her debut single failed to breach the all important *Billboard* Top 100 pop chart, but it did bring Madonna her first magazine cover. In the December issue of *Dance Music Report* she and another band, Jekyll and Hyde, were nominated for awards in the 'Sales' category of a readers' poll. It was Madonna's picture that appeared on the cover, however. As with every one of her press clippings, she carefully labeled and saved the item. It was work that would expand with her success, for over the next couple of years she was to amass an entire portfolio of stories about herself.

Certainly the word was out on the street. Fab Five Freddie remembers walking along Houston Street one day after the single's release, behind a couple of hip Puerto Rican girls, boombox in hand, singing and grooving to the sound of 'Everybody.' 'That impressed me,' he admits. 'They were hot, she was hot. Madonna was attracting those who were more street, more savvy, more flavorful.'

At that time the epitome of downtown cool was another black graffiti artist, Jean-Michel Basquiat, who would become the James Dean of the art world, a young rebel who played hard and died young. Now the subject of several biographies and films, Basquiat, the Brooklyn-born son of a Haitian father and a Puerto Rican mother, was a wild genius who was introduced to Madonna by Ed Steinberg at the Lucky Strike Club just as her single was taking off. He was then making a name for himself as an artist, creating, with apparently effortless ease, striking semi-abstract works of art that synthesized the sights and sounds of the inner city, paintings that today attract widespread critical notice and very high prices.

'You will never guess who I slept with last night,' he told his roommate, stretcher-maker and general assistant, Steve Torton, one day in November 1982. 'Madonna.' Torton was unimpressed, but realized that if Basquiat was attracted to her, she must be special. 'He was a study in exuberance,' recalls Torton. 'He was excited because he had identified her as the coming person.'

Their three-month love affair, which occurred just as both were being catapulted from obscurity to celebrity, gives a real sense of Madonna as an individual and as a developing artist. The manner in which she expressed her personality in this brief relationship reveals the qualities that combined to create her eventual popular appeal. Yet in many respects their affair was one of the attraction of opposites. He was everything that she was not: Madonna ambitious, ascetic, focused, self-aware and controlled; Basquiat prodigal, reckless and otherworldly.

For her every day had a direction, every meeting an outcome, every conversation a purpose. By contrast, life for Basquiat, two years her junior, was without calculation. Careless of opportunities and indifferent to career, utterly confident in his own talent and effortless ability, for him success was assured. He would paint all night, watch the sunrise, and might then spend all day in a hired limousine, sleeping, snorting coke and handing out money to eager street kids through the blacked-out windows. If one of his paintings sold, he might take a suite at the five-star Waldorf-Astoria Hotel on a whim and perhaps never use it. An enduring image is of Basquiat standing naked in his bathtub, a bag of cocaine in one hand, worrying about a party he was just about to throw for his friend and promoter Andy Warhol. Charismatic, spontaneous yet self-destructive, Basquiat emerged as one of the towering artistic geniuses of his generation. Yet he was not the easiest of free spirits, often falling prey to moods of depression, or rages in which he hurled accusations against those close to him. Like so many of the artists of that time, he expected to die young and did so, of a heroin overdose in August 1988, aged just twenty-seven.

Nothing mattered more to Basquiat than the next canvas – or the next line of coke. He and Torton would mock Madonna as she talked, endlessly, about her career, for the artist had known instinctively that success was his for the taking, not the making. As a result, it baffled him that when they went to clubs, the three of them crammed into his black 1950 Plymouth convertible, Basquiat simply wanted to hang out, while Madonna would work the room, ceaselessly talking up her single. 'It was in a way a lot easier for Basquiat than Madonna,' Torton observes, perceptively. 'He was a uniquely talented artist, she constantly had to work at making it. His genius assured him of success, she was uncertain of her talent.' Indeed, it can be said that Madonna is accessible as an artist precisely because her status is deemed to be as much a product of hard work, grit and determination as of any latent ability. She epitomizes the American dream, the idea that anybody can be somebody, an idea deeply rooted in the hearts of those descended from immigrants to the United States, whose forebears had so often been driven by the same dream. She might have been any ordinary Midwestern girl-next-door, and yet she is one in a billion, through her own efforts to fulfill her potential – from high-school cheerleader to international superstar. Conversely, Basquiat's genius set him apart, an exotic bird even amid the colorful plumage of so many of his contemporaries.

The lovers were, however, united by a quality often overlooked in assessments of Madonna's career – artistic courage. Neither was afraid to take artistic risks, neither was afraid to fail. Both had the nerve, metaphorically speaking, to expose themselves in public. There was, too, a very human, rather vulnerable innocence about their relationship that has been lost in the caricature of Madonna as a sexual grotesque. (Surprisingly, in view of her sexually voracious image, the word 'innocent' is used of her by several of her former lovers.) For much of the time they behaved like excited children, giggling in bed, tickling each other, telling each other stories; or listening to Torton as he sat on the edge of the bed and spun one of his yarns in rapid-fire sentences, like a tobacco auctioneer on speed. One afternoon, for example, Madonna came round to Basquiat's apartment just for a kiss – and to try to get his day going. Torton's photographs of the couple, taken in that apartment, capture something of the guilelessness of the relationship.

Ultimately, the relationship foundered on the elemental divide between them: his dark moods and paranoia, as against her essentially positive, life-affirming spirit. 'How can you stand him? He's so depressing,' she moaned to Torton after returning from Los Angeles, where she and Basquiat had spent New Year at the beach house of art dealer Larry Gagosian. 'He never wakes up until the sun goes down and he didn't even see the sea all the time we were there,' she complained. Yet even after they split, she remained on good terms with him, as she did with other boyfriends, helping him when, inspired by Madonna's success, he decided that he too would make a record. If she could do it, so could he – as a seventeen-year-old, he had played in a local punk-rock band – and proved it by recording a rap song called 'Beat Bop,' which featured New York hip-hop artist Rammell Zee.

Just as she maintained her friendship with Basquiat when their relationship ended, so there was a reasonably amicable parting from Mark Kamins. While their love affair had been over for some time – he was then seeing the woman he would marry – they still had a working relationship. With the success of 'Everybody,' record companies were clamoring to sign her, and because Sire Records had only placed her under contract for a singles deal there was a danger she could go elsewhere. It was then that Madonna was whisked to Seymour Stein's hospital bedside, where he was recovering from heart surgery; the canny music executive was 'freaked' by the realization that she might be snatched from under his nose. Resplendent in dressing gown and jockey shorts, and with an IV tube still in his arm, the man responsible for signing The Pretenders and Talking Heads now exchanged contracts with Madonna. The $5,000 advance she secured on her new deal, this time for a single and an album, enabled her to buy a Roland synthesizer that would allow her to compose in the new apartment she was now renting in Broome Street, in fashionable SoHo.

By now it seemed that everyone was eager to capitalize on the success of her first hit. Not unreasonably, Mark Kamins expected to be asked to produce her second single, 'Burning Up,' which was recorded in early 1983. Like Steve Bray before him, however, Kamins was turned down; Michael Rosenblatt explaining that they wanted a producer who had more experience in direct-ing singers. A Warner Brothers producer, Reggie Lucas, who currently had a number-one hit with singer Stephanie Mills, was brought in as producer, and penned the 'B' side, 'Physical Attraction.' As far as Kamins was concerned there were no hard feelings. He was working with other artists, his deal with Sire and Warner gave him a percentage point on everything Madonna released for the foreseeable future, and he was inundated with remix produc-tion work. 'I was a happy boy,' he recalls. 'My career was taking off at the same time as Madonna's.'

Those of her New York friends whom she had involved in the production of these early records and their attendant videos were equally happy. Indeed, her efforts to help her 'crew' seem at odds with the long-accepted image of a young woman who stepped on everyone to reach the top. She asked Martin Burgoyne to design the cover for the 12-inch dance single of 'Burning Up,' while Debi Mazar was hired as makeup artist for the music video Sire com-missioned to promote the second single. Maripol, who had first introduced the singer to her trademark fashion-item rubber bracelets, was the stylist, and Madonna's occasional lover Ken Compton appeared on screen. The video, directed by Steve Baron, was America's first introduction to Madonna's sex-ual politics and became a minor hit on MTV, which by then had begun to show dance-music videos. In one scene Madonna seems about to be hit by a car driven by a handsome young man, played by Compton. By the end of the song, she is driving the car and has ditched the young man. The message, which would be repeated throughout her musical career, was that she was the one in charge.

When her second record was released in March 1983 Madonna was indeed in command, almost immediately setting out on tour with the other members of her crew, dancers Erika Belle and Bags Rilez, to promote the single. Like dozens of other new dance groups, Madonna and her company performed 'track' dates at numerous clubs, Madonna singing to a background recording while the three of them went through their three-song routine. Then they would travel on to the next venue and repeat the twenty-minute performance.

This was the grueling, unglamorous side of show business. At one club in Fort Lauderdale, Florida they came on after a dancing pantomime horse, while at another gig, at the Copa in Key West, off the south-western tip of Florida, they performed before a handful of bored youngsters after driving all day through torrential rain to reach the club. Even so, before they went on Madonna insisted on rehearsing their routine in the single hotel bedroom they shared. 'It was funny watching them dance between the beds,' Sire's record promoter Bobby Shaw, who accompanied them on the trip remembers. 'She was a perfectionist and I admire that.'

What was both more glamorous and more fun was when they took the show to the clubs in New York. They got to ride in the limo the record company provided, playing with the multi-colored lights, fiddling with the switches, cranking up the music, and inviting friends and virtually anyone else nearby to join them as they cruised round the streets of New York after finishing their shows for the night. For a girl who had usually rattled round New York on an old bicycle, the luxurious car was a real treat. 'It was playful, it was a blast,' recalls Erika Belle, who denies the myth that they cruised round in order to pick up teenage Puerto Rican boys, and would have sex with them in the back of the car. 'There was lots of flirting, lots of fun and that's all as far as I'm concerned,' she continues. 'Sure those were the days when girls were having sex on the dance floor of the Pyramid, but Madonna never wanted to be known for that. She was always self-aware, in control. That story just doesn't fit with the person she was and is.'

When they were out of town, Madonna would go out to interviews with radio stations or local newspapers after the show while the others were relaxing. Driven, professional and energetic, during her time on the road she also proved that she was a young woman with a strong will and attitude to match. After they had gone through their three-song set in a club, the manager would often plead with them for an encore. She always refused, preferring to leave the crowds begging for more. On one occasion they performed in a club at Sag Harbor on Long Island. The mainly preppy crowd was rowdy and unresponsive, something most singers experience at one time or another, simply gritting their teeth and carrying on with as good a grace as they can muster. Not so Madonna. Halfway through their act, she suddenly stopped singing, shouted 'Fuck you!' at the audience, and walked offstage. Erika and Bags followed, ending the performance. While her gesture infuriated the management, it impressed at least one member of the audience that night,

Frances Grill, the chief executive of the Click Model Agency. Used to spotting talent in unlikely circumstances or situations; she immediately recognized that she was watching a performer with genuine star quality.

The embryonic diva was beginning to understand that for herself. One night as she, Bags and Erika were returning from a gig in Brooklyn, Madonna stretched out in the limo and looked over at the Manhattan skyline, glowing in the setting sun. 'I'm going to own this town,' she said, matter-of-factly.

That burning ambition brought its own limitations, of course, not the least of them the fact that she only had one way of operating – her way. In the studio she was constantly at loggerheads with producer Reggie Lucas, as they tried to put together her first album to capitalize on the success of 'Burning Up,' which went to number three in the dance charts. 'On one occasion they couldn't agree so they turned to me and asked, "What do you think?"' recalls the keyboard player Fred Zarr, who had once again been brought in to provide backup. She didn't have much material to play – nor did she have much time. Halfway through the recording she and her little troupe, together with Mark Kamins, flew to London to promote the single. She appeared at Heaven, a fashionable gay club, as well as Camden Palace and the Beatroot Club, and traveled north to play the Hacienda Club in Manchester. While they enjoyed meeting The Smiths, The Fall and Jools Holland, their act failed miserably with audiences. 'It was a disaster,' Kamins remembers. 'People just didn't get it. I was shocked.'

Back in New York, a different kind of disaster was looming. Madonna had planned to use her unreleased song from the first unreleased single, 'Ain't No Big Deal,' to launch the album. Crucially, Steve Bray had sold it to another label, which meant that she had to find another song quickly. At the same time, she was concerned that Reggie Lucas had over-produced other songs on the album, changing them from the rather sparse form of the demos, which she had preferred. A rapid first-aid job was needed.

By chance, her new boyfriend, Jellybean Benitez, had a demo of the song 'Holiday,' written by Curtis Hudson and Lisa Stevens of the group Pure Energy. He had already offered it to Supremes star Mary Wilson and singer Phyllis Hyman but they had turned it down. Madonna, anxiously looking for a song, was more than happy to accept when he offered 'Holiday' to her. She quickly laid down the vocals and Benitez, despite the fact that he had never produced a song before, set to work on the sound, laboring night and day in the studio to knock it into shape before the April 1983 deadline. He then set about reworking several of the tracks recorded earlier under Lucas's direction in the style that Madonna preferred. Just before 'Holiday' was completed, she and Benitez took the tape over to Fred Zarr's apartment in Brooklyn to see if he could add any of what Madonna called 'Zarrisms,' creative flourishes that would provide the finishing touches. Zarr tinkered around on the keyboard in his front room and came up with the distinctive piano solo that gave the song its final polish.

Although Madonna has since admitted that the songs on her debut album, released in July 1983, were 'pretty weak,' and that her inexperience led her to dwell too long in the disco mold, the album was an astonishing success, selling nine million copies worldwide. The second single from one of the album's tracks, 'Lucky Star,' gave Madonna the first of her fifteen American top-five hits, more than either The Beatles or Elvis Presley, while the first, 'Holiday,' in truth little more than a scissors-and-paste recording, was to dominate the charts from Thanksgiving through Christmas that year. Indeed the album's incredible success took everyone by surprise – including Warner executives, who had to hold back the release of her second album, *Like A Virgin*, for months, until the demand for her debut album, *Madonna*, had tailed off.

That first album made Madonna a household name. Yet when it was released in November 1983, she did not have a manager, an accountant, or a lawyer, nor even a bank account. Now, however, with a little help from her boyfriend, Jellybean Benitez, she set about building around herself what was to become the most formidable professional team in the business. Benitez, a shrewd businessman as well as a respected and highly successful DJ, introduced her to music accountant and business-affairs advisor Bert Padell, a colorful New York character who writes poetry and was once a batboy to the great Joe DiMaggio. For the next fifteen years his firm, which has handled countless pop legends from The Beatles to Britney Spears, managed her business affairs with supreme competence.

Just as importantly, she was in dire need of a music manager. Mixing romance, former or current, with career, she had already signed short-term deals with both Mark Kamins and Jellybean Benitez, deals that would in the end prove to be expensive as her success continued. Seymour Stein, who had by now recovered from his heart operation, suggested that she fly to Hollywood to meet one of the world's leading managers, Freddy DeMann of Weisner-DeMann Entertainment, who had just parted with Michael Jackson. Raising its head yet again in Madonna's story, romantic legend has it that she auditioned in his office and that he was so bowled over that he later told the media that 'she has that special magic few stars have.' Others remember it differently, however, recalling how after that first meeting DeMann wondered aloud who on earth this girl, in her rags and tatters, thought she was. Certainly their partnership had rather more to do with the business relationship DeMann and Stein enjoyed than with any input from Madonna. As they signed a deal cementing a relationship that would last for fifteen years, Stein couldn't resist joking: 'What are you going to call yourselves: "DeMann and DeWoman?"'

The pun had its echoes elsewhere, for the man and woman really turning heads in New York that summer were Madonna and John Jellybean Benitez. After weeks of flirting and warily circling around each other's characters, they began to be seen together regularly, arriving as a couple at the trendiest restaurants, hip venues and hot parties around Manhattan – when their busy schedules allowed. As Benitez concedes, speaking of their careers and business interests, 'We kept trying to set up a meet, then make a plan, and ended up canceling because I had to be in the studio and she had to go to Europe or something.'

In this relationship, however, it seemed that Madonna had for once met her match. Unlike her former lover Jean-Michel Basquiat, Benitez was as consumed with ambition as his girlfriend, each taking from and learning equally from the other. 'We're both very career-oriented, very goal-oriented,' he has said. Although by nature a quiet, even shy, young man, his hunger for fame was every bit as great as Madonna's, as was shown by his decision to hire his own publicist, David Salidor, when he landed a DJ job at the Funhouse. It was a shrewd move; Benitez was invited to those parties and meetings that would normally be closed to a DJ. Once again Madonna proved a quick study, quizzing Benitez's publicist closely about the mechanics of dealing with the media. 'She took that knowledge and applied it to her own career,' Salidor observes.

Just as Benitez had introduced Madonna to Bert Padell, so he was now instrumental in giving her a sense of the social and commercial possibilities open to her. He showed her how to manipulate and exploit the downtown scene in a way that was cool and hip. In short he conducted for her a daily seminar on how to be a star – or at least behave like a star. As she once acknowledged, 'I always acted like a star long before I was one.'

When they were not busy trying to add themselves to the stars glittering in the New York scene's firmament, they would steal away to a cliff-top beach house in the Hamptons, which had been rented the year before by the actor John Belushi, not long before his tragic death from drugs. The party, usually comprising Jellybean, Madonna, her brother Christopher, the record producer Arthur Baker and his singer wife Tina, and session musician John Robie, would arrive in the early hours of Saturday morning after Benitez had finished his stint at the Funhouse. If they didn't crash out they would go swimming, watch the sunrise and feed the ducks. Other friends would arrive and sleep out on the porch, and the whole group party all night. Cocaine and other drugs were in plentiful supply; Arthur Baker, then at the peak of his career with five records in the Top Twenty, remembers that they spent most of the time 'totally off our faces.' Everyone, that is, except Madonna. 'I always got the impression that this wasn't what she wanted to be doing,' Baker adds. 'Things were happening for her then. She wanted to be working.'

Not that she had much opportunity to party, for things were indeed happening for her. Her new association with Freddy DeMann soon began to pay dividends, as the Hollywood manager secured a meeting for her in September, with film producer, Jon Peters, who asked her to play the part of a club singer in a movie he was making, a romantic comedy called *Vision Quest*. A few weeks later she found herself, 'cold, bored and lonely,' in Spokane, Washington, for the shoot. It didn't seem fair, especially as that month she was celebrating the fact that 'Holiday' was now the number-one dance song in America, a song, as one critic remarked, 'as infectious as the plague.'

True, there were compensations. Only a year earlier she had been 'the black Madonna,' scarcely acknowledged by her record company when her first single was released. Yet the following November she was in a Chinese restaurant chatting about her music, her crucifix jewelry and her life in Detroit with Peters's girlfriend and business partner, Barbra Streisand.

It was a meeting, if not of soul sisters, then of two women who were each driven by an almost visceral desire for mass adulation, for universal love, acclaim and acceptance. Theirs was not an act, a performance to be switched on and off at will, but a deep-seated craving to be the center of attention every day, in every way. It was, and is, a feature of Madonna's personality, which left her father, a self-effacing and private man, simply baffled. 'Do you always dress like that? Is that a costume?' he asked quizzically when, later that month, his flamboyant daughter arrived at his home for Thanksgiving, with Jellybean Benitez in tow.

She remained unabashed by such criticism, her self-belief as powerful as a force of nature. A few weeks later she met up with another name from her past, budding actor David Alan Grier, joining him at Studio 54 where she was due to perform at a birthday celebration for the Italian fashion house Fiorucci. Surveying the room, she told Grier, now a well-known actor, 'You and me and are going to be big stars, baby, and leave these other suckers in the dust.'

Until now, only her friends and a handful of acquaintances had witnessed her vaunting ambition at first hand. That was soon to change. In January 1984, the success of 'Holiday' earned Madonna her national television debut, a spot on the world's most famous teenage dance party, *American Bandstand*. When the show's evergreen host, Dick Clark, asked her what she wanted to do when she grew up, she replied without hesitation, 'Rule the world.'

Clark was amused, but her reply had been breathtakingly honest, a precisely truthful statement of her deep-seated desires and needs. The pathology of her ambition, primal and unyielding, made her willing, even eager, to sacrifice anything– love, affection, friendship, stability, anonymity– on the altar of stardom. Perhaps more accurately, she was prepared to pursue her longing for love by pandering to the fickle, dark-hearted god of fame. Her psychology made it inevitable that she would enter wholeheartedly into this Faustian pact, anxious to see her name in lights and her picture on magazine covers, to watch her screaming fans adoring her.

As it turned out, she did not have long to wait.

Chapter Eight

'I'm a Sexy Woman,
Yeah, Yeah, Yeah!'

A GIANT WHITE WEDDING CAKE stole the show at the first ever MTV
Video Music Awards on September 14, 1984. Or rather, the young singer
perched on top of the cake did. The ceremony, which was being broadcast
live from Radio City Music Hall in New York, had been carefully rehearsed,
but even its host, Bette Midler, seemed taken aback when Madonna, dressed
in a tight white bustier with a skirt and veil of white tulle, and accessorized
with her trademark 'Boy Toy' belt buckle, strings of pearls, crucifix jewelry
and rubber bangles, launched into the title song of her yet to be released
second album, *Like A Virgin*. If the word 'virgin' was not in itself enough to
make the audience sit up, the sight of this far from coy-looking bride
writhing on the stage in unmistakable simulation of sexual intercourse,
certainly was. They had seen nothing like it.

While Bette Midler made a couple of weak jokes following the
performance, the audience at Radio City was bewildered. A bemused Arthur
Baker and his wife Tina, who were sitting near the front row, could not
believe their eyes. 'Afterwards we all said that her career was over, that she
had simply lost the plot,' Baker recalls. What they didn't know at the time
was that, while they may not have enjoyed Madonna's raunchy act first-
hand, it looked great on camera, and TV viewers loved it. The single of 'Like
A Virgin' was set to be Madonna's biggest hit so far, going multi-platinum
and staying at the number-one position for six weeks from December 1984.
'It was the performance that made her career,' Baker had to concede. 'It
showed that she was savvy enough to know how to use the camera to her
advantage.'

If there had been any doubt at Sire Records that Madonna was more than
a one-album wonder – the company had held back her second album while
trying to reap maximum profits from the first, and were still pushing singles
from the now million-selling *Madonna* album into the charts as the singer
introduced 'Like A Virgin' – these were now swept aside. Rather, the record
company found itself in the enviable position of promoting the newly
crowned Queen of Pop.

It was not a role that everybody was happy to see Madonna in. While many fans seemingly couldn't get enough of the song, outraged moralists were quick to condemn 'Like A Virgin,' which they saw as undermining traditional values and encouraging sex outside marriage. The controversy was one that she herself had anticipated when she chose to record the track, predicting that the resulting 'virgin or whore' debate would win publicity for her and the song. 'I was being provocative,' she said. 'I like irony. I like the way things can be taken on different levels. "Like A Virgin" was always absolutely ambiguous.'

With its accompanying video set in Venice and featuring a slutty-looking Madonna singing in a gondola, alternating with rather romantic scenes in which she wears a wedding gown, the song actually owed its success to the fact that it appealed both to the sexually inexperienced, who were happy to see it as a celebration of true love, as well as to those who saw it as being about sexual desire and fulfillment.

Meanwhile, Madonna's public persona – indomitable, sexually unashamed, supremely confident – had begun to strike a chord with a new generation of teenage girls. Many of these young women had been brought up, like their heroine herself, with old-fashioned stereotypes of women as virginal brides or as whores, or with feminist values that rejected the use of a woman's looks for her self-advancement. To these girls, Madonna was saying that it was okay to show off your body as well as your brain; that one could be sexy and successful. Here was a woman who dressed wantonly and behaved badly, yet who, far from being punished for this behavior, was instead richly rewarded.

In addition, at a time when eighties fashions were promoting flat-chested, stick-thin women as ideals of beauty, the more curvaceous Madonna made average girls feel that it was fine to be the shape they were. The new word 'wannabe' perfectly described the thousands of girls who tried to emulate the singer's look. At one point Macy's allotted an entire floor area to the sale of Madonna-look clothing, including cut-off gloves, rubber bangles and lacy leggings.

The Madonna phenomenon was now such that university professors, gender-studies experts and feminists earnestly discussed her influence as a post-modernist cultural icon. Yet, in the words of Angie Bowie, the former wife of Madonna's hero, David Bowie, Madonna's creed was simpler: 'I'm a sexy woman, yeah, yeah, yeah.'

Although she had now achieved the success and adulation she had craved for so long, 1985 was to be a year of very mixed emotions as Madonna the individual struggled to cope with her new life as a modern icon. At first she reveled in her celebrity status. Ever since Madonna had first appeared in a fashion spread in the *Village Voice,* she had saved every press clipping about herself, carefully labeling and dating each one. Each morning she read the New York tabloids and the *New York Times,* scouring them for stories about herself. Then she would look over clippings sent by her press secretary, Liz Rosenberg. While publicly she feigned indifference when a critic wrote a withering review or when a reporter made up a negative story about her, she was frequently hurt by such coverage, often losing sleep if a particular remark hit home. She took, and takes, the position that those who judge her negatively, since they neither know her nor have ever been in her position, artistically or personally, have no right to throw stones. It would take several years before Madonna truly began to feel comfortable with her star status, with the adulation and the isolation.

She came to understand that constant limelight was both a blessing and a curse. Gone were the days of getting around New York on her bicycle, taking the subway, or visiting the local laundromat unrecognized. When she went to restaurants, other diners would talk about her or just stare, while paparazzi photographers waited for her outside, the more daring walking up to her table and snapping a picture as she ate.

She was disconcerted to find that universal recognition was not something that she enjoyed. 'It really bothered me,' she recalls, and admits that, at times, she felt 'caged' in her own room. As Steve Bray commented laconically, 'She always wanted to be the center of attention. Now it's her job.' Her changed circumstances were witnessed one evening by video producer Ed Steinberg, whose path and Madonna's had first crossed in 1981 when she was a struggling unknown. He spotted her at the Lucky Strike Club, trying hard to be inconspicuous at the back of the room, and surrounded by bodyguards and other assistants. 'I thought that it must be great to have her money, entrée and fame, but I would not want to be her. She looked very lonely. Who could she now trust? Did people want to be her friend because of who she was or what she could do for them?'

Certainly, some of Madonna's closest acquaintances were having trouble coming to terms with her rise to fame. Her ex-lover from 1983, Jean-Michel Basquiat, went into a deep depression when, in May 1985, her face appeared on the cover of the prestigious *Time* magazine. His artistic sensibilities outraged, he felt that he was more talented than she, and that it should be his face fronting such publications, not hers. Even Madonna's younger sister Paula complained to Steinberg, who had employed her at the time, that she was a better singer than her sister and should therefore be the star of the family. Steinberg sympathized. 'It was very hard on Paula always living in the shadow. She was a nice kid, used by the New York crowd as a kind of substitute for her sister.'

Some felt walked over by Madonna on her route march to stardom, others carelessly discarded. Madonna herself was typically unapologetic. 'I'm tough, I'm ambitious and I know exactly what I want,' she argued. 'If that makes me a bitch, that's okay.' When her former boyfriend Mark Kamins discovered that 'Into The Groove,' which Madonna had specifically written for his latest protégée, Cheyne, had been recorded instead for the film *Desperately Seeking Susan*, he hit the roof. It was only after he had paid to record the song that he learned that she herself had recorded it for the film's soundtrack. While 'Into The Groove' would come to be described as Madonna's 'first great single,' it left an angry Kamins out of pocket. 'I was pissed at her,' he says – more angry that she had not taken the trouble to tell him than about the cost.

While some relationships fell by the wayside, other friendships strengthened and deepened. Thus her creative collaboration with Steve Bray, now drumming with the re-formed Breakfast Club, yielded half the songs for the *Like A Virgin* album, which had been produced by Niles Rodgers. Bray describes the process of working with Madonna thus: 'I've always kind of made the rib cage and the skeleton [music] of the song already – she's there for the last things like the eyebrows and the haircut [lyrics]. She writes in a stream of mood really.' It was a process witnessed first-hand by their mutual friend Erika Belle, who watched them at work at the Sigma Sound studio. Bray was struggling with the 'bridge' for 'Into The Groove', when, undeterred by his obvious difficulties, Madonna stepped up to the microphone and sang the words 'live out your fantasy here with me.' 'It just seemed to come out of her,' Belle remembers, adding, 'I was awestruck.'

Diplomatically, her then boyfriend of two and a half years, Jellybean Benitez, acknowledged that people felt 'exploited' by Madonna, but argued that their expectations of her were too high. 'If there is any cooling of that friendship, it's taken as rejection,' he said. Eventually he too became a victim of her success. In the beginning many had expected that Madonna and Benitez would marry, especially when they became engaged and began living together in SoHo. 'He was in love with her,' observes the DJ's close friend, Arthur Baker. 'I knew he was really into her. They were both very ambitious people and they were a great team. But she was the one in charge. She's a diva – man, they like to command attention. All singers are like that.'

Jellybean, too, liked to command attention, and that was at the heart of the issue. They both had too much ambition, so intent on pursuing their individual agendas that they never had the time to nurture their mutual growth as a couple. 'He's a Scorpio and we both want to be stars, so it's tough-going all the way,' Madonna admitted at the time. They were undoubt-edly at their best when they were working on her musical career, discussing new songs or exploring angles, whether creative or business. Yet even that partnership had its limitations, as Madonna herself acknowledged: 'When you're working and your private life is falling apart, it's hard to carry on. When you're getting on, you can't stop talking about the record business and then you wonder if you have anything else in common.' These limitations were further exposed when Benitez discovered that, behind his back, Madonna was seeing Steve Neumann, a journalist who was in a long-term relationship with Madonna's friend Erika Belle. While it was a short-lived fling, perhaps because of Benitez's actions – on one occasion he burst into Neumann's apartment looking for his fiancée – her behavior did little to cement mutual trust. Erika Belle, however, is calmly dismissive of the situa-tion. 'He could be a little jealous around the edges,' she says of Benitez. 'It was his Latin blood. But you should never underestimate how close Madonna and Jellybean were.'

Perhaps the greatest contribution Jellybean Benitez made to Madonna's life at this time was simply his presence at her side as she tried to cope with her new celebrity. As he later told the writer Mark Bego, 'I think it was really good that we ended up meeting when we met – because we helped each other through some very difficult times.' Besides dealing with fans asking for auto-graphs, many of whom felt at liberty to make such remarks as, 'Oh, you're shorter than the pictures,' or offered comments about her hair, he tried to shield her from photographers, and was there to reassure her when she attracted media criticism. After a time, however, even Jellybean tired of being Mr Madonna, an understandably galling position for a successful DJ and producer in his own right, a man who had employed his own publicity agent when his girlfriend was still an unknown. In an attempt to restore their rela-tionship, in December 1984 they took a Christmas break in the Virgin Islands. Yet the holiday only served to underline their growing social disparity. On the flight home, Jellybean found himself playing both the role of his girlfriend's public-relations officer and her security guard, shooing away the constant procession of hopeful fans who approached her.

Less than a month later, in January, Madonna flew to Los Angeles to film the video of her latest single, 'Material Girl,' a three-minute film directed by Mary Lambert, who had also directed the *Like A Virgin* video. The *Material Girl* video was to become a modern classic, Madonna reinventing herself as an archetypal fifties Hollywood sex goddess, reprising Marilyn Monroe's role in the Howard Hawks movie *Gentlemen Prefer Blondes*. It was a punishing schedule – they had only two days to film the video, and matters were thrown into crisis when, while in California, Madonna discovered that she was pregnant by Benitez.

For a woman determined to be in control of her life, her pregnancy came as a tremendous shock. After discussing matters with her lover, Madonna, upset and apprehensive, decided that it would be best if the pregnancy were terminated. Her manager, Freddy DeMann, was on hand to make the necessary arrangements. As Melinda Cooper, DeMann's assistant, told Christopher Andersen, 'She came to Freddy and me and she was very upset – just this scared young girl who didn't want her family to know. Madonna loved Jellybean very much, but she wanted a career and so did he. So we arranged for Madonna to have the abortion, drove her to the doctor's office, everything. She seemed so innocent at the time.'

It has been said that during her affair with Benitez she had three abortions, her friend Erika Belle cited as the sole source. Belle herself says that, while they discussed contraception, periods and other intimate matters, abortion was never on the agenda. 'For all her self-protection, she is human, she loves children, has hormones and is a prisoner of her biology,' she says. 'Abortion, however, is not something we ever talked about.'

Years later, however, when Madonna and her lover of the time, Jim Albright, were discussing plans to have children together, she told him about the abortions she had had in her life, including the termination of her pregnancy by Jellybean Benitez when she was in California. 'It was a very traumatic time for her,' Albright says, reflecting that her ferocious longing for fame was balanced by her maternal feelings and her sense of guilt, partly as a result of her Catholic upbringing.

In early 1985, however, there were few moments in which to dwell on the matter. After filming in Los Angeles, Madonna flew to Hawaii, where she posed on the beach for celebrity photographer Herb Ritts for a Madonna calendar. Meanwhile, *Like A Virgin* had toppled Bruce Springsteen from the top slot in the album charts, so that when she jetted on to Osaka in Japan for a short promotional trip, she had become the hottest property on the planet, her records and tapes selling at an astonishing 80,000 copies a day worldwide.

Yet although she had every reason to be on top of the world, Madonna felt 'lonely and upset' after the abortion and in the light of her realization that she was losing Benitez, a state of mind not helped when a hoax caller told her that her father had died. Even though she informed her aides that she wanted her boyfriend to be flown out to the West Coast to be with her, the couple were not reunited until January 28, 1985, when he escorted her to the American Music Awards in Los Angeles – only for Madonna to lose the title of Favorite Female Pop Vocalist to Cyndi Lauper. It was to be their last date

Previous page and above: Madonna posing for Linda Alaniz. In New York she often earned money modeling nude for art students and photographers; some of the photographs would later come back to haunt her

emmy

clean up

AT botany

show at 11

THURSDAY DEC 11

6 Ave AND 27

741 9182

Above: A rare handbill for Emmy, the band Madonna put together in 1980. She sang lead, Brian Syms played lead guitar, Gary Burke bass guitar, and Steve Bray (left) drums

Right: Madonna practicing with her $300 guitar on the tenth floor of the Music Building, New York, a grungy downtown space where her band Emmy rehearsed

Above and left: More punk than New Romantic now — Madonna on the roof of the Gramercy Park Hotel in New York, 1981

Left: Madonna performing in men's pajamas with the fly sewn up during a gig at Max's Kansas City in Manhattan. Her one-time Michigan boyfriend and musical collaborator Steve Bray is on the drums

Right: Going through her paces at Max's Kansas City, the club that launched the careers of Blondie, The Talking Heads and The Ramones

Left: In June 1981 Madonna signed a deal to record a demo tape at the Media Sound studios, New York. *Left to right*: Adam Alter, Madonna, John Roberts, Susan Planer and Madonna's manager, Camille Barbone

Below and right: In her early career Madonna wore anything that came to hand when she appeared on stage, borrowing her manager's denim jacket and a second-hand frilled top. In the background is guitarist John Kaye

Left: Madonna's showcase gig at the trendy Underground Club, November 1981. The club was filled with exotic flowers for the occasion, and numerous record-company executives were invited to see her perform

Right and below: A twenty-four-year-old Madonna at the time of her first record release, seen here with Jean-Michel Basquiat, the famous Brooklyn-born artist with whom she was briefly involved. The most troubled of her lovers, and a heroin addict, Basquiat died of an overdose in 1988, aged twenty-seven

The camera just loves Madonna and she loves the camera. 'She doesn't want to *live* off camera, much less talk,' was Warren Beatty's famous observation of his one-time lover. There has always been a chameleon quality about her photographic image, so that her look is constantly evolving. Even when she became a star, she was able to sit outside in street cafés, passers-by only half wondering if it was the real Madonna.

For much of her career Madonna has played on her obvious sex appeal, vamping it up for the camera, on and off stage. Her book *Sex* was essentially the summation of her love affair with the lens, a modern-day collection of raunchy pin-ups. These seven rarely seen portraits (*these two pages and following*), taken in her New York days around 1980 and 1981, show the many faces of Madonna: quizzical, haughty, friendly, thoughtful and indifferent, the human face of a young woman who would soon dominate the music scene, blazing a trail around the world as an emblem of the strong, sexually confident woman

together – although, as with many of her lovers, Madonna remained on good terms with Jellybean, even singing on his dance single, 'Sidewalk Talk,' in December that year.

Already she was moving to pastures new. Indeed, her fateful first meeting with the man who would become her husband had actually taken place just as the relationship with Jellybean Benitez was ending. Legend has it that, as she stood nervously waiting at the top of a staircase on the set of her *Material Girl* video, Madonna looked down and saw the man she would marry. Director Mary Lambert had invited her friend Sean Penn, the son of television director Leo Penn and former actress Eileen Penn, along to watch the shoot. Hard-drinking, violent and abusive, if immensely talented, Penn was a member of the so called 'Brat Pack' of young Hollywood actors that included Rob Lowe, Tom Cruise and James Foley. As Madonna stood poised for descent, and looking every inch the 1950s movie queen in her fuchsia sheath dress, she noticed Penn hovering in the shadows off-set, wearing a leather jacket and sunglasses. At that moment, she later claimed, she 'immediately had this fantasy that we were going to meet and fall in love and get married.'

If so, she gave the fantasy little thought during the first few weeks of her stay in Los Angeles. Never one to stand still, she was determined to make the best of the opportunities now opening up for her in Hollywood. Yet for all her metropolitan sophistication and pop success, during her first visits to the West Coast she was just a starstruck visitor from the Midwest thrilled to be rubbing shoulders with Hollywood royalty. Within a matter of days she had met Keith Carradine, who played a sleazy Hollywood mogul in her *Material Girl* video, Jack Nicholson, Warren Beatty and Prince, who invited her to a concert of his after she presented him with an award at the American Music Awards. 'She was like a kid in a candy store,' recalls Erika Belle. 'She was utterly star-struck. In no particular order she told me that she had met Elizabeth Taylor, Sean Penn and a popcorn magnate. It was exciting for her, but she was serious about making a name for herself.'

Prince squired her around town, taking her for dinner at various Japanese restaurants and sending over a limousine to collect her when he played his concert date at the Los Angeles Forum. While the tabloids talked of a 'red-hot romance,' Madonna, focused as ever, was more interested in how Prince was going about his career – in the previous twelve months he could boast a top single, album and movie, as well as an Academy Award for the soundtrack for the film *Purple Rain*. In the event, the 'red-hot' romance failed to ignite, but their friendship would prove to be a fruitful musical and business collaboration; although they discounted writing a musical together, they performed a duet, 'Love Song', on Madonna's album *Like A Prayer*. She also later took an interest in his Paisley Park recording studios.

It seemed that Prince was the creative template for her own career as she embraced the world of music, video and film. In the first six months of 1985 Madonna had six separate singles in the charts, with no fewer than five separate music videos on television as well as two films in which she had parts, *Vision Quest* and *Desperately Seeking Susan*, vying for public – and critical – attention. She had always seen herself as the queen of the big screen and, never one to rest on her laurels, had began to turn her thoughts towards Hollywood. Her small part as a singer in the film *Vision Quest,* shot on location in Washington State in November 1983, in which she sang 'Crazy For You' (the title used for the film in Britain) and 'Gambler,' had helped her to win the part of Susan – ahead of established actresses like Kelly McGillis, Ellen Barkin and Melanie Griffith – in a low-budget film that turned out to be a surprise box-office smash. Directed by Susan Seidelman and featuring Madonna's song 'Into The Groove', which she co-wrote with Steve Bray, *Desperately Seeking Susan* was released on March 29, 1985, and went on to take $27.3 million at the box office in the United States alone, making it the fifth highest-grossing film of that year.

This light and funny social satire, about a bored housewife who, after losing her memory, changes places with the free-spirited and sexually liberated Susan, was intended as a starring vehicle for Rosanna Arquette, who won a British Film Academy award for her role, but the star of the film was undoubtedly Madonna. Of the character she played, the singer remarked: 'She has no roots, she represents freedom and adventure and all the things that normal people think they can't do,' although, in an aside, she also observed that Susan was a conniving opportunist. Interestingly, and perhaps revealingly, she continued, 'But she really did care about people. Anybody who goes around acting like nobody matters obviously is protecting themselves and hiding what they really feel.'

The critics judged her performance a success, although many remarked that it was that of an actress playing herself. Her former manager, Camille Barbone, thought she was 'brilliant' in the part, revealing that Madonna 'used to lie on my living-room floor taking pictures of herself just like in the film.' To her former lover, Mark Kamins, the part of Susan 'wasn't a character, it was Madonna. A wisecracking, smart-ass, gum-chewing, savvy, streetwise chick. She was the original club kid, riding a bicycle around New York, always off to the next place.'

For Madonna, the next venue had to be Hollywood, her eyes always on the prize of acting success. It was on the West Coast, too, that she found the man of her dreams, embarking on a whirlwind romance that became a whirligig of headlines, heartache and regret. While the tabloids were feasting on the headline-making liaison between Madonna and Prince, Sean Penn was quietly making his moves in the background. The first signs were propitious. Birth dates are important to Madonna, so when she discovered that she and the actor had been born a day apart, her interest in him sharpened. There was also something about the mean, downward curve of his mouth, the eyes set slightly too close together and the luxuriant head of hair that reminded her of someone: her father. A glance at a photograph of the young Tony Ciccone immediately confirms the likeness.

Like Madonna, Sean Penn had just emerged from a serious long-term relationship. For the last two years he had been engaged to the actress Elizabeth McGovern, the couple starring together in the film *Racing With the Moon*. Short-tempered and wildly jealous, Penn had pounded on the side of her trailer when she was being interviewed alone by a male reporter during a break from filming. On another occasion the tempestuous star had allegedly shot the watch off her wrist. Whether such displays had anything to do with the decision or not, by 1985 the couple had decided to go their separate ways, calling off their engagement shortly before Madonna arrived in Los Angeles.

Penn drove Madonna around town, showing her the sights, including Marilyn Monroe's grave at Westwood Cemetery. She was also shown his gun collection, the actor not only revealing that he kept a weapon in his four-wheel-drive pickup, but also pointing out the shooting range at his home. On their first night out together Penn took Madonna over to the home of his friend Warren Beatty, where, among other Hollywood celebrities, she met Penn's acting mentor Jack Nicholson, Mickey Rourke and the stand-up comic Sandra Bernhard, who would become a close friend.

The path of the budding romance was hardly smooth, however. Early in March, before it had even become a romance, the pair allegedly quarreled over Madonna being seen out with Prince, while Penn's encounter with his former girlfriend, Elizabeth McGovern, at a Manhattan restaurant led to a tirade of very public abuse from Madonna. Penn was not used to having his love life played out in the media, but where there was Madonna, there were always plenty of reporters.

In many ways Sean Penn – chain-smoking, short-fused and frequently abusive – was a strange choice of lover for Madonna. There can be no doubt, however, about the effect he had on her. 'I'm inspired and shocked by him at the same time,' she told the entertainment journalist Fred Schruers. When she arrived back in New York her friends were amused to see that her casual wear now consisted of rugged outdoor clothes more suited to the mountains than to Manhattan. On being told about the new relationship, several of her circle thought that it was the Hollywood tag that came with Penn that was the real attraction. After weeks of 'Sean this' and 'Sean that,' however, it became clear to them that Madonna was seriously smitten.

Her friends' confusion was matched only by their concern. Penn's first visit to New York was not a success, mutual suspicion merely exacerbating the cultural gulf between the East and West Coasts. It seemed to her circle that he could barely contain his revulsion when he met homosexuals like Andy Warhol, Keith Haring and Martin Burgoyne, their dress, values and sexual orientation alien and intimidating to him. 'He was horrified,' Erika Belle remembers. 'He sat there mortified at this crowd of freaks. We made his skin crawl, he couldn't wait to get the fuck out. He didn't communicate, he just sneered.' The truth was, of course, that neither side gave the other a chance, each prepared only to have their own prejudices and preconceptions confirmed. From then on Madonna, sensitive to her boyfriend's feelings, was careful to keep him away from her New York set.

Yet beneath the immature persona, there was a good deal more to Penn than the spoiled rich kid who had enjoyed a sheltered and overprivileged upbringing. Like Madonna's New York friends, he was passionate about his art, prepared to take creative risks while having the courage to thumb his nose at the Hollywood establishment. As the writer Lynn Hirschberg has observed, 'He is a throwback to the sort of men – tough, thoughtful, somewhat dangerous, full of inchoate feeling – who haunt the songs of Bruce Springsteen and the writings of Charles Bukowski.' Throughout his career he has demonstrated and maintained an almost permanent sense of outrage and moral principle as a means to keeping his art pure. 'A cowboy poet,' is the way Madonna once put it, a phrase which, although an oversimplification, still manages to convey something of Penn's straightforwardness and integrity as an actor.

For her part, Madonna was attracted not only to the bad boy in Sean Penn, and to the wild side of his nature, but also to his basic decency and old-fashioned chivalry. More cynically, there was, too, as some of her acquaintances had suspected, the not insignificant fact that a union with Penn could open many doors to her for a future career in Hollywood. Nonetheless, her close friends accepted that she was in love with Penn. 'She had very genuine feelings for him,' noted one. 'For a woman who wants to be in control of everything, she made herself vulnerable to accommodate his feelings and well-being.'

Such was not the case, however, when it came to her career, and work was once again in the way of romance. Madonna spent time in New York and Los

Angeles madly rehearsing for her first nationwide tour, which kicked off in April 1985. Meanwhile Penn was preparing for two months' filming in Nashville, Tennessee for the movie *At Close Range*, which also starred his brother Chris and Christopher Walken. Thus the relationship now became dependent on long-distance telephone calls and weekend visits when the lovers' schedules allowed.

For the Like A Virgin Tour Madonna and her manager, Freddy DeMann, plundered talent from Michael Jackson, as well as props and stage designs from Prince. After weeks of remorseless rehearsals, overseen by Madonna, the show opened in Seattle with Sean dutifully watching his lover go through her paces. He was in the audience again in May when the Madonna roadshow rolled into the town of her birth, Pontiac, Michigan. In Detroit she performed a toned-down version of the show, out of respect for her family, particularly her father, and Penn found himself being introduced to Tony Ciccone, Christopher Flynn and various teachers from Madonna's days at Rochester Adams High. The tour was a huge success, hundreds of thousands of young girls turning up for the concerts dressed exactly like the woman they had come to see.

When she arrived back in New York in June 1985, at the end of her sell-out tour, she received a rapturous welcome from her circle. They had watched her rise to fame avidly, seeing her as a torch bearer for their lifestyle in a country where conservatism ruled. 'We were just thrilled for her,' says Jimi LaLumia, former star of Max's Kansas City. 'She was one of us made good.' Nor did it go unnoticed that her choice of backup act, The Beastie Boys, showed loyalty to her roots – the band had been part of the Danceteria club crowd in those early, hardscrabble days.

At a party hosted by her designer friend Maripol at the end of the tour, Madonna hooked up with friends from the old days. For once, she wasn't in the mood for schmoozing with hip trendsetters; more than anything at that moment, she wished to be the old, anonymous Madonna. She just wanted to party. After a brief chat with Andy Warhol, she, Fab Five Freddie and others jumped into her chauffeur-driven limousine and headed off to seedy Alphabet City. She was eager to find a young Latino named Pedro whom she knew. They stopped the car, she opened the sunroof and yelled out his name. When he didn't appear they headed off to the Palladium Club to go dancing.

Madonna was no longer just another club kid, however, and the days of her anonymity were far behind her. When they arrived, the paparazzi were waiting for her, and, as flashguns illuminated the scene, there was a scuffle between the photographers, a bodyguard and a couple of her party. On this night though, even such unlooked-for intrusion failed to dampen her high spirits. Inside the club, the DJ was playing her record, 'Into The Groove,' and she, Freddie and the others immediately hit the dance floor. She even found it funny when a couple of guys who came over to check her out decided that she was definitely not Madonna. 'She was as happy as she could ever be,' recalls Freddie. 'We bounced around and she was just the same as ever. But at the same time, you know, different.'

She was soon to be very different. That month, after spending only a few weeks together as a couple, Penn asked Madonna to marry him. He popped the question one Sunday morning in Nashville, as his bride-to-be bounced naked on their hotel bed. She, of course, accepted. At the time rumors were already rife that Madonna was pregnant; indeed, one anonymous well-wisher even sent to their hotel room a bunch of balloons with a card that read, 'Sean and Madonna, Congratulations Mom and Pop.' The couple chose to remain silent about the matter, but, years later, Madonna confided to her friends that she had indeed been pregnant and had had a second abortion that year. Once again she decided that it was not the right time, either in terms of her career or, despite her impending marriage, of her relationship, to have a child. For a woman who so desperately needed to be in command of her destiny, Madonna was once more exercising her right to control her life, albeit in rather drastic fashion. Certainly, to have two abortions within a matter of months suggests that in some areas, her life was not altogether under control.

It was an issue that clearly troubled Penn almost as much as it did his fiancée, as a friend notes: 'The second abortion was traumatic for both of them, especially as their relationship had progressed so far. He looked on it as an opportunity to settle her down. She used to tell me, "Barefoot and naked in the kitchen," that's how he wanted her to be. But she definitely loved him. She always talked about him in a good light.' Indeed, it can be argued that the issue of children was to be one of the main stumbling blocks in the forthcoming marriage. As Penn conceded in a later interview for *Fame* magazine, 'I wanted to have a kid, she didn't.' The strain of the abortion could not have come at a worse time, for more trouble was just around the corner.

To the casual eye, Ed Steinberg, Freddy DeMann and Seymour Stein were enjoying a boys' night in at Steinberg's Manhattan apartment, savoring balloon glasses of cognac and illegal cigars that their host had just brought back from a trip to Havana. As usual, however, business was not far from their minds, and tonight, like many other people in the world, they were discussing the effect that the publication of nude photographs of Madonna would have on her career.

The photos in question were those taken in New York in 1978, when Madonna, desperate for money, had modeled nude for Bill Stone and Martin Schreiber. Now, they were about to be published simultaneously in *Playboy* and *Penthouse* magazines. There was little that anyone present in Steinberg's apartment that night could do about it, for at the time when the pictures were taken, Madonna had signed the appropriate release forms in return for as little as $25 a session. All she and her team could do now was sit back and watch the furor, as those lucky enough to have taken nude shots of her cashed in their photographs for $100,000 a time, and the two magazines entered into a desperate race to be the first to publish.

I am not ashamed of anything, was Madonna's message to the world, delivered in a statement given out by her press agent, Liz Rosenberg. Yet when she performed before some ninety thousand fans at the Live Aid concert in Philadelphia that July, just as the magazines were hitting newsstands everywhere, she belted out her hits in a brocade coat in temperatures of over 90 degrees. In reply to Bette Midler's introduction, 'Here's a woman who has pulled herself up by her bra straps and who has been known to let them down occasionally,' Madonna yelled to the waiting fans, 'I ain't taking shit off today. You might hold it against me in ten years.'

'Doesn't all this upset you?' Ed Steinberg asked Freddy DeMann. In response, Madonna's manager looked at the video producer as if he were an imbecile. 'Ed, don't you get it?' he replied. 'What would it cost to get that kind of publicity? You can't *buy* that kind of promotion.' Thoughts of engineered publicity had occurred to others, too. *Rolling Stone* magazine, for instance, was skeptical that, even given the fierce competition between the publications, both *Playboy* and *Penthouse* had managed to uncover a cache of naked Madonna photographs at exactly the same time. 'If it isn't a fix then God clearly likes bad Catholic girls,' was *Rolling Stone*'s view.

While, in general, most people doubted that Madonna had been involved in 'planting' the photos, few saw her as a victim in the situation, and there was much media talk about her opportunism. *Penthouse* publisher Bob Guccione stirred the debate by announcing that he had offered Madonna a million dollars to pose naked for the magazine. Had she agreed, he would, he said, have withdrawn from publishing the earlier photographs, but she had turned him down.

Nor had her past yet finished its sport with Madonna. In addition to the publication of the nude photographs, Stephen Lewicki had seen his chance to cash in on the star's success by releasing video copies of *A Certain Sacrifice*, the low-budget underground movie he had made with her in 1979. He had offered distribution rights in the film to Ed Steinberg's company, Rock

America, seeking to sell video copies of the film, with its copious nudity, sex slaves, rape scene and human sacrifice, for $59.95 each. Steinberg now told Freddy DeMann that for a few thousand dollars he could secure an exclusive deal and effectively suppress the film, but the latter was certainly not interested. 'Distribute it, go ahead,' he told Steinberg. As far as DeMann was concerned, any publicity was good publicity. Lewicki distributed the videos and, it is said, made hundreds of thousands of dollars from his otherwise worthless film.

For all her manager's confidence, however, Madonna was not happy about the circumstances in which she now found herself. While her offer to Lewicki of $10,000 to withdraw *A Certain Sacrifice*, which he rejected, was always unlikely to have made him change his mind about distributing the film, and the half-hearted and ultimately unsuccessful lawsuit that followed only gained her more publicity, she found it difficult to cope with the fact that her fiancé and her family – and in particular her maternal grandmother – were upset by the publication of the nude photos. She also genuinely resented that she was unable to intervene. 'I think when I first found out about it, the thing that annoyed me most wasn't so much that they were nude photographs but that I felt really out of control,' she said.

As Freddy DeMann had predicted, the publicity did Madonna no professional harm, although it certainly put a damper on her excitement about her wedding. With the announcement of her engagement, the media had gone crazy, and the couple were involved in high-speed chases through the streets of New York and elsewhere, pursued by photo-hungry paparazzi. Intensely private by nature, Penn had already got on the wrong side of the press when, while still in Nashville, he had attacked two British journalists with a rock. He was duly charged with two misdemeanor counts of assault and battery. He did not defend the charges, and received a short suspended sentence and a fine. Madonna, who usually co-operated with the media, saw his behavior as an example of his chivalry, insisting that he had been trying to protect her from unwanted attention. As she was soon to find out, it was not, perhaps, a good idea to get on the wrong side of the press.

By now, the couple had decided to marry on her birthday, August 16, at a secret location in California, and Madonna turned her prodigious energies, her eye for detail, her desire for perfection and for control, upon her wedding. She wanted to make this a special day, one to be cherished by her family and friends, and spent hours each day on the phone making arrangements, from the guest list to the catering, the decoration to the dancing. Such was her concern that she would speak to her sister Paula, who was to be her maid of honor, at least half a dozen times a day.

In keeping with the rags-to-riches history Madonna attaches to herself, she themed the wedding around the tale of Cinderella and Prince Charming. Gold Cinderella slippers formed the centerpiece for each table, and her wedding dress designer, Marlene Stewart, was instructed to create a fifties-style concoction fit for a princess, such as 'Grace Kelly would have worn.' Certainly, the world had proof, if it had needed any, that the girl from the Midwest had come a long way as she now planned the wedding of the year, with a guest list that included the Hollywood stars she had watched at the movies or on television as a young girl.

The couple went to elaborate lengths, almost to the point of paranoia, to keep the media at bay. In a nod towards the rather unsavory public image they were now acquiring, they sent out witty, if cryptic, wedding invitations to 220 guests, poking fun at themselves as the 'Poison Penns.' The illustration on the card, drawn by Penn's brother Michael, showed a demonic-looking Sean and Madonna, the latter wearing a 'Sean Toy' belt buckle. In the interests of privacy, however, details of the time and place of the big event were deliberately omitted. Yet despite these elaborate precautions – even staff at the Spago restaurant, who provided the catering, were not told the whereabouts of the reception until just hours before – the media discovered that the couple were to marry in an open-air ceremony at the Malibu home of the millionaire developer Kurt Unger, a long-time friend of the Penn family.

Thanks to the media, Madonna's fairytale wedding rapidly degenerated into a nightmarish farce. Unger's cliff-top house was surrounded by journalists and photographers, while the noise of low-flying helicopters, also full of press reporters and cameramen, made it impossible for anyone to hear the couple as they took their marriage vows before Judge John Merrick; indeed, before the ceremony, a furious Penn ran down to the beach and scrawled 'FUCK OFF' in giant letters in the sand, and even fired warning shots at the aircraft from a .45-caliber pistol. Madonna, who was in the middle of a photo session with Herb Ritts when Penn began shooting, broke away and stood at an upstairs window shouting at him to stop. But control had been snatched from her, and she could only watch helplessly as the day she had planned so carefully rapidly descended into chaos.

Not only had the press taken over the airspace, but some had managed to infiltrate the wedding guests and had to be forcibly evicted. Meanwhile, the guests were not exactly mingling. The Hollywood crowd, which included Cher, Martin Sheen, Diane Keaton and Carrie Fisher, kept well away from Madonna's New York friends, among them Andy Warhol, Keith Haring, Debi Mazar and Steve Rubell. 'A lot of shade was being thrown,' recalls Erika Belle.

Matters were not helped when the nightclub-owner Steve Rubell vomited into the swimming pool, or when the maid of honor burst into the powder room and declared to everyone within earshot, 'This should be my wedding day, not hers.' Utterly careless of what she was saying, Paula Ciccone went on to inform embarrassed guests, 'I should be the famous one. This should be my career. All this attention should have been mine.' Andy Warhol was heard to remark, 'I can't believe this,' shaking his head in wonder at being present at such a bizarre event.

The mood was hardly celebratory. Madonna's friends disliked Penn, and his were convinced that he should not go through with the marriage. As the couple danced to the strains of Dinah Washington's soulful rendition of 'Mad About The Boy,' many thought that 'mad' just about summed up the union. Now, however, it had been made official; Madonna had turned her back on the free-spirited New York girl. She was a Hollywood wife now.

Chapter Nine

Desperately Seeking Hollywood

WITH THE CHAOS OF HER WEDDING DAY mercifully in the past, Madonna now had to adapt to life as Mrs Penn, and to get to know the man she had married. After the honeymoon at the exclusive Highlands Inn in Carmel, California, her marriage was at first a great adventure to her, a self-conscious exercise, both in public and in private, in how she should mold herself as a wife, and especially as the wife of a Hollywood bad boy. Yet although it was a role she enjoyed – and she continued to convince those close to her that she was a woman deeply in love – from the beginning she struggled with the limitations it imposed on her, not so much in the sense that she now had someone other than herself to consider, but rather more because she craved the more spontaneous lifestyle she had enjoyed in New York.

It was not long before she had grown bored with the luxuries of Los Angeles. Whereas in New York anything and everything had seemed to be happening virtually on her doorstep, in LA the social life seemed to her to be too carefully planned and orchestrated to be fun. Like a creature newly taken from the wild, she chafed against the apparent limitations of her new life, even though they were largely self-imposed.

To cheer herself up, she invited some of her New York friends for a weekend house party at the Malibu home she now shared with her husband. It was not a success. Her guests were guarded and on their best, and therefore least typical, behavior; nervous of Sean, no one really felt inclined to party in the old way in his company. 'There was much less room to be impulsive,' recalls Erika Belle. 'Nor did it help that Sean barely tolerated us.'

Her social life may not have been as stimulating as Madonna desired, but by the autumn of 1985 work on her third album was proceeding well. This time she had decided to co-produce the album, and she also co-wrote all but one of the nine tracks. She went on to name it *True Blue* – a favorite expression of Sean's – and although only the title song is a direct tribute to her husband, the whole album is inspired by her feelings for him at this time. 'She was very much in love,' confirmed Steve Bray, who worked with her on the album. 'If she's in love she'll write love songs. If she's not in love she definitely won't be writing love songs.' She had learned her trade well, for although *True Blue* failed to win rave reviews from the music critics when it was released at the end of June 1986, it sold over five million copies in the United States alone and another twelve million worldwide, reaching the number-one slot in twenty-eight countries. Whatever else Madonna was trying to be at this time, the album's success undoubtedly reinforced her status as the hottest new thing in pop.

For the truth is that she did want to be something else, over and above what she had already achieved. She may have got the man she wanted and the success she craved, but Madonna also wanted to be a movie star. As she was to admit later, 'Music was still very important to me, but I always had a great interest in films, and the thought that I could only make records for the rest of my life filled me with horror.' Then, in 1985, a script for a comedy movie, *Shanghai Surprise,* was sent to her by the producer John Kohn, a long-time friend of the Penn family. Madonna was intrigued by the storyline about a female American missionary who goes to work in China in the 1930s, during the Sino-Japanese War, and who becomes involved with a handsome young racketeer. She found the idea of herself as the heroine and her husband as the gangster irresistible, and although Sean did not entirely share her enthusiasm, they agreed to meet Kohn to discuss the script.

In fact, Sean had already worked with the producer on two other films, *Racing With the Moon* and *Bad.* Kohn met with the Penns in a Hollywood restaurant, partly in an attempt to persuade Sean to take the part, and a few minutes after they had sat down, his co-producer, the former Beatle George Harrison, who now ran the company behind the project, HandMade Films, turned up to greet the couple. 'They nearly fell off their chairs with surprise,' Kohn remembers. 'He left after fifteen minutes and when he had gone Madonna said to me: "There goes a legend. In all my time I've never met a legend and he's a real legend."'

The word seems to have received a considerable airing, for when he returned home, Kohn told his wife Barbara that he, too, had met a legend in the making. As he admits, speaking of Madonna, 'I thought we had the next Judy Holliday on our hands. She reminded me also of Raquel Welch, whom I worked with. She knew all about makeup, publicity and costumes but didn't know how to act. I thought though that she had the potential to be a terrific actress.'

Sean finally agreed to take on the part of the racketeer, and contracts were drawn up and signed. At first, the auguries seemed good. John Kohn, the director, Jim Goddard, and the Penns got along well on the occasions when they met before shooting began in Hong Kong in January 1986, and thereafter the couple endeared themselves to the film crew when they eschewed their grand suite at the five-star Regent Hotel in Hong Kong in favor of the more modest establishment in which everyone else was living. For once, too, they managed to maintain virtual anonymity, able to walk through the streets of Hong Kong unrecognized.

Sadly, the auguries proved wrong. Nine days into shooting the 16 million-dollar movie, the on-set producer knew that the film was not working. Above all, it was not developing into the charming and sensitive comedy it was supposed to be. There were problems of direction. As far as Penn was concerned, he knew better than Goddard, refusing to take instruction to the point where he would even argue about the framing of a shot. Every scene became a struggle, not helped by the fact that Penn either could not, or would not, abandon his dour demeanor and act the jaunty character he was supposed to be playing. The crisis point came when, during one scene, the severely tested Goddard walked off set, leaving Penn squinting through the camera lens, at which point Kohn intervened, telling him that unless he fell into line, he would be in breach of his contract.

In complete contrast to her husband's, Madonna's behavior was extremely professional; always on time, always ready with her lines. She was, too, always happy with her first take – and therein lay yet another problem for the harassed film-makers. As she was to show time and again in her acting career, she invariably believed that her first take was the best, and became unhappy when asked to shoot a scene again, or to play it differently. Furthermore, her lack of acting experience soon caused concern. It seemed that, while she liked the idea of herself in the role, she had not given any real thought as to how she should play the character of the missionary Gloria Tatlock. Cocky and difficult as ever, Sean was only too happy to offer his views on how he saw the part, but since these clashed with the director's, they proved, for everyone concerned, more of a hindrance than a help.

John Kohn has good cause to remember his leading lady's failings, though he does so without bitterness. 'Before a scene she would never ask questions about the character's inner motivation or how she related to the other characters. So on set the minute the guy shouted "Action!" she didn't have a clue what she was doing. She was only good in the love scenes with Sean because she really loved the guy. That was her, not the character. In the rest she was very wooden because she was so inexperienced. She would just walk through a scene and think she had given a fine performance when it was nothing of the sort. It was a very funny part but she didn't carry it off.'

Since that perceptive comment by a reviewer of *Desperately Seeking Susan*, the criticism that she cannot act unless she is playing herself is one that has very much haunted Madonna. While her on-stage concert performances can be mesmerizing, and she has won praise for her acting in some of her videos, and particularly in the 1986 *Papa Don't Preach* video, in which, aged twenty-eight, she convincingly plays a pregnant teenager, she has not found it easy to transfer her skills to the big screen. As ever, the message was ambiguous. Some critics thought she was pro-life, others that she was encouraging teen-age pregnancy.

Madonna herself has admitted that her struggle to come to terms with her part in *Shanghai Surprise* was largely because the innocence and repressed personality she was required to portray was so at variance with her own character. Yet when the film was released in August 1986, to poor reviews and even worse box-office figures, she was quick to blame anyone but herself. She described the making of the film as a 'hellish nightmare' and announced that she was 'extremely disappointed with it.' Without a trace of irony, she added, 'The director didn't seem to have an eye for the big screen. He seemed to be in a bit over his head.'

It wounded her deeply that a film in which she had seen such promise should have become an object of derision, and she herself pilloried when she had believed she would be fêted. Years later, when a friend casually mentioned to her that she had been weak in the film, she snapped back, 'You've got a lot of nerve. At least I took a chance. You have to start somewhere.'

While every single taken from her *True Blue* album would find its way into the Top Ten, getting her film career off the ground continued to be a struggle. True, there were plenty of scripts, but Madonna was now uncertain of her ability to make a good choice, and producers were even less sure about backing her. Nonetheless, the period did at least bring her first acting performance on stage. In the last week of August she again teamed up with Sean in a play by David Rabe called *Goose and Tom-Tom*, in which she played the part of a gangster's moll. Although the play, staged as a work-in-progress in the Mitzi Newhouse Theater in New York's Lincoln Center, was only open at this time to an audience of celebrities, the public waiting outside got their share of the drama when Sean assaulted two paparazzi photographers, hitting Vinnie Zuffante several times and spitting on Anthony Savignano, as well as punching him. On the night of her debut stage performance, this was hardly the publicity Madonna was looking for, a situation made worse when both photographers pressed charges.

For her next screen project, she picked another comedy, originally entitled *Slammer*, but later renamed *Who's That Girl?* since its release in 1987 would have coincided with a 60-day jail term Penn was to serve, having violated the probation he received for assaulting a friend of Madonna's in 1986 by attacking an extra on the set of his latest film who was taking snapshots. The part she wanted to play was that of a wisecracking street urchin named Nikki Finn, who has been jailed for a crime she did not commit. In the light of the bad publicity surrounding her and Sean, and also of the very public failure of *Shanghai Surprise*, she had to fight hard to persuade the producers, Warner Brothers, that she was up to the part. In addition, Madonna wanted an old friend, James Foley, Penn's best man at their wedding and the director of her *Papa Don't Preach*, *Live To Tell* and *Open Your Heart* videos, to be the director, proclaiming him to be a 'genius.' The combination of a dubiously talented movie star and a first-time movie director hardly guaranteed a box-office hit, but the film received the go-ahead from Warner.

This time around, there was a lighter atmosphere on set when filming began in New York in October of 1986. Madonna was approachable, signing autographs for children of the film crew, joining in with the wisecracking, and on one occasion even dancing around a boombox with fellow star and long-time friend Coati Mundi (real name Andy Hernandez), one of the original members of the group Kid Creole and the Coconuts. Her idea of preparing for her part, however, was hardly studied; for example, before a scene in which she needed to appear badly out of breath, she did a series of push-ups before going on set. Once again she was always punctual and professional, and once again she always felt that her first take was perfect. It was a source of conflict. Her co-star Griffin Dunne, who played the male lead, observed; 'She likes her first take best. I think my best is around the fourth. She always says, "You got it, you got it," and she was driving me crazy, just the way her character would.' On one occasion James Foley mockingly went down on his knees and kissed her feet to encourage her to do a retake. Afterwards he noted, not without irony, 'She's very instinctual, what comes out is unencumbered by analysis.'

Although Coati Mundi recalled getting on well with Madonna, and was particularly impressed that when one scene they were rehearsing, which involved a live cougar, went wrong, she stayed calm, even he admitted to being 'flipped out' by her on occasion. 'She doesn't rest,' he noted. 'She's got a bit of that perfectionist thing in her. She was doing the movie, and the sound-track album for the movie, and also planning her Who's That Girl? Tour at the same time. She's doing all this stuff, plus she's got the lead in the film!'

In spite of a glitzy launch, in front of thousands of screaming fans, at the National Theater in Times Square in August 1987, and even though the single of the title song from the soundtrack album reached the top of the charts, once again a Madonna movie bombed. This time, however, there was some comfort. Reviews were poor rather than damning – 'In Madonna Hollywood has a potent, pocket-sized sex bomb. So far, though, all it does is tick,' noted Vincent Canby in the *New York Times* – and although critics were not overly impressed by her performance, Madonna's comic talent was acknowledged. Even so, cinemagoers in the United States stayed away in droves. The movie fared rather better abroad, however, leading Madonna to defend herself, rather weakly, by saying that her ideas were more appreciated in Europe and Japan than in her own country. Yet with a number-one single in America and with her nationwide Who's That Girl? Tour a sell-out, it seemed that it was only her acting that her home country didn't appreciate. Americans didn't want another actress; they just wanted Madonna.

There were other problems, too, for the relentless speculation in the media about the state of her marriage was a low point of Madonna's life at this time.When Sean failed to visit her on set during the filming of *Who's That Girl?* it fueled rumors that they were about to split. While she accepted that as a Hollywood couple they were bound to attract attention, media interest merely exacerbated existing difficulties. 'A lot of times the press would make up the most awful things that we had never done, fights that we never had,' Madonna recalls. 'They couldn't make up their minds: they wanted me to be pregnant, or they wanted us to get a divorce. That put a lot of strain on our relationship after a while.'

The Penns fought back where they could, Sean often with his fists. For her part, Madonna had appeared in a skit about their wedding on the American comedy show *Saturday Night Live*. As the strains of Wagner's 'Ride of the Valkyrie' – used in a famous scene in the Vietnam movie, *Apocalypse Now* – faded into the background, along with a clip from the film showing the helicopter invasion, Madonna impishly told the audience; 'We have a great show . . . I'm not pregnant and we'll be right back.'

In the early days of their marriage, their running battle with the press drew the couple together in mutual rage. Yet, although Madonna initially viewed Sean's displays of aggression as a form of chivalry, she soon grew weary of his behavior. It diminished her image, and proved costly. During the filming of *Shanghai Surprise*, for example, Sean had scuffled with local photographer-cum-publisher, and influential local Hong Kong politician, Leonel Borralho, who filed a $1 million dollar lawsuit against him. Then, one evening in April of 1986, as Sean and Madonna were relaxing in a Los Angeles nightclub, one of her friends, the songwriter David Wolinski, walked over to greet her and kissed her on the cheek. By all accounts, Penn flew into a rage and began beating the hapless Wolinski, only stopping when the club's owner, Helena Kallianiotes, and a visibly shaken Madonna dragged him outside. Shocked, Wolinski pressed charges, and Penn was fined $1,000 and given a year's probation.

Penn may have been on probation for his attack on David Wolinski, but thereafter it seemed that rarely a week passed without his being involved in some incident or other, as the couple played hide-and-seek with the media. When Madonna bumped into Dan Gilroy in Hollywood, where he was busy shooting his own video for the first and only Breakfast Club album, they fell to talking about the old days. Commenting on the media's near obsession with her and her volatile husband, she told Gilroy wistfully, 'Do you remember the time when I would do anything to get noticed? Now I spend all day hiding.'

While Madonna managed to rise above the media taunts, knowing that any reaction from her merely played into the hands of journalists and photographers, Sean was too easily provoked. By mid-1986 matters were getting out of hand. He found himself taunted by paparazzi cameramen every time he went out, his tormentors hoping that their foul-mouthed abuse, directed either at him or his wife, would push him into an attack, thereby providing a juicy story and a lucrative front-page photograph. In New York in August 1986, shortly after they had celebrated their first wedding anniversary, he allowed himself to be drawn into a fistfight with a group of photographers as he and Madonna were walking home to their apartment. The resulting pictures were plastered over all the front pages, and so, just a day later, were others of Penn spitting on a crowd of photographers and fans from the second floor window of a downtown restaurant.

For her part, Madonna had more to worry about than her husband's behavior. She had reached another low when in June of the same year, her close friend Martin Burgoyne had been diagnosed as suffering from AIDS. This was a devastating blow, not just to Burgoyne, who was only twenty-three years old, but also to all those who knew him. At that time there was considerable hysteria and ignorance about the AIDS virus. What was known was that AIDS was a death sentence for those who contracted it, and that they, on top of their physical suffering, faced the likelihood of being shunned socially, a situation made worse by the strident outpourings of many vociferous would-be moralists, from churchmen to senators, who proclaimed the disease to be a 'gay plague'.

While those in Martin Burgoyne's circle struggled to come to terms with the news, many of them no doubt fearful for their own health, or even survival, Madonna put aside her own problems and seized the opportunity to do what she could to make her friend's remaining days more comfortable. Her friendship with Burgoyne had been utterly unshaken by her rise to fame, and now, unbidden, she paid his considerable medical expenses, and also rented an apartment for him just round the corner from Saint Vincent's Hospital, New York, where he was receiving treatment.

The press lost little time in sniffing out a story. By the first week of August, there were reports of Madonna being seen in New York buying books for a sick friend, and on October 13, 1986, a photograph of Sean and Madonna appeared on the cover of the *National Enquirer*, along with the headline, 'Madonna's Former Roommate Has AIDS – Sean Is Terrified & Furious. It's What's Really Ripping Their Marriage Apart.' Burgoyne was devastated by the lurid exposure of his illness.

Certainly there had been other reports of Sean's fear of contracting the disease, and of the fact that he had repeatedly urged Madonna to take an AIDS test, which she steadfastly refused to do. In the circumstances, however, he found the strength to put aside his personal fears, as well as his concerns about his wife's relationship with Burgoyne. When Madonna, who tirelessly explored every avenue that might give her friend the chance of a few more precious months of life, learned of an experimental drug which, although not licensed in the United States, was available in Mexico, it was Sean who took the trouble to fly across the border to bring back supplies of the medication. Not only did his efforts mean a lot to his wife, but for a time they also raised his standing among her friends. Interestingly, Burgoyne was one of the few among Madonna's set who was comfortable with her relationship with Penn. 'She can learn from him, and he can learn from her,' he had said at the time of their marriage.

As Burgoyne's condition deteriorated – friends who saw him at the end of August were shocked to see his face covered with sores – Madonna did her utmost to raise his spirits. She telephoned him most days, her lively, positive manner helping to keep him cheerful, and she also spent time shopping for books and presents that might amuse him. When she was in New York she visited him regularly, and, perhaps most importantly, and ignoring others' concern for her own well-being, she continued to hug and kiss him as she had always done – once even offering him a bite of her chocolate bar, which she then resumed eating. 'He really looked forward to her visits, it sustained him,' recalls a mutual friend. She and Andy Warhol were guests of honor at a benefit for Burgoyne at the Pyramid Club, where the young designer had worked for a time, and on November 10, Madonna was one of several celebrities who took part in an AIDS benefit at Barney's clothing store, modeling a denim jacket decorated with a picture by Burgoyne.

The end came on the Sunday after Thanksgiving. By then, Burgoyne's every breath was an effort, and he was slipping in and out of consciousness. Although his family were at his bedside, he wanted Madonna – who was on her way to New York from Los Angeles – to be with him when he died, and was seemingly fighting to hold on to life until she could be there. It was an unbearable wait for all concerned, as first her flight was delayed and then her limousine became stuck in traffic. When she finally walked into the room, he was able to give up his struggle. She took him in her arms, whispered a few words, and stayed with him until he was finally at peace. The memory of that moment is still fresh in Erika Belle's memory: 'They had a very deep and profound love. Once he heard her come into the room he knew he could die. It was very beautiful, very moving, and I still cry about it now.'

Burgoyne's death at such a young age badly affected his friends. Although she told the actress and writer Carrie Fisher, in an interview for *Rolling Stone*, that Burgoyne's rage at dying haunted her, Madonna, then twenty-eight, displayed great strength in the face of the tragedy, not only in looking after her friend, but also comforting his family and even organizing a wake in his honor. For her, though, the death marked the start of a terrible era, but one to which she responded both energetically and effectively. Over the next few years she would lose many of her closest friends – notably Christopher Flynn, Keith Haring, Steve Rubell and Haoui Montaug – to AIDS. In response to their deaths, she has quietly donated considerable sums to AIDS research and to the care of those suffering from the virus. She is also a champion of safe sex and gay rights, as well as a staunch advocate of the promotion of greater public awareness about the disease. To this end she has attended numerous charity events, freely lending her name and support to AIDS-related causes. In 1991 she became the first recipient of the AmFAR (American Foundation for AIDS Research) Award for Courage for her charitable work and AIDS-awareness efforts, while even conservative estimates put the money she has raised for AIDS charities at over $5 million.

Yet while such celebrities as Sir Elton John and the late Diana, Princess of Wales, have been widely praised for their efforts in raising public awareness and money in the fight against AIDS, Madonna's good works have been overshadowed by the controversy that so often surrounds her. Certainly the coming of the AIDS era did little to tame her performances, for on stage she continued unashamedly to use sex and sexuality as her tools. In December 1986, she caused a storm when she released the video to 'Open Your Heart,' playing an exotic dancer in a peep-show booth, who reappears dressed in a man's suit and kisses the lips of an obviously underage boy who has been spying on her through the booth's peephole. Directed by Jean-Baptiste Mondino, not only was *Open Your Heart* Madonna's most overtly sexual video to date – and a sign of her future artistic direction – but the single, which hit the number-one slot, was in stark contrast to the cutesy 'True Blue,' described by one source as an 'unabashed valentine' for Sean Penn.

While Penn had briefly redeemed himself in his wife's eyes during Martin Burgoyne's illness, he did not remain her valentine for long. In the spring of

1987, while relaxing with friends in the West Beach Café in Venice, California, he spat at a photographer, Cesare Bonazza, as he prepared to take Penn's picture. The paparazzo also claimed that the actor had 'gone crazy' and further alleged that he had threatened to pull a gun on him. By now Penn was drinking heavily and his behavior was out of control.

It was not long before Penn's hair-trigger temper brought him into real trouble. Sure enough, in April 1987, on the set of Dennis Hopper's film, *Colors*, in which he was playing the part of a police officer, Penn spotted an extra, Jeffrey Klein, taking his picture. As Hopper and co-star Robert Duvall looked on in amazement, Penn went over, screamed at the extra and then spat in his face. A fistfight broke out which, after it had been stopped by security staff, left Klein with cuts to his face, and determined to press charges. Still on probation for hitting David Wolinski, Penn knew that he was heading for a jail sentence.

Even with that knowledge, the wild acts continued. On May 25, he was arrested for speeding and running a red light in LA. He was breathalyzed, which confirmed that he had been drinking, and he was duly arrested and charged. On June 23, in a ten-minute court hearing, he pleaded no contest to the charges of assault and of reckless driving, and was duly sentenced to sixty days in jail with two years' probation. He was also instructed to undergo counseling. When, after the hearing, Madonna's publicist Liz Rosenberg met with the press, in response to questions about the marriage, she told the eager reporters, with masterly understatement, 'They are having some problems and they're taking some time to think things through.'

Penn began his sentence on July 7, but served just thirty days in the Mono County Jail in California, even being allowed out to film in Germany. While he missed his second wedding anniversary, he was sent nude pictures of his wife, courtesy of *Penthouse*, which published another set of portraits taken when she had been a struggling dancer. Madonna was furious with the unknown individual – she blamed *Penthouse* – who sent the men's magazine to her husband. Not that she was overly impressed by him. On his release in September 1987 he took a pizza home to her, but, by his own admission, she was not particularly pleased to see him; as he observed, 'Going to jail is not good for any marriage.' Indeed, weeks later, Madonna instructed realtors to begin the search for a house of her own, although it was a quest that she soon abandoned.

There had been one consolation for Madonna as her husband whiled away the hours in his cell, reading books by James Thurber and writing a play, *The Kindness of Women*. At least he was out of trouble. Like everyone else, she had heard the rumors of his wild behavior in bars and hotels around Los Angeles, drinking into the small hours and spending the night with different women, sometimes, it was claimed, booking into local hotels. Inevitably, it played on her mind. For while she likes to exude an air of sexual insouciance, seemingly indifferent to the behavior of the men in her life, Madonna is chronically insecure about relationships, reacting to them in the same way that she does, in private, to media criticism.

While cracks were appearing in their marriage, Madonna was busy consolidating her career. In April her song 'La Isla Bonita,' also from the *True Blue* album, had become her twelfth consecutive top-ten single and her greatest success to date internationally, and in the summer she threw her energies into her Who's That Girl? concert tour.

The Hispanic look Madonna adopted in the song's accompanying video, in which she appears dressed both boyishly in wide-brimmed Spanish hat and bolero jacket and as a flamenco dancer, started a fashion craze for bolero jackets and tiered skirts. The wannabes who had slavishly followed her early look were now having a hard time keeping up with their idol, for her image had changed frequently and dramatically since her first album. She turned her back on glamour by sporting a new gamine look for the video of *Papa Don't Preach*. Gone was the sex siren and in its place was an impish tomboy with a bleached-blonde crop, outfitted in jeans and a black leather jacket.

Her focus, though, was not just on fashion but on her first ever worldwide tour. She prepared for the 'Who's That Girl?' concerts as if she were embarking on a military campaign, starting her day with a two-hour workout, including a 25-mile bike ride, before going on to direct every aspect of the 90-minute show, which she called a 'theatrical multi-media spectacular.' It had everything – sex, sensation and, of course, controversy, including images of the Pope and President Reagan projected on screens during her rendition of 'Papa Don't Preach,' and an erotic frisson when she kissed a young boy, Chris Finch, on the lips at the end of 'Like A Virgin.'

The outfit that stole the show – a crazy, Marlene Stewart-designed costume encrusted with material objects such as toy watches, ashtrays, and a plastic lobster – was typically Madonna, indicating both her awareness of surrealism and her tongue-in-cheek style, for when she bent over in this ensemble she revealed a pair of panties with the word 'KISS' emblazoned on them. Another outfit was Andy Warhol-inspired, and featured a tin of Campbell's soup on the side, the letter 'U' on the front, and the word 'DANCE' on the back, so that when she turned around the audience were able to read 'U [Can] Dance.'

As she threw her prodigious energies into the tour, the only person who seemed in any doubt as to the identity of 'that girl' was the star herself. Although she conveyed a new confidence on the stage, managing to glide through her performances seamlessly, she later admitted to thinking, 'Oh God. What have I done? What have I created? Is that me, or is that me, this small person standing here on the stage?'

Whatever her doubts, the fans and the critics loved it. 'No big messages, no revelations, familiar sounds and images, plenty of catchy tunes – the show was easy to enjoy,' said a review in the *New York Times*. Certainly her fans thought so. In Japan, where the tour opened on June 14 at Osaka Stadium, 1,000 troops had to hold back a crowd of 25,000 when Madonna landed at the airport. Again, when she arrived in France such was her popularity that the French Premier, Jacques Chirac, stepped in to overrule a local mayor who had threatened to cancel a concert because of potential crowd problems.

She closed her tour in Turin, in northern Italy, declaring before 65,000 cheering fans that she was proud to be Italian. While in Italy, she met some of her relations from Pacentro, the village in which her grandfather and grandmother, Gaetano and Michelina Ciccone, had been married. It was hardly a glorious homecoming. Although they were intrigued by her fame, and there was talk of her being made an honorary citizen of Pacentro, it was obvious from comments made at the time by some of her relations that they were scandalized by her appearance and behavior.

As her first world tour it was a resounding success, although by its finish Madonna was declaring that she didn't want to hear any of her songs again and that she didn't know whether she'd ever write another one. 'I returned feeling so burned out and I was convinced I wouldn't go near music for quite a while,' she said at the time.

Although the film of *Who's That Girl?* had disappeared from cinema screens before Madonna played her last concert in the tour, her dreams of movie stardom remained undimmed. Before the end of the year the word was out that she was to star in *Bloodhounds of Broadway,* an art-house film with a formidable cast that included Matt Dillon, Randy Quaid and Jennifer Grey. Sadly, however, its director, Howard Brookner, was taken ill with AIDS during filming and did not live to see the finished movie. This time the movie, based loosely on the stories of Damon Runyon, was not a Madonna vehicle, but neither was it to be a success, reviewers finding it too theatrical and somewhat plodding. Madonna had hoped that in choosing a film with artistic integrity her status as an actress would, by association, be treated more seriously. But the film, which had been shot in New Jersey on a tiny budget, did not go down any better with cinema audiences than it had with reviewers; indeed, when a reel of the movie went missing for two weeks during its New York run, no one even noticed. Nevertheless, *Bloodhounds of Broadway* was one movie for which Madonna did not have to take the blame.

The critical and commercial failure of her latest film, coming as it did after the catastrophic *Shanghai Surprise* and scarcely less disastrous, in the United States at least, *Who's That Girl?* do not seem to have caused much soul-searching in Madonna. It may be that she suffers a lack of critical faculty when it comes to judging her own acting performances, something suggested by her almost invariable preference for first takes of her scenes. Certainly, and ironically, the characteristics at the heart of her ambition, her obsessional quest for perfection, her need to be in total control and her reluctance to reveal her vulnerability, were the very qualities that betrayed her in her attempts to be an actress. What was unquestionably true is that Madonna is at her most appealing on those rare occasions when she lets down her guard and reveals her humanity. Her dramatic difficulties in her early films were due as much to her personality as to her actual performances. After *Desperately Seeking Susan*, she instinctively chose characters that she could mold into a likeness of herself, strong women who triumphed by virtue of their wits, their sexuality or their courage, or a combination of these features. Thus, seeing these characters as reflections of herself, she always tried to make them likeable, whether to do so was believable or not; indeed, a decade later it was a trick she would try to pull off when she played Eva Perón, the wife of the Argentine dictator. If this was yet another manifestation of her desire to be loved, one result was that the interaction of, say, Gloria Tatlock, the missionary in *Shanghai Express,* was not so much with other characters in the movie, but with Madonna herself. It is no coincidence that her most successful film after *Desperately Seeking Susan* was *Truth or Dare* (outside the USA, released as *In Bed With Madonna*), the documentary about herself.

While her assault on the heights of Hollywood had not yielded the breakthrough for which she had hoped, still Madonna did not give up her quest for the role that would finally win her praise, and make the world take notice of her as an actress. She decided to devote 1988 to acting, and having released her fourth album in the autumn of 1987, she recorded no music in the following year.

Her willingness to take a chance and her desire to broaden her artistic horizons saw her begin the year by turning to the stage once again. When she heard that the actress Elizabeth Perkins had pulled out of David Mamet's latest Broadway play, *Speed-the-Plow*, she immediately called the director, Gregory Mosher, with whom she had worked on *Goose and Tom-Tom*, and asked if she could read for the role of Karen. A great admirer of Mamet's work – she had written to congratulate him on producing 'stimulating cinema' when his film *House of Games* was released in 1987 – she was inspired by his latest work.

[151]

The play was a three-hander, featuring two high-powered and sexist Hollywood characters, Bobby Gould, a film magnate, and his producer, Charlie Fox, played respectively by stage veterans Joe Mantegna and Ron Silver, and Karen, an outwardly demure temporary secretary whose ultimate vision and strength of character result in a kind of epiphany for the hard-boiled Gould. After winning a $500 bet with Fox that he will be able to get Karen to sleep with him, he is ultimately persuaded by her to change his mind and make a film based on a life-affirming book she has been reading, rather than the sleazy commercial offering of his friend. The appeal of Karen's character for Madonna was obvious. 'She is a sympathetic, misunderstood heroine who speaks the truth at any risk.' (Her manager, Freddy DeMann, was not so impressed, moaning that her $1,200-a-week pay wouldn't even keep him in cigars.)

When she won the role in the face of intense competition from thirty other actresses, she went into six weeks of rigorous rehearsals, only ever complaining, typically, when Mosher ended rehearsals early one day. Ever the professional, she learned her lines assiduously, was always on time, thoughtfully sent flowers to everyone involved with the production before it opened on Broadway in May. Yet, once again, it was not her attitude that ultimately caused difficulties, but her artistic interpretation.

The problem came when, a few days into the read-through, Madonna realized that the character she was to play was not quite the angel of mercy she had initially envisaged. As far as Mamet and Mosher were concerned, Karen's nature was more ambiguous, both writer and director seeing her as a cunning schemer as much as an innocent idealist. 'Everybody else saw me as a vixen, a dark, evil spirit,' Madonna lamented. 'That didn't dawn on me till halfway through rehearsal, when David kept changing my lines to make me more and more a bitch, a ruthless, conniving little witch. So in the middle of this process I was devastated that my idea of the character wasn't what she was at all. That was a really upsetting experience.'

Given that she was playing the pivotal role in the drama, it was in fact Madonna's job to keep the audience guessing, using her character's femininity to explore the different ways men and women disguise raw ambition, the former more obvious and direct, the latter subtle and sly. She did not see it that way, however, ungraciously complaining in *Cosmopolitan* magazine that: 'It was devastating to do that night after night. I saw her as an angel, an innocent. They wanted her to be a cunt.' Thus she saw the role wholly in terms of herself, going home each night in a miserable mood because her character failed in the context of the play, and sometimes walking offstage in tears.

The critics noticed her similarity to Judy Holliday, but yet again complained that she lacked experience. 'There is genuine reticent charm here but it is not yet ready to light the lamps of Broadway,' noted the *New York Post*, while the headline in the *Post's* tabloid rival, the *New York Daily News*, yelled: 'No, SHE CAN'T ACT.' This time Madonna blamed David Mamet, griping that the Pulitzer Prize-winning playwright was 'not interested in collaborating. I think he's interested in fascism,' although that did not prevent the play from breaking Broadway records for advance ticket sales for a serious work.

For a star so utterly convinced of her innate talent, and who had been so successful in so many artistic endeavors, to trip continually on the slopes of theater and film during her relentless ascent to stardom was both perplexing and galling. After all, she had undoubtedly mastered the art of the three-minute video, the compressed drama encapsulated in her performances of songs like 'Papa Don't Preach,' undeniable in their social impact and artistic quality. Of this conflict between her acting on her videos and her stage and screen performances, Michael Musto, *Village Voice* columnist and Madonna camp follower, observes: 'She has the perfect talent for the highly visual, snappy video format. When it comes down to inhabiting a character in film and interacting with other characters she is usually extremely self-conscious. She is too aware of the camera and trying to look good. Too aware of herself. Unlike Cher and Courtney Love, she fails to radiate natural screen magnetism.'

Whatever her feelings about her acting, by the time her run in *Speed-the-Plow* ended in September 1988, Madonna had reached a pinnacle in her career. By any standards, hers was a remarkable artistic achievement. Just turned thirty, she had appeared in four Hollywood movies, and a Broadway play, while her music had resulted in twelve hit singles and four hit albums. She had also masterminded two sell-out concert tours, the first around America, the second taking in Japan and Europe, as well as the USA; both helping to establish her as a national and international superstar. These were only the outward manifestations of her impact, however. Her courageous and indomitable persona had truly revolutionized feminist politics, offering millions of women around the world the sense that they could be strong, sensual, in control, and yet retain their essential femininity, their gender no barrier to achievement. At the same time, her crusade for AIDS awareness and her empathy with the gay and black communities had shaken gender and race relations. It is little wonder, therefore, that she constantly featured in magazine lists, along with President Reagan and the Russian Prime Minister Mikhail Gorbachev, as one of the top twenty individuals who had shaped the decade. At the end of 1987, she had also been cited in *Forbes* magazine as seventh in a list of top-earning showbusiness personalities, with a gross annual income of $26 million. This made her the top-earning female in entertainment.

Apart from her disappointment over her acting engagements, Madonna had made it to the very top in just five years. Sadly, though, while she was willing to go on fighting for a movie career, she had given up on fighting to save her marriage. By mid-1987 she had accepted that she could no more bend Sean to her will than she could bow to his, and she finally lost interest in the role of Mrs Penn. Proud, strong-willed and competitive, Sean had wanted Madonna to play the part of a domesticated goddess, a woman prepared to slow down her career as they started a family. A star in his own right, he also came to resent bitterly being dubbed 'Mr Madonna' as his wife's career reached new heights. As he pithily observed of his marriage, 'At twenty-four I didn't realize the difference between a great first-time date and a lifetime commitment.'

As far as Madonna was concerned, she could be forgiven for thinking that marrying one of Hollywood's leading actors would further, rather than tether, her career. Stubborn and headstrong, she was unwilling to compromise her commitment to her work, even if that meant alienating her husband. As a close friend explained: 'While she is definitely into bad boys he was more than she could handle. He made the fatal mistake of trying to put himself in front of her career at a time when it was about to explode.'

Ultimately, she wanted a relationship based on a complex dynamic in which she never gave up control, either of her career or herself, and yet maintained the illusion of being controlled by her husband. In the event, however, she found herself with a man who was out of control in private as well as in public, and yet who wanted to restrict her. In short, she tried to tame Penn, and he tried to domesticate her. It proved to be a recipe for emotional trauma and, ultimately, divorce. 'We were two fires rubbing up against each other. It's exciting and difficult,' Madonna later observed. The last comment was nothing if not an understatement.

Like her former lover Ken Compton, Sean Penn possessed the ability to get under her skin, driving her wild with anxiety and uncertainty. They had made a pact to call each other every day at a certain time no matter where they were in the world. When she was away she religiously called him first thing in the morning and last thing at night, not just to keep in touch but to make sure he was where he said he would be, and on his own. More often than not she could not reach him, endlessly reduced to leaving frustrated messages on his answering machine. 'I've got big phone bills,' she joked.

Madonna's insecurity and her husband's heavy drinking, wild behavior and alleged womanizing combined to create an atmosphere of mutual distrust and anxiety. It was an insupportable situation, and one in which, eventually, something must give. At last, just ten weeks after Penn was released from jail in September 1987, Madonna had had enough. On December 4, she filed for divorce, instructing her attorney that she wanted to revert to her maiden name and invoking the pre-nuptial agreement under which their earnings were treated separately. There was a poignant symmetry to the moment she chose to serve papers on her husband, for she was losing the man she loved at the same time as she reflected on the anniversary of the death of the mother she had lost, so many years earlier. Such poignancy was wasted on Penn, who characteristically went off on a drinking bender with his Hollywood cronies.

For Madonna, as was by now almost a romantic reflex, there was always another man waiting in the wings to keep her company. As one of her former lovers noted, she had become the mistress of the 'soft landing,' invariably making sure that she had another place to go, another shoulder to cry on, another rung of the social ladder beneath her foot. That December, if she was ruefully contemplating the end of her marriage, she was also quietly considering her elevation from Hollywood celebrity to American royalty. Ever since her 1985 hit single, 'Material Girl,' Madonna's name had become synonymous with that of Marilyn Monroe, a sex symbol of the eighties paying homage to the blonde bombshell of the fifties who wowed a nation and wooed a president, John F. Kennedy. The difference between these two icons, however, was that Madonna's ethos was remorselessly life-affirming whereas Monroe's was vulnerable and self-destructive, drawn to the fall. Nevertheless, when word got out that Madonna had secretly been dating the late President's son, John F. Kennedy, Jr, in New York in the weeks before Christmas 1987, the symbolism was as uncanny as it was obvious.

They had met earlier at a party in New York, the late President's son subsequently seeing her backstage after her Who's That Girl? Tour performance at Madison Square Garden, and then meeting up with her again in December at a downtown fitness center, after which they sometimes went jogging together in Central Park. With his craggy saturnine features, well-toned body, and keen intelligence, as well as his family pedigree, the charming John Kennedy, Jr, was an eminently suitable squire for one of the world's most glamorous and exciting women.

Beyond that, however, Madonna was interested not just in Kennedy, but in his mother too, Jackie Onassis, an American icon to match, perhaps to outshine, even Marilyn Monroe and Madonna. 'She was one of the few people in the world she really admired,' recalls a friend, adding, 'Madonna was impressed by her style.' Unfortunately, those feelings were not reciprocated. A stilted meeting at Jackie O's elegant Fifth Avenue apartment, at the end of which Madonna signed herself 'Mrs Sean Penn' in the visitors' book, left her under no illusion that her charm had failed to win over her hostess. It was clear that Jackie O did not want her son to be seen with, let alone to date, such a controversial character, especially as Madonna was still married. That John Junior was something of a mother's boy did nothing to help her cause. Although they were lovers for a brief period, the affair was not a success, John Junior as intimidated by Madonna's reputation as he was by his mother. For all her outward aggression, explained one of her former lovers, Madonna is a woman who expects her man to take control, more of a kitten than a tigress in the bedroom. Rather ruefully, she explained to friends after the end of her affair with Kennedy that he was just too nervous for them to click sexually. The chemistry simply wasn't there. 'Some guys can handle the fame, others can't,' says a former lover. 'He couldn't.' What the affair did do, however, was annoy a husband always prone to jealousy. Even after their divorce, her fling with John Kennedy, Jr, rankled with Sean Penn. Indeed, when the two men met years later at a party in New York, Penn told Kennedy bluntly that he owed him an apology.

In reality, the affair proved to be as short-lived as her decision to divorce her husband. A week before Christmas 1987, just two weeks after she had filed for divorce, she withdrew her suit. The arguments of concerned friends, a charm offensive launched by Sean Penn – among other blandishments he sent her balloons and a singing telegram – and their agreement to work harder at making their marriage endure all helped to build a bridge between the estranged couple.

Nevertheless, neither could do anything about the demands of their respective careers. Madonna threw herself into her work, starting filming *Bloodhounds of Broadway* on Christmas Eve 1987 and later, as soon as shooting had wrapped, embarking on six weeks of grueling rehearsals for *Speed-the-Plow*. Sean Penn missed the opening night in May because he too was working, filming *Casualties of War* in Thailand with his co-star and friend Michael J. Fox. From the point of view of his marriage, the opening performance of *Speed-the-Plow* was to assume a significance out of all proportion to its importance as an event.

In the audience that night was a stand-up comedian, Sandra Bernhard, a woman who would have a powerful impact on Madonna's life, her marriage and, ultimately, her future relationships. Bernhard's one-woman show, which included a skit about Madonna's iconic pop-star status, was running in a downtown theater at the time, and when the two women met backstage they immediately struck up a friendship. 'It seemed like the right thing at the right time,' recalls Bernhard. She and Madonna and a third member, *Bloodhounds of Broadway* co-star Jennifer Grey, made up a boisterous threesome who called themselves the 'Snatch Batch' – an ironic reference to the 'Brat Pack' tag given to Penn and his clique of young actor friends.

Throughout that summer they terrorized the city's most fashionable spots, going to parties, restaurants, gallery openings and clubs together, beating up the town in best Brat Pack fashion. For Madonna, it was just like the old days. Their behavior was juvenile and uninhibited, on one reported occasion seeing them stage a belching competition in a downtown restaurant. Meanwhile, teased and tormented by the trio, the media now speculated that Madonna and the openly bisexual Bernhard were more than just friends. Contemptuously amused by these allegations, the two women merely added fuel to the rumors. Their appearance on *Late Night with David Letterman* for which they wore matching jeans, tee-shirts and clumpy shoes, gave the gossips a field day. In a raucous, now infamous chat, the terrible twosome claimed that they frequented the Cubby Hole, a lesbian hang-out, while Bernhard boasted that she had slept with both Sean and Madonna.

Theirs was a notorious double act that was to continue for the next few years, long after Madonna's marriage had ended in divorce. In 1989, for example, before she and Bernhard went on for an AIDS 'Dance-a-Thon' in Los Angeles with Stacey Q and their other dance partner, *Who's That Girl?* co-star Coati Mundi, they discussed how they were going to freak everyone out. 'It was like a game,' recalls Coati Mundi. 'They went out together, hugging and dancing in step.' Again, at a charity benefit in New York in June the same year they performed a hilarious pastiche of the 1965 Sonny and Cher song 'I've Got You Babe,' grinding their hips together and fondling themselves in front of a delighted audience.

Behind the light-hearted banter and the deliberate sexual ambiguity, however, there had been an intriguing change in the dynamic of Madonna's relationships. As she entered her thirties, she took to ensuring that there was always another woman, invariably a lesbian, by her side. Sandra Bernhard at first, then, later, nightclub owner Ingrid Casares and model Jenny Shimizu. They were her *doppelgänger*, shadowing her every move, advising her, shopping with her, or simply spending time with her. Whatever the sexual chemistry between Madonna and these friends, their constant presence helped create an emotional buffer between herself and the current man in her life. Since those to whom she had given her heart, notably her husband and mother, had, for whatever reason, let her down, the presence of these 'shadows' in her life now gave her, in some way, protection, from hurt, from commitment and from emotional intimacy.

When Sean Penn returned home from filming in South-East Asia in June 1988, he discovered that there were now three of them in their marriage: Madonna, Sandra and himself. As Madonna has admitted: 'I'd say that my friendship with Sandra was just beginning as my relationship with Sean was dying.' They went everywhere together, Sandra tagging along, for instance, when the Penns joined their friend, the artist Peter Max, on his yacht for a cruise up the Hudson to celebrate the Fourth of July. It was an arrangement that did not sit well with the temperamental actor who, like several of Madonna's future male paramours, had little time for Bernhard or her involvement with his wife. As far as Madonna was concerned however, her bisexual friend provided a raucous, girly counterpoint, or even antidote, to Penn's endless petulance.

That petulance had certainly not abated. When he arrived back in the States he began where he had left off, abusing photographers and fans at a Mike Tyson fight in Atlantic City in June, and a couple of weeks later kicking in the car door of a photographer in New York. Nor was it long before he turned his anger on his wife, inevitably over her friendship with Bernhard. Sandra had been hanging out with Madonna in Hollywood as she worked on her latest album, *Like A Prayer*, and while Penn was rehearsing a new stage play, *Hurlyburly*. Worried about his behavior towards photographers and his heavy drinking, Madonna would drive to the theater at the end of the day to collect him, mainly to ensure that he didn't get into any more trouble. By now, however, relations between husband and wife had hit a new low.

It was not long before evidence of the rift became visible in public. The opening-night party for Penn's play in the Twenty-20 club, saw a very public altercation between the virtually estranged couple. When Madonna arrived with Bernhard as her 'date' for the evening, Penn exploded in fury. 'You cunt, how could you do this to me?' he screamed, his outburst witnessed and reported by several alarmed bystanders, including the actor Sylvester Stallone. For Penn, red-blooded male cast in the Hemingway mold, his wife's behavior seemed to add injury to the greatest injury of all: the fact that she insisted that her career came before children. Years later, Madonna admitted; 'Sean wanted to have a child. It wasn't the right time, you know everything is about timing.'

Although the conflict over children and career lay at the heart of their difficulties, Penn's suspicions about his wife and her friend can only have exacerbated the divide between them. Were they lovers? While she and Bernhard have kept the public guessing, privately Madonna answered in the affirmative when asked point blank about her relationship. Jim Albright, who enjoyed a stormy three-year relationship with Madonna during the 1990s, certainly believed that they had slept together. 'I asked her why, because I can't stand her [Bernhard]. She didn't give me an explanation.' It cannot have been very surprising, therefore, that as their marriage careened out of control, Sean Penn moved back in with his parents, while Sandra Bernhard stayed at the couple's Malibu home with Madonna.

The end, when at last it came, was as dramatic as the beginning, although it was accompanied by the sound of a police bullhorn rather than the pounding of helicopter rotor blades. On December 29, armed police surrounded the Malibu house, and an officer's amplified voice demanded that Penn should come out, Madonna having apparently complained to the local sheriff's office about an alleged assault. Penn, eating from a bowl of Rice Krispies, sauntered out into the morning sunshine, to be confronted by what he later described as a SWAT team of armed police who had taken that extreme action because they knew he had guns in the house. 'I had made a threat that I would literally cut her hair off,' Penn told the writer Chris Mundi. 'She took it quite seriously. It was pretty dramatic.'

A rather more lurid, and hitherto uncontested, version has been widely published, and contends that Penn, drunk and out of control, had burst into the marital home the previous afternoon, overpowered his wife and then 'trussed her up like a turkey' before gagging her. He left her alone for nine hours before she was able to make good her escape, eventually calling the police from the phone in her car, before driving to the sheriff's office to file charges.

Neither version, of course, is entirely true to what really happened. In fact, the actuality of the incident symbolized the fundamental fault line in their marriage. Penn wanted Madonna 'barefoot and naked in the kitchen,' she wanted to explore her artistic career. After hours of arguing and fighting that fateful night, an exasperated Penn grabbed his wife, threw her down and sat on her, pinning her arms to the floor and refusing to let her move. In spite of her screams and tears, he kept her like that for what she later told friends was about four hours. After a while, her sobbing ceased and as the hours ticked by, she just quietly lay there, utterly traumatized by the experience.

'She is never still for a minute, so to do that was like death to her, like Chinese water torture,' says a friend to whom Madonna related the true story. 'There was a lot of symbolism in the actual act, him wanting to hold her back, to stop her career, to have control, to keep her in her place. It was probably a desperate attempt to get his way. It must have been smothering for her.'

In those few fateful hours, any hope of a reconciliation died. In her heart, Madonna realized that, as much as she might love her husband, they were, to use his phrase, 'reading from different scripts.' A month later they were divorced, Sean Penn going on to father two children by the actress Robin Wright, whom he then married, Madonna storming on with her career, while at the same time beginning a period of sexual exploration that would both titillate and unnerve her fans and detractors alike.

A few months after the breakup of her marriage, Madonna was sitting with a girlfriend outside a New York café, soaking up the spring sunshine. Unrecognized by passers-by and without a photographer in sight, she was for once able to relax for a moment and reflect. A self-confessed 'old-fashioned girl' who revered the institution of marriage, Madonna truly believed that she had put her heart and soul into trying to make the relationship work. That it had failed so spectacularly was a source of pain and regret. Nevertheless, as with almost every significant event in her life, it was an experience from which she was able to learn. She had emerged a wiser, more mature woman, determined never to make the same mistakes again. Even if she was not especially happy, at least she was at peace with herself. Perhaps, she reflected, it all had been for the best.

Chapter Ten
Nice Ice Baby, Don't Go

BOOM. *Boom.* BOOM. Man, that was a heavy sound. Just the way he liked it. He boasted that you could hear his car coming from three blocks away, the deep thud of the bass making window frames and doors vibrate as he passed, his blond head nodding with the pumping rap music. Fitted the speakers in the back himself. Eight-oh-eights – best on the market. And here's the thing. No matter how loud you pushed those suckers, they wouldn't hurt your eardrums. At least, not permanently. He knew. Vanilla Ice had done a special study. He was cool about the sound. IT WOULD NOT HURT YOUR HEARING. Got that. You sure? You deaf or something?

So when his manager, Tommy Quon, quietly pointed out that they could be sued for damages if one of the kids who came to watch his sell-out concert tour suffered medical injury, Vanilla Ice turned – so to speak – a deaf ear. Stack them speakers high, man, stack 'em high. We're going to rock the house tonight. Quon knew better than to argue with his star. Vanilla Ice – born Robert Van Winkle in Miami in October 1968 – was riding higher than any bank of speakers. Ice was a sky rocket. In 1990 his anthem 'Ice Ice Baby' was the first rap single to hit number one in the pop charts, while his debut album, *To the Extreme*, sold an incredible 15 million copies worldwide.

When his fans crowded into a New York club Vanilla Ice was determined to crank up the music, bigtime. As the kids grooved to his rapping lyrics, the music boomed out, those giant woofers working overtime. Plaster dropped from the ceiling on to a few heads. Thinking lawsuits, Tommy Quon was a worried man. But it was chill. Everyone went home happy. No one went deaf or sued anyone. It stood to reason. Vanilla Ice had made a study that said loud music was cool.

Backstage after the concert things started to heat up, as though they weren't hot enough already. Charles Koppelman, the head of their record label, SBK, pushed his way through the crowd tailed by an entourage that included Madonna and a sexy girlfriend. Vanilla Ice didn't catch the girl-friend's name in the hubbub, but he remembers that she told him she was a porn-movie actress. He expressed his skepticism, but she left him in no doubt when she showed him photographs she pulled from her handbag. 'Whoa baby, want to ride in the limo?' he asked. The result was that Vanilla

Ice, Madonna and her porn-star friend got to talking, and finished off the evening swapping telephone numbers. He never did see the porn star again.

He saw plenty of Madonna, however, for the meeting marked the start of an unlikely love affair between the rap artist and the pop icon that would last, on and off, for more than a year. In truth, it was a familiar pattern in Madonna, a latter-day hunter-gatherer seeking out that season's latest trend and biggest name, her hunger for love and validation matched only by her addiction to publicity. From the end of her marriage to Sean Penn in 1989, the men in her life had served either as counterpoint or complement to her celebrity, social pygmies like model Tony Ward lending scale to her gigantic status, while her superstar menfriends like Warren Beatty and Michael Jackson confirmed and endorsed her status as a legend. In 1991 they didn't come much bigger than Vanilla Ice.

Or, for that matter, Madonna. Since her divorce she had amply demonstrated that she needed no help from Hollywood royalty to be the undisputed queen of popular entertainment. When she met Vanilla Ice, Madonna was at the zenith of her career.

By 1989 Madonna had found the formula, an artistic alchemist who was able to blend creativity and controversy in equal measure, and so create commercial gold. Ironically, it was a lesson learned in part from her ex-husband. She had been inspired by him to confront the demons in her marriage and her childhood, openly and honestly. The result was distilled into her critically acclaimed album, *Like a Prayer*, which was dedicated to her mother, who she said, 'taught me how to pray.' Indeed, Madonna's frenetic activity seemed to be a manifestation of her awareness of the shortness of her mother's life, and of a feeling that every day had to be lived to the full.

Not only did the album, released in 1989, explore the breakdown of an abusive relationship, it touched on other sensitive subjects; the death of her mother, the unresolved relationship with her father and her confused feelings about her Catholic faith. Her ability to express, through her music, the burdens that she carried in her heart, showed her growing stature as an artist of some eloquence and power, a performer who was prepared to reveal her doubts and vulnerability to the world. 'It's taken a lot of guts to do this and I've taken more risks with this album than I ever had before and I think the growth shows,' she would later admit.

She took more risks with the video of *Like A Prayer*, a dark, disquieting film, directed by Mary Lambert, which was released simultaneously with the first showing of the sunny, sentimental commercial based on the same song she made for Pepsi. In her video Madonna witnesses a murder, falls in love with a black man who is falsely accused of a crime, and eventually rescues him from a racist mob. In this feminist fairy tale, a bold inversion of the traditional damsel-in-distress story, Madonna, dressed in a black slip, is seen dancing in front of burning crosses, kissing the black saint Martin de Porres, in church, and experiencing Christ-like stigmata on her hands. The message of racial tolerance was, however, buried in the subsequent controversy, particularly the outcry from the moral majority and the Vatican at what they saw as the blasphemous use of religious iconography in a pop video.

The hapless soft-drinks corporation, which, in 1989 had paid the singer $5 million to appear in the much publicized commercial, was caught in the crossfire. Faced with a boycott of their products by religious groups concerned that Madonna was 'ridiculing Christianity,' Pepsi withdrew the commercial, although the company agreed that the singer should keep the fee. Madonna had squared the circle, occupying the artistic high ground while achieving a stunning commercial success. Indeed, in 1990 she was the world's top earning female entertainer, grossing an estimated $39 million. Unlike Michael Jackson, Paula Abdul and Britney Spears, who have all been willing to endorse commercial products, Madonna endeavored to give the impression that her ventures into the world of advertising were simply art by another name. 'I do consider it a challenge to make a commercial that has some sort of artistic value,' she says, constantly at pains to disguise her keen head for business and commercial opportunities.

For example, during negotiations that year for a potential personal endorsement of Nike running shoes Madonna took control and issued personal invitations to senior company executives – 'the suits,' as she calls them – to her Los Angeles home to try to seal a $4.25 million deal. They balked when she argued that she wanted to keep her endorsement to a bare minimum; that is to say, she would not even wear their sports shoes. When the company pulled out, Madonna telephoned Nike chairman Philip Knight, fighting to get the deal up and running again. She was unsuccessful although that did not stop 'Team Madonna' negotiating with Nike's rival, Reebok, for a similar deal. As her lawyer, Paul Schindler, has said, 'She has an excellent sense of sell.'

In what was to become a familiar pattern Madonna enjoyed her artistic cake while taking a good chunk of the commercial pie. So, when she was cast as the sultry nightclub singer Breathless Mahoney in the 1990 Disney movie *Dick Tracy*, it was announced that she was so enthralled by the opportunity to work with the actor Warren Beatty, who was both directing and starring in the film, that she was accepting the standard union rate of $1,440 a week. However the public relations equation omitted the fact that she was to take a percentage of the box office gross and the rights to the film soundtrack. In all, she made an estimated $13 million, and change, from the deal.

Artistically though, it was worth every cent. In her role as a modern-day Mae West, the saucy platinum blonde earned plaudits for her brassy, sassy style: 'Quivering with lust, double entendres and bad intentions, Madonna is smashingly unsubtle as the *femme fatale*,' noted one reviewer. Given her all-time best-selling single, 'Vogue,' which paid homage to the stars of the 1930s, Madonna appeared to be simply unstoppable, an artist at the top of her game. Warren Beatty, by then her lover, seemed to be stating the obvious when he observed, 'She is funny, smart, beautiful, musical. She has everything, she's an actress, a singer and she's great at it all. She has irony and wit. She has sexuality, she's generous-spirited. She's going to be a huge movie star.'

Her sexual chutzpah, eye for controversy and commercial instincts came together again in her 1990 video *Justify My Love*, an erotic fantasy in which a sultry Madonna encounters a sensual netherworld in a Paris hotel. It was banned by MTV, particularly for its focus on same-sex kissing, one such scene showing Madonna with the model Amanda de Cadanet. Undaunted, the singer marketed the five-minute video herself, selling a remarkable 800,000 copies.

She continued to explore and develop her own ideas about ambiguity in gender and sexuality, a feminist agenda in which a woman is in control of her body, her role and her life. Although she examined this theme in her *Like A Prayer* video, it was most fully expressed in her audacious four-month, twenty-seven-city Blonde Ambition Tour, which established her as a modern-day Amazon, her erotic and exotic routines invariably ending with the woman on top. She strutted the stage in contemporary armor, Jean-Paul Gaultier's cone-shaped bustier, presenting an enduring image of Madonna as superwoman, her dancers playing musclebound slaves utterly subservient to her will. Yet the French designer's description of the garment that will be for ever identified with the singer can also be applied to her own psychology; as he said, 'A tough outer shell protects hidden vulnerability.'

As it happened, the vulnerability Madonna had exposed in her songs for the *Like A Prayer* album was clearly evident in her life away from the stage. Undoubtedly, she had become the epicenter of the entertainment world, and yet she still wanted more. Her emotional need for mass adulation and accept-ance existed in stark contrast to her image of effortless female ascendancy and control. It was a contradiction that Vanilla Ice would come to experience at first hand, struggling to square the strident stage persona with the woman who complained when he didn't call, or who phoned very late or early in the morning wanting to know if he was with another girl.

From the beginning, it was she who pursued him, intrigued by the success and personae of white rapper Vanilla Ice, but he was not the easiest of conquests. She flattered him, telling him that he reminded her of Elvis, but he was not particularly impressed with her at the outset. He didn't much like her music – 'friendly-assed corny shit' – and he was concerned about the ten-year difference in their ages. Yet in the end he lost his caution. 'She started calling me,' he remembers. 'We started talking, feeling each other out. Real personal and in-depth conversations.'

When, that summer, Madonna went to Evansville, Indiana, to film *A League of Their Own*, a comedy about an all-female baseball team, she and Vanilla Ice would meet up, often adopting a series of light disguises, usually wigs and hats, to keep their assignations secret. They went to movies and restaurants, invariably arriving separately and without their chauffeurs or bodyguards so as not to attract attention. 'What was really cool was that we kept it quiet for a long time and we bought ourselves a lot of time to get to know each other,' he recalls. He expected a 'snotty, rude' star, and instead discovered a 'sweet, innocent, but sexy girl.' As he says, with more than a nod to her stage performances at that time, 'She's not about whips and chains at all. She was very romantic, very sexy, but not in a slutty way.' At the same time he was beginning to enjoy being with a woman who seemed genuinely interested in the direction of his career and life, and to like having a girlfriend who sent him flowers and love letters.

As the relationship deepened, Madonna would sometimes visit him in Florida when she wasn't filming, recording or on tour. They would lie on the deck of his boat, which was moored off Star Island on Florida's west coast, and as he watched the stars he would chat to her for two or three hours at a stretch. 'It was like going back to high school and talking to your sweetheart,' he reflects, the intimacy created by their meetings and their long-distance conversations forging a growing bond between them. 'She really dug me a lot and told me she loved me. Madonna was everything you would want to marry. There is no doubt that if she had stayed that person we would be married and have kids today. The way she was talking she was really desperate to have kids. I knew that. Her biological clock was ticking and she was ready to have a kid when we were going out.'

As the months passed, however, he began to see a different side of her character, a needy, anxious side, insecure and suspicious. It was perplexing. She didn't seem to understand that Vanilla Ice, whose own life was by this time a haze of touring, publicity and cocaine, was trying his best to act the regular boyfriend. 'Hey, it isn't like that sweetie,' he would soothe her. 'Everything is cool, calm down.' Paradoxically, it was her very insecurity, waking him in the middle of the night or leaving pleading messages on his answering machine, that began to push him away. He realized that the woman who seemed to have everything was at heart an unhappy soul, a sad figure searching for love and contentment. 'I was digging her,' he recalls, 'but there was a desperate neediness about her, an impatience to get married.' Soon he began to see sides of her personality that he didn't 'dig,' all too often finding her self-obsessed, selfish and snappy.

Just two years since her divorce from Sean Penn, it was clear to her latest beau that the hard-drinking actor was still very much on her mind – and in her heart. 'I felt that she still loved him,' says Vanilla Ice. 'In fact, I know she did because she told me. But it didn't work out between them.' When Sean's lover, the actress Robin Wright, gave birth to girl, Dylan, in April 1991, Madonna fell to wondering distractedly what might have been. As well as sending gifts for the new baby, she reportedly sent a note to her ex-husband that read, 'Silly boy, if you'd given me a baby, we'd still be together.' Given their history, and especially her choice of career above motherhood, the sentiment seems more than a little disingenuous. A month later, when she launched *Truth or Dare*, the documentary film of her Blonde Ambition Tour, at the Cannes Film Festival, observers speculated as to whether her spectacular invasion of the French resort to premiere her film was done more to impress Sean, who was there to promote his own film, *The Indian Runner* (his debut as a director) than the judges, the critics and the media.

Ironically, the most revealing moment in *Truth or Dare* was when Madonna confessed that the love of her life was Sean Penn, a moment of vulnerability which, typically, she wanted edited out. 'Over my dead body,' Harvey Weinstein of Miramax, the film's distributor, told her. Yet her frequent and at times impassioned declarations of affection for her former husband drew only pity from her rival, Robin Wright. 'I feel sorry for Madonna. I think she is a very sad and rather lost soul. Yet deep down there is a real person who is as sensitive as the rest of us.'

Ostensibly the documentary, directed by first-timer Alek Keshishian, was a behind-the-scenes look at her sell-out Blonde Ambition Tour. In reality, it was a film about Madonna. 'It's like being in psychoanalysis and letting the whole world watch,' noted Keshishian, who first came to her notice when he sent her his college thesis. That she was prepared to take a risk with a talented novice says much about her artistic courage. That everyone who appeared, from her father Tony Ciccone to her then boyfriend Warren Beatty, was merely a prop to support the star, says more, a point the director made time and again as he juxtaposed her comments about them with their own behavior. So, for example, when she revealed how she and a childhood friend, Moira McPharlin, had indulged in mutual masturbation during puberty, he filmed Madonna's former friend denying her story. He then set up an excruciatingly embarrassing interlude in which, to Madonna's evident discomfort, McPharlin asked her to be godmother to her youngest child and Madonna's namesake.

In another scene Madonna mock imitated fellatio with an Evian bottle while her father and stepmother waited in the adjacent room, and later said to her lesbian friend Sandra Bernhard that as a little girl she could only get to sleep after her father fucked her. 'Just kidding,' she added. During the documentary she also revealed that her brother Christopher was gay, and that her elder brother Martin was an alcoholic. In one mawkish scene she lay by her mother's grave while her younger brother bashfully hid behind a tree. At the time even the chief cameraman, Robert Leacock, had been embarrassed, although it is now one of his favorite scenes. He says, 'One of the things that I will forever love her for is that she trusted us and let us do it. That's amazingly brave. Most people will not let their life be that invaded.'

Certainly not everyone was willing to be grist to her publicity mill. Three of her dancers – two of whom she encouraged to French kiss on film – were so upset at the way they were used by Madonna that they sued her for invasion of privacy, fraud and deceit. The matter was settled out of court. Madonna was also shown in the film moaning about her lover, Warren Beatty – on one occasion calling him 'pussyman' – to the actor's discomfort; eventually the point was reached when his attorney took out a court order to stop her from using their private telephone conversations in the documentary. 'It was a long, very loving conversation that portrayed him in a warm way,' Madonna argued. 'But it is illegal to tape someone's conversation without their knowing about it.'

If her feelings about Penn exposed her vulnerability, then Beatty's laconic observations about his girlfriend, twenty-two years his junior, suggested another aspect of the girl he called 'Buzzbomb' – her insatiable narcissism and exhibitionism.

Beatty, a product of the old days of Hollywood, when publicity had been as much about illusion as revelation, found himself continually taken aback by her apparently total addiction to celebrity. During filming he was happy to be photographed visiting restaurants and clubs with Madonna, displaying the traditional complicity between star and media that ensured his current movie was publicized in return for banal glimpses into his private life. That she was prepared to go far beyond that, however, displaying a willingness, throughout their year-long affair, to use every fragment of her private life, however personal, in order to provide her with her next publicity fix, whether a magazine cover or a newspaper headline, left him bemused, and occasionally furious.

At times he would call her publicity agent, Liz Rosenberg, in exasperation at the way Madonna willingly exposed herself and used the private lives of others, including him, to feed her craving to be the center of attention. Sometimes her statements could be very personal. When she was asked by one interviewer about the size of Beatty's manhood she responded, 'I haven't measured it but it's a perfectly wonderful size,' while she boasted to chat-show host Arsenio Hall, on his late-night TV show *Arsenio!* that she was able to satisfy the legendary stud in bed. Of Beatty and his concerns, Liz Rosenberg says dismissively, 'He was into the publicity game of another era. It's just not the way publicity is any more.' That might, perhaps, be put more accurately as meaning that it's not the way publicity is for Madonna.

As far as *Truth or Dare* was concerned, her exhibitionist qualities were perfectly matched to the voyeuristic urges of her audience, but her craving for exposure revealed the extent to which she defined herself by her image, a kind of desperate scorning of the soul. On one occasion during the filming of the documentary she visited a throat specialist, who asked her if she wanted to discuss anything off-camera. Watching out of shot was Beatty, whose shrewd observation serves as a telling commentary on her life. 'She doesn't want to *live* off-camera, much less talk,' he noted. 'There's nothing to say off-camera. Why would you say something if it's off-camera? What point is there in existing?' Her former lover, Dan Gilroy, wryly reflected on the truth of Beatty's remark, recalling Madonna's early days in New York, when she would spend hours capturing her thoughts and feelings on his tape recorder. He once joked that she even wanted to take the tape recorder with her when she went to the bathroom. There was a difference, of course, for in those days she did not have a wider audience. Now she did.

That Madonna's romance with Warren Beatty died almost as soon as *Dick Tracy* was released in 1990 seemed to confirm the feeling that the whole affair had been carried out for the cameras, for publicity. To her, Beatty's celebrity was the hook, but also the catch, for while his stardom had been the original source of his appeal, it proved to be the cause of the failure of their relationship. Madonna admitted that she was in love with Beatty, but realized that he would never play second fiddle to her. As a close friend of the actor observed, 'It was hard for him being so successful in the past and her being so successful in the present. It was role-reversal for him. There was love there, but it wasn't a deep relationship. It was a symbolic love affair.'

If Madonna's search for a life partner, even a soul mate, also included a large dose of celebrity hunting, she was not to be disappointed for long. Nor were the media and her public, for a few months after the demise of her affair with Warren Beatty, another superstar took his place at her side. Just as she had learned from the movie master, she was now about to take a musical seminar from Michael Jackson, the most successful solo singer of the decade. Following the critical acclaim that greeted *Dick Tracy* on its release in June 1990, Madonna was asked to perform the Oscar-nominated song from the film, 'Sooner or Later' by Stephen Sondheim, at the Academy Awards ceremony on March 25, 1991. The Gloved One was her date. She and Jackson had met a week earlier in The Ivy, a fashionable Los Angeles restaurant, where the staff had tried in vain to stop paparazzi from taking pictures of the two stars, even though both were happy to be photographed together. In addition to agreeing to be each other's dates at the Oscars ceremony, they also discussed collaborating on a duet for Jackson's forthcoming album, *Dangerous*.

As speculation about the relationship between the androgynous singer and one of the world's sexiest women reached fever pitch, Madonna played her part to perfection, suggesting that she was going to give him a makeover and hinting that he was a closet gay who, she felt, needed to meet her gay dancers to encourage him to come out. Jokingly, she described a night out with Jackson: 'First I beg him not to wear his sunglasses and of course he complies, because I'm stronger than he is. Then we exchange powder puffs – we both powder our noses – and we compare bank accounts.'

Their appearance at the Oscars together – Jackson in a white sequined jacket and white gloves (two, rather than the single glove he usually affected), Madonna in a glittering white Bob Mackie gown and 20 million dollars' worth of loaned diamonds – caused a sensation. Even observers as seasoned as Barbara Walters were impressed, the TV-show hostess remarking, 'They looked like caricatures, they seemed untouchable, larger than life.' It was a good night for *Dick Tracy*, too, 'Sooner or Later' winning the award for Best Original Song; the film had also won six other nominations, including Best Supporting Actor for Al Pacino.

Madonna may have given the impression in public that Michael Jackson was some kind of exhibit in a freak show, winking with complicity when questioned by journalists about their relationship, but that did not stop her from trying to add him to her growing list of high-profile conquests. She later told one of her lovers that she had indeed tried to seduce Jackson shortly after the Oscars – but confessed that her bedside manner failed to arouse his interest. The same lover recalled her description of the scene: 'They were on the couch at his place and she would put the moves on him and he would stick out his tongue for a second. When they touched he would start giggling, like a little boy. Nothing happened because he was giggling so much. That was one man she was not able to conquer.'

If her celebrity boyfriends enabled Madonna to keep capturing the headlines, her relationship with Sandra Bernhard kept the public guessing about her sexual orientation, further stoking the fires of media interest surrounding her. Away from the cameras, Bernhard was always the third wheel in her friend's love affairs, an invariable feature at restaurants and house parties to which Madonna and her escort of the moment went. Just as Bernhard had always been on hand during the collapse of Madonna's marriage to Sean Penn, so she was around throughout her affair with Warren Beatty, accompanying the couple to clubs and theaters, or just hanging out with them.

It was natural, therefore, that Bernhard would be present to watch with amused approval when Madonna encountered a bisexual model, transvestite and aspiring actor named Tony Ward at her thirty-second birthday party, thrown for her by the photographer Herb Ritts in August 1990. The handsome, musclebound actor was teasingly offered as her 'birthday present' by her half-brother Mario, although she had in fact met Ward before when he worked on her 1989 videos, *Like A Prayer* and *Cherish*. Legend has it that Madonna stubbed out a cigarette on his back, a story that prompted the witty riposte from her spokesman, 'Madonna doesn't smoke, she sizzles.'

On the rebound from her failed romance with Warren Beatty, who was by this time squiring the actress Annette Bening, around town, friends considered the good-looking younger man to be the perfect pick-me-up, especially as, at twenty-six, he was half the age of her previous lover. Madonna duly obliged, and picked him up. Perhaps inevitably, they became lovers, Ward moving into her Hollywood mansion a month after the party. For a time, in a rather self-conscious reversal of roles, he became her 'arm candy,' his well-muscled body by her side when she went to restaurants or gala events. She flew him to New York to be her date for the film premiere of *Goodfellas*, as well as her escort at a benefit in honor of one of her idols, the legendary dancer, choreographer and teacher Martha Graham, perhaps the most important and influential figure in modern dance.

There was more to the relationship with Ward than simply exorcising the end of an affair, however. Hurt rather more than she cared to admit about the failure of her romance with Beatty, Madonna was also out to prove a point. Or, more accurately, she was hurt that the media focus seemed to be permanently transferred to Beatty and Annette Bening, whom he met in 1991 when he auditioned her for a role in his film *Bugsy*. A year later they were married. 'It took all of thirty seconds to fall in love,' he said later, rather sententiously. 'I knew instantly that she was special.'

In a matter of months, Madonna had gone from dating a Hollywood hero to being squired by a Tinseltown toyboy. While that may have seemed a comedown for her, it was quite the reverse for Tony Ward. A former waiter, he had first fallen for Madonna when he served her and Sean Penn as they dined at the Los Angeles restaurant where he was working. 'I was totally ga-ga over her,' he admits. 'I was really hurt when she married Sean, really hurt.' In every way he was the opposite of Warren Beatty or, for that matter, Sean Penn. While the two actors, both noted sexual swordsmen, were cut from vigorous heterosexual timber, Tony Ward had a reputation for cross-dressing and sexual submission. Just as her ex-husband and Beatty may have reminded Madonna of her father, so Ward, quiet, unassertive and passive, seemingly brought out the maternal instincts in her. It was not a side of her she necessarily wished to engage. 'At one point she asked me to leave because she just ended up being a mother to me,' Ward recalls, with admirable candor.

As a couple they enjoyed, as he says, a 'very odd connection,' although excited tabloid reports claiming that just days after he met the singer, Ward married his existing girlfriend, fashion stylist Amalia Papadimos, at a secret ceremony in Las Vegas, turned out to be wildly inaccurate. So too were stories – emphatically denied by Liz Rosenberg – that Madonna had miscarried Ward's child in December 1990. In actual fact, Madonna was so 'devastated' when a fortune teller told her at a New Year's Eve party that she would never have children that she promptly got so drunk she was sick for days afterwards.

The media were right in one matter, however: Ward's fondness for cocaine was no tabloid exaggeration. During the time he was with Madonna he twice voluntarily entered rehabilitation clinics, the treatment paid for by his fond patroness. Not only did she encourage him to try to kick his drug habit, she also urged him to pursue his acting career, doing what she could to help – if that is the right word – by featuring him in her erotic video, *Justify My Love*, which was banned by MTV for its sexual content.

Indeed, a comment she made about her relationship with the gay dancers on her Blonde Ambition Tour could be applied equally well to her affair with Tony Ward: 'I've chosen people who are emotionally crippled in some way and need mothering from me.' Damaged herself by her mother's death, she has, perhaps subconsciously, quite often chosen flawed lovers, men impaired by drink problems, like Sean Penn, or drugs, like Tony Ward, Vanilla Ice, and others, or suffering from personal difficulties of one kind or another. Even her second husband, Guy Ritchie, is severely dyslexic.

For Madonna at this time – successful, rich, and with a huge international following – there remained a yawning gap in her life: someone to love, and who would love her in return. It had become a quest, with the result that during her search for love – 'I'm not sure who I'm looking for,' she confessed – she was playing the field. Her model toyboy was not the only man to share her bed, for by the summer of 1991 she was also seeing Vanilla Ice, as well as briefly dating the young Hollywood heartthrob Luke Perry, the star of the teen-cult TV show *Beverly Hills 90210*, after he presented her with AmFAR's Award of Courage for her AIDS work at a ceremony in Hollywood. Indeed, when she was in Evansville that summer filming *A League of Their Own*, Madonna, a master at juggling people and relationships, managed to arrange matters so that both Tony Ward and Vanilla Ice flew to the Midwest location to keep her company. She organized the timetable so that they would not meet.

Her juggling act continued during the shooting of her now notorious book *Sex*. The conception and rude birth of this curious amalgam of aluminum and paper offer a telling insight into the world of Madonna, businesswoman, artist and woman. It was the first offering from Maverick Entertainment, the multi-media venture, started in April 1992, which gave Madonna what she had been striving towards for years – total control.

Born after a year-long negotiation between her manager, Freddy DeMann, and her record company, Time-Warner, Maverick was truly Madonna's creation, enabling her to dabble in the world of books, film, video, merchandising and, of course, record production. Even the name, Maverick, was her idea, reflecting her vision of herself as an outsider and non-conformist. That may have been her perspective – the men in suits who backed her venture to the tune of $60 million were more impressed by Madonna's extraordinary ability to transform the creative and the controversial into real commercial success.

Typically, Madonna gathered a strong team around her, with DeMann as manager, Seymour Stein as record scout and a young Israeli, Guy Oseary, who became a close friend, as head of A and R. However, she was the one in charge. 'Warner didn't hand me this money so I could go off shopping at Bergdorf's,' said the singer, six months after the deal had been signed. 'I have to work and come up with the goods.'

While the star label is nothing new – The Beatles and The Rolling Stones had their own imprints – Madonna's vision owed as much to her old friend Andy Warhol as to anyone in the music industry. Over the years his factory in New York had produced a dazzling array of underground talent, from artists to singers and movie makers. As she herself said of her new venture. 'Maverick will be an intellectual thing. It started as a desire to have more control. There's a group of writers, photographers, and editors that I have met along the way in my career who I want to take with me wherever I go. I want to incorporate them into my little factory of ideas.'

The genesis of *Sex* – originally known as *The Rock* – fitted that philosophical template perfectly, Madonna the star and *raison d'être* of the whole enterprise. Artistically, the concept behind the book incorporated and developed previous highly successful and equally provocative enterprises, namely her video *Justify My Love* and the documentary *Truth or Dare*.

Sex, then, was the logical extension of her creative and commercial vision, an audacious piece of pop culture, conceived, designed, directed, written, and marketed by Madonna; iconoclast, sex goddess and company chairman. As an exercise in vanity publishing it took some beating, the CEO indulging in an illustrated sexual journey, a story that was part autobiography, part fantasy. For a woman who wanted the world to love her, it was a high-risk strategy in which she attempted, by sleight-of-hand, to be the multi-millionaire company executive who presents herself as a knowing but lovable sexual subversive.

During her frenetic career she had successfully aired the issues of teen pregnancy, blasphemy and gay rights. Now she was aiming to tackle sexual taboos in strait-laced America. As befitted Maverick's first high-profile venture, Madonna was in total control. She carefully selected pictures from the 20,000 shots taken by the photographer Steven Meisel on location in New York and Florida, discussed the design with the art director, Fabien Baron, and debated the text with the laconic writer Glenn O'Brien. Her hand was in everything, from the famous silver Mylar bag used to cover the aluminum-bound book, to the volume's size and shape – she originally wanted it to be circular, so that it would be 'different' – and the obsessive secrecy surrounding its production.

In the incongruous setting of the Vault, a seedy fetish club in the meatpacking district of New York, the two faces of Madonna were on display, the scantily dressed sex object and master of ceremonies, her persona changing from biddable model to haughty auteur with the speed of a whipcrack. Dressed only in a borrowed blazer and a pair of high heels, she was every inch the pocket-sized tyrant, complaining vociferously about the heating, the food and the lighting. Her bodyguard, Jim Albright, who had just started working for her, noted her behavior with keen interest. 'In a split second she became the boss and everyone on the set was on tenterhooks. My first impression was that she was bitchy and demanding but as time went on I realized how much power she had over these people, how absolutely everything revolved around her. She had total control.' Even when the *Sex* circus moved to Florida she never relinquished her grip for a moment. When the owner of the house they were renting was spotted covertly taking pictures of the frolicking star, Madonna called a halt to shooting. The woman, who collapsed in floods of tears, was forced to hand over the camera and made to sign a confidentiality agreement before filming could continue.

Madonna was right to be cautious. Stars like model Naomi Campbell – who was worried about what her mother would think – the rapper Daddy Kane and the actress Isabella Rossellini were on the set, and it was only the force of Madonna's personality that encouraged these celebrities to shed their inhibitions. When she wasn't reassuring nervous stars, Madonna was calming nerves in the Time-Warner boardroom, already under siege from moral crusaders like Tipper Gore, the wife of the Vice-President, for signing rapper Ice T, some of whose lyrics appeared to advocate cop killing.

As if this was not enough, Madonna the sexual ringmaster was not only juggling stars and boardroom executives, but was still trying to keep her boyfriends apart. In the winter of 1991–2, when she was shooting scenes for the book in New York, Tony Ward went through his paces as a model, playing a rapist to Madonna's Catholic schoolgirl and a foot worshipper to her dominatrix – a persona she called 'Dita Parlo' – for Meisel's camera. A few weeks later, in February, she invited Vanilla Ice to join her at the house she and her team had rented in Florida for the second stage of the shooting. The heavily tattooed white rapper was clearly out to impress, arriving in his brand-new customized Porsche, complete with white kid-leather upholstery and a serious sound system that could deafen people streets away. So he was flattered when Meisel asked to use his car for some shots of Madonna.

He was rather less impressed, however, when, after the shoot, he saw that she had left his upholstery stained brown with the fake-suntan cream that she had used to protect her alabaster-white skin from the Florida sun. 'That was my dream car, man,' he recalls. 'She ruined my interior for nothing, they never used a picture.' She made it up to him when they went back to his house for the night. Before they went out for dinner, he and Madonna cavorted before the camera, Vanilla Ice under the impression that they were posing for a magazine.

Silently watching from the sidelines was the tall, lithe figure of Jim Albright, her new bodyguard. He was trying to figure out the true nature of her relationship with Vanilla Ice. For when she was posing in the Florida sunshine with her rapper lover, Madonna was surreptitiously making eyes at – and suggesting a good deal more to – at the young man who would soon graduate from bodyguard to suitor, and finally to serious marriage prospect.

Chapter Eleven

Looking for Love in All the Wrong Places

I T WAS HARDLY love at first sight. 'One more fucking person stands on my fucking dress and I'm going to kill somebody,' were the first words he heard from the woman who would one day dominate his life. Her invective was in full flow that night, at the New York premiere in 1991 of her documentary, *Truth or Dare*, where Jim Albright was working on bodyguard detail for a security company. He was not to see her again until he was assigned to be her personal bodyguard for the duration of the *Sex* shoot in New York and Florida.

It was while she was getting ready for the book's 'rape' scene at the YMCA in New York that he first noticed her making eyes at him. She was in her dressing room with Tony Ward, but the twenty-two-year-old bodyguard noticed that she kept glancing in his direction. Of mixed Native American, Afro-Caribbean, Polish and Italian antecedents, Albright's lightly tanned good looks and sleek physique – he is a martial-arts specialist – had clearly caught her eye. As the day progressed Steven Meisel joked with him, 'She's going to have you.'

He thought no more of it until he was detailed to accompany her to a party at the Palladium Club to launch the single by vogue dancers José and Luis, who had featured strongly in the *Vogue* video and the Blonde Ambition Tour. As Albright pushed a way for her through the crowd, she grabbed his hand. A tingle of electricity went through his body. He had felt the Madonna connection for the first time. That night, though, she only had eyes for her date, Nick Scotti, a handsome young Italian model turned singer whom Madonna was grooming for stardom. She and Scotti would go on to sing a duet together for the soundtrack of the film *Nothing But Trouble* starring Demi Moore, and a version of the song also appeared on his first album. Albright hung around during the party, and then ushered Scotti and Madonna into a limousine in which they headed back to her apartment.

The shooting of the photographs for the book continued in Florida in February 1992, Madonna flying to Miami and a suite in the Fontainebleau Hotel, where she stayed for the duration of the shoot. In spite of the misgivings of his girlfriend Melissa, who was worried about Madonna's man-eating reputation, Albright went along as her personal bodyguard – at the singer's express request. His room was next to her penthouse suite and every morning at dawn he would accompany Madonna and her girlfriend, Ingrid Casares, as they ran for six miles along the beach. Noticeably Madonna, who has an abiding fear of breast cancer, which killed her mother, wore three training bras to stop her breasts from bouncing. The women teased him that he couldn't keep up, and despite boasts he had made earlier, he had to admit he was 'pussy whipped,' exhausted by the time they had run up the thirteen flights of hotel stairs back to her room. Then he sat and watched in admiration as Madonna went through an hour-long workout with her gym equipment.

Next day he was so stiff that when they went running he bummed a ride from a patrolling policeman, who generously let the bodyguard sit next to him on his dune buggy while Madonna and Ingrid jogged ahead. Throughout the day he was the butt of their jokes, teasing that became ever more flirtatious. Over dinner there was a conversation about tattoos, and Albright admitted that he had one on his back. He coyly refused to reveal all, however, in spite of the urgings of the other people at the table, including Madonna. It was only when he escorted Madonna to her room that he offered to show it to her. In reply she gently touched his back and said, 'Do you want to kiss me?' 'I guess so,' he stuttered. In almost a parody of a movie cliché, the phone in her room rang just as they were about to embrace. After taking the call, they finally kissed. Then Madonna told him bluntly, 'You know, I'm not going to fuck you.' Startled and somewhat breathless, Albright's response was to tell her that he didn't fuck on the first date. 'This isn't a date,' she replied tersely.

The next day Madonna, hot and sweaty after her morning run, grabbed Jim in the kitchen of her penthouse suite. This time the electricity really did flow. Wet with sweat from her morning workout, Madonna touched a faulty electrical appliance and both were jolted as the electric shock passed through her to him. Nearly electrocuted or not, Albright was now hooked. Throughout the shoot, their mutual flirtation intensified, Madonna stealing a kiss from him when there was no one around, or holding his hand in the back of the limo. It was not long before the inevitable happened, despite her bold statement after their first kiss, the two lovers sharing a romantic night together in her penthouse, with just the sound of the breakers and the stars in the jet-black sky as accompaniment.

Yet for Albright, that night signaled rather more than simple romance. Besides the usual first-time nerves, he found himself both alarmed and dumbfounded by the turn events had taken. Everything that his girlfriend Melissa had warned him about was coming true, and yet he could not help himself from being caught in the web spun by the singer. Here he was, a young guy from Hackensack, New Jersey, who had strayed on to the wrong side of the tracks, falling for one of the world's biggest sex symbols, a multi-millionaire with a fabulous Manhattan apartment. 'I could feel myself being sucked in,' he remembers ruefully. 'I knew I was going to break my girlfriend's heart and yet how far, realistically, was I going to go with Madonna? Looking back, it was like I was making a pact with the Devil.'

The story of the relationship between the young bodyguard and the world-famous singer, eleven years his senior, not only allows a vivid insight into Madonna's makeup, but also serves as a modern-day fairy story, the mirror image of the tale of Cinderella, in which a humble youth is whisked away by the princess of pop and offered the keys to her kingdom.

Madonna had other matters on her mind, however. While Jim Albright was struggling with his feelings for the singer, she was falling in love with Florida, with the ambience, the clubs, the people. She adored the house on Biscayne Bay where they were shooting, and which was close to homes owned by Cher and Sylvester Stallone. After making enquiries, she discovered that the house was owned by department-store magnates, the Nordstrom family. They had no plans to sell, but when Madonna made them an offer in the region of $5 million, it was a price even they could not refuse.

Her enjoyment of life in the winter sun inspired a mood of risk-taking frivolity on set. She was game for anything, something that gave her bodyguard a professional headache – how to save her from arrest. So when she impulsively decided to be photographed hitchhiking naked along the highway, he stood a couple of yards away with a coat to cover her modesty in case the police came by. While that escapade went without a hitch, she nearly gave the Italian owner of a pizza parlor a heart attack when she dropped her coat to the floor and, wearing a smile and nothing else, calmly asked for a slice of pepperoni. 'Get out, get out or I call the police,' the woman owner yelled as Madonna and company beat a hasty retreat, Albright throwing a coat over her as, almost hysterical with laughter, she ran out of the restaurant.

This devil-may-care mood merely added to the exhilarating sexual and personal chemistry developing between them. They could not wait until the end of that day's shoot so that they could sneak a kiss together or retire to her penthouse suite. It seemed that the bodyguard was more than just a passing fancy, for Madonna talked about the two of them coming back to Florida to spend time together if she bought the house. Then, on the night before they left for New York, she told him that she loved him. 'That blew me away,' Albright admits. During the three-hour flight back to New York Madonna constantly made eyes at her bodyguard, and when they landed she asked for him to be her security detail at a Lenny Kravitz concert that night. Albright agreed, and during the course of the evening she told him that she and

Kravitz, who co-wrote her 1990 hit 'Justify My Love' for her, had been lovers. At the end of the show, Madonna took Albright back to her apartment on West 64th Street and asked him to stay the night, knowing that his girlfriend was waiting for him in New Jersey. Sure enough, at three in the morning his pager went off; it was Melissa, wondering where he was. He left the apartment, but it was a pattern that was repeated virtually every night for the next month, until he decided to leave Melissa for Madonna.

They were soon enjoying a 'hot and heavy' affair, although, like Vanilla Ice and others, Jim Albright scoffs at the legend that Madonna is a woman with whips and chains hidden in the closet at her New York apartment, but knows her instead as a 'normal,' if rather passive, sexual partner. Whatever happened in bed, however, he noticed that as soon as he left his long-time girlfriend, the dynamics of their budding relationship subtly changed. It seemed to him that it had been a little game for Madonna to encourage him to leave Melissa. Yet now that he had done her bidding, she was reluctant to let him come and live with her. Instead, he moved in with his mother for a time until he could find a place of his own. That too caused a certain amount of friction, the hip singer not wanting to be seen dating a guy who lived with his mom. Eventually Albright found himself in a one-bedroom apartment in Hackensack. Perhaps feeling she was going slumming, Madonna came over one evening and he cooked pasta for her.

That, though, was an exception. For the most part it was Jim Albright who drove over the George Washington Bridge from New Jersey to join her at her apartment. Even though he was now living only a few miles away, it was as though he was entering a different world. They ate out every night at midtown sushi bars or at restaurants near the 54th Street studio where she was recording her *Erotica* album, and she took him to shows and plays, often going backstage to meet the stars, especially those she admired.

He was by her side when she congratulated Alec Baldwin and Jessica Lange, one of her heroines, after seeing them in the Tennessee Williams drama *A Streetcar Named Desire,* and he accompanied her to watch another of her idols, Peggy Lee, sing at the Hilton Hotel's Club 53. Madonna, who covered the famous Peggy Lee song 'Fever' on her *Erotica* album, was all smiles when she presented Lee with a bouquet of red roses at the end of her show, which she performed from a wheelchair. It was a bittersweet evening, Madonna thrilled at meeting someone she had admired since childhood, yet saddened at the toll age and illness had taken, the younger singer perhaps seeing in Peggy Lee intimations of her own mortality.

Not everything was wine and roses, however. In the summer of 1993 a night out at a pizzeria in SoHo exposed Madonna's lover to the darker side of fame. They had gone out in a group that included a couple of Albright's friends and two of her male dancers. As they were leaving the restaurant, they were confronted by a posse of paparazzi. In the ensuing mêlée a couple of punches were thrown before Madonna and Albright made good their escape and headed back to her apartment. The following morning the headline in one New York tabloid read, 'Testy Titans of Testosterone,' the accompanying article blaming the bodyguards for the fracas. The singer, who had valiantly tried to keep her latest paramour out of the headlines, was mortified. Later, one of the cameramen, Kenneth Katz, sued Madonna, his damages suit eventually being settled out of court.

The incident marked a watershed. Albright was still technically her bodyguard, both of them deriving some amusement from deciding when the billing stopped, the point in any day when he changed from hired bodyguard to unpaid lover. For the last few months he had been a regular visitor at her apartment, her staff now shopping for his dietary needs since his six-foot-two-inch frame was hardly sustained by Madonna's diet of ricecakes and fruit juices. Nonetheless, the clash between his duty as her employee and their emotional relationship was an accident waiting to happen. Realizing this, he quit working as Madonna's bodyguard, taking another position as head of security for the Palladium nightclub.

It proved a change for the better, as Albright recalls: 'We just got closer. The relationship seemed so rosy, it was new and fresh. I had an overwhelming feeling of love for her which I felt was reciprocated.' Indeed, in an interview at the time Madonna cryptically suggested that she was in love, that it was love at first sight, and that it would last for ever. Yet if she would not publicly name the man in her life, she and Albright were on the phone to each other almost constantly. On every day of their three-year relationship she either called or paged him using a secret code. As often as not she would be calling to tell him that day's joke, gleaned from a joke book or a member of her entourage. For Albright, 'That was one of the best parts of the relationship. She has a great sense of humor.'

When he could afford it, he bought her tiger lilies, her favorite flowers, or scoured antique markets for little trinkets that might amuse her. A silver charm bracelet he found for her was a particular favorite. For her part she was always sending him flowers, especially when she was out of town. When he moved into a bigger apartment in North Bergen she bought him a microwave and a quilt as housewarming gifts. Indeed, during their three-year affair she was always concerned about his well-being, 'like a mother sending her child off to school,' he says, adding that, 'She has a need to be mothering to her men and the people she cares for in her life. Obviously losing her own mother at such an early age has brought out her own maternal instincts. She is a very caring person with a lot of love in her heart, which she kept bottled up during her childhood.'

He was not the only one in her 'family.' There was always someone she was 'mothering,' trying to help, whether it was Tony Ward and his problems with cocaine, her friend Ingrid Casares and her drug addiction, or any one of a host of other waifs and strays in her life. Her strength of character, as well as her fame, gave her friends the strength to fight their various problems or addictions, the carrot being the fact that they could continue be part of her circle if they recovered, the stick the knowledge that Madonna's support would be of limited duration if they did not help themselves.

Of even more immediate concern to her, however, was her own desire to have a family. To Albright, it was clear from early on in the relationship that Madonna wanted children, especially a child of mixed race. As he says, 'She just loved my skin color and she was always fascinated by interracial children. Quite frankly that was part of my attraction to her. Her biological clock was ticking, she has this incredible maternal instinct and I think that in her eyes it would make her life complete. It would give her the thing she cherishes most in life – unconditional love and admiration.' They had even chosen the names for the children they planned to have, Lola for a girl and Caesar for a boy. In letters to him she would sign herself 'Lola,' and playfully sent her love to their two putative offspring. When she bought the Nordstrom house in Florida she even named the boat she kept there *Lola, Lola.* Yet whatever her hopes, it was to be another four years before her dream became reality.

If planning their family together was one indicator of the close bond between Madonna and Albright, another was when he took her home to meet his librarian mother, Jane, and other members of his family for a Sunday lunch in Hackensack. They chatted in the kitchen, Madonna charming and careful to put everyone at ease, aware that entertaining a living icon is a daunting prospect for most people. Then she and Albright walked hand in hand through the local park and along the main drag, colloquially known as Burgerland Avenue, stopping to buy Terigo, a Cuban wheat drink she likes, from a local store, and admiring a pitbull they encountered (they talked about buying one together). It was the very normality of the day that appealed to Madonna's lover. No one recognized them, and even when he introduced her to an acquaintance in the street, his friend couldn't quite believe that she really was Madonna.

Having become close to a woman whose life is so organized and controlled, Albright came to cherish those times when she relaxed a little, showed her humanity, her humor and, at times, her vulnerability. On one occasion they went to a retrospective of the work of the graffiti artist Keith Haring, which was staged in a New York gallery. Haring, another old friend of hers from her time in New York in the 1980s, had died from AIDS in 1990. For the first time, Albright saw her collapse in tears, astonished to find this woman, normally in complete command of her feelings, sobbing in his arms as she reflected on the roll call of friends from those early New York days who had died either from AIDS or from drugs.

She let the mask slip again when she was immersing herself in the character she was to play in the film *Dangerous Game*, which her company, Maverick Entertainment, was producing. There was a scene in the film in which her character smoked marijuana, so Madonna, ever the perfectionist, decided that she needed to experience what that would be like so that she could portray it accurately on screen. So she, Jim Albright and a music-industry executive went to an underground club in the meatpacking district of New York and smoked several joints, the would-be method actress taking a notebook with her in which to write down her thoughts and feelings. As what she calls the 'dabble weed' took effect, Madonna slipped into a state that was far from the woman in charge of herself and everyone around her. She became forgetful, continually losing her notebook, amusingly silly and so laid back that she was soon horizontal. 'It was refreshing to see a control freak so out of control,' Albright remembers.

She showed her hidden side yet again when she and her lover flew to Detroit in Time-Warner's private jet to spend Christmas with her family. While the manner of her arrival was entirely suitable for a sophisticated superstar, when she was with her father, stepmother and the other Ciccones she became just another Midwest girl-made-good. Her father loaned them a battered minivan to drive around in, and gave them the use of an empty house he owned. So Madonna, icon of feminism, adopted a new persona, 'Madge in the Minivan,' driving Albright round the city like a mother on her school run. They slept in sleeping bags on an airbed in the empty property, huddling together for warmth. For once they were on their own – no Ingrid, no secretary, no publicity agent, no phones or television. They played Scrabble with her family, amid the usual sibling rivalry common to all families, the simmering undercurrents of jealousy and disapproval subdued in the atmosphere of Christmas cheer.

For Madonna, the most enjoyable moment about that trip home was the chance it brought for her to sit on her father's lap. It made her feel like a little girl again. 'At home nobody brings up the fact that I'm a star,' she told the writer Lynn Hirschberg. 'Not one word. At first I thought: "Well, how come I'm not getting any special treatment?" But even though I had to sleep on the floor in a sleeping bag, even though I didn't know who else had slept in that sleeping bag, the trip was really such a joyous thing for my father.' It was joyous for Albright, too, who admits, 'These were the moments I cherished with her.'

Besides sharing the good times, Albright was also by her side during what became for her a dark journey of the soul, when the controversy over her book, *Sex*, was at its height in the fall of 1992. Published in October by Warner Books, *Sex* ignited a nationwide controversy, albeit one that did little, if anything, to slow its sales. 'I've really bitten off more than I can chew, I really wish I hadn't done this,' she confessed to him one day in a moment of utter despair. Every morning when she read the corrosive reviews, sent in the daily clippings service from Liz Rosenberg, her mood would palpably darken. Even though he would devote the day to reassuring her that for everyone who hated the book, there were a thousand who loved her, it did little to lighten her spirits.

When the book was published, amidst frenetic scenes as fans choked the bookstores, clamoring for the copies, there was an immediate – and personally devastating – backlash. For the first time feminists, liberals and the Christian right were united in their condemnation of a book which, they argued, dealt in pornography, rape and degradation for the singer's personal profit. The humorous juxtaposition in many of the images – notably the shots of her hitchhiking naked down a Florida highway, or pumping gas wearing nothing but black lace leggings – and the erotic, witty and, at times, self-deprecating text were submerged in the tidal wave of criticism. 'I think I'm treated that way because people find it hard to believe that an ordinary little lady can become rich and powerful and stay sexy and disrespectful,' Madonna argued.

Brave words in public, but in private she was distraught. *Sex* proved to be a watershed in her career and her personal life. For the first time there was no way of sliding out from under the controversy – no director, playwright or cameraman to blame for the bitter emotion and biting criticism she had aroused. She was learning that the handmaiden of absolute authority is total responsibility. For once, she was completely exposed, even the caveat in her book, in which she wrote, 'Nothing in this book is true. I made it all up,' giving her no room for maneuver, and far less escape.

To feel so utterly out of control was a searing experience, especially for a woman who so badly needed to be in control. She received sackloads of hate mail – at one time running at 200 letters a day – from furious individuals and groups, as well as vicious death threats from groups and individuals, which naturally concerned her, her friends and her staff. Looking back on that period, she reflected, 'I divide my career from before and after the *Sex* book. Up until then I really was just being a creative person working and doing things that inspired me and I thought would inspire other people. After that I suddenly had a different point of view about life in general. *Sex* was my fantasy and I made money off of it. That is a no-no. I was involved on every level and that is unacceptable. It's all part of the strong woman in control terrifying people.'

At the time, not only was she was under pressure to finish off the *Erotica* album, whose sales suffered as a result of the backlash, but she had to try to stave off the constant criticism. After the publication of *Sex*, she went on to star in the erotic thriller *Body of Evidence*, and then *Dangerous Game*, the first film funded by her own company. Coming as they did on the heels of the controversy over her book, the failure of these movies, both critically and commercially, would make 1993 a year that was to test her to the limit. Nonetheless, she could at least comfort herself with the commercial success of *Sex*, which went on to sell 1.5 million copies around the world, a triumph of marketing for the fledgling Maverick group.

During previous controversies she had drawn comfort from the experience of the man she sees as her spiritual guide and talisman, Elvis Presley, the anniversary of whose death falls on her birthday. She had always been consoled by the fact that he was ultimately accepted by society when initially he had been vilified as a rebel, a cheap performer whose sexually provocative poses outraged moral America. This time, however, Elvis was no consolation.

Nights were the worst. Always a restless sleeper, Madonna could only sleep if Albright rubbed her forehead or stroked her hair. Even then the singer, who has persistent nightmares about death, was not at peace, her eyes beneath the closed eyelids flickering in constant agitation. 'She was a mess,' her former lover states categorically. 'It was the darkest time in her career. She was haunted by the criticism. My role was as a supporter, to take the pressure off her and constantly reassure her that what she was doing was right, and not to let the negative energy from the media and others affect her. She is a very, very sensitive and insecure person and I just had to let her know that she was a great entertainer, one of the most famous people in the world, and there was a price to be paid for that.'

Madonna was concerned about more than bad reviews, however, although Albright didn't know it at the time. While he was comforting her, she kept to herself the reaction of one of the participants in the book, Vanilla Ice. Still under the impression, not yet confounded by her, that they had a relationship, the rapper was furious when he found out that she had plastered his face –

and much else – all over her book without having the courtesy to ask his permission or, for that matter, considering the consequences to his own career.

Vanilla Ice, who beat his drug habit and is now a born-again Christian,
remembers how he very ostentatiously burned the signed copy of *Sex* she
sent him. 'I was so displeased that she put me in this whole slutty package.
That was the end for me and her. When she rang I told her that the book
belittled and embarrassed me. People looked at me as though I was this big
slut and I got bad headlines for it.' What saddened him as much as anything
was that by publishing the book, the Madonna he had come to know was
demeaning and degrading herself. 'I knew her,' he observes sadly, 'and what
she was portraying was phony, it was fake. She was not this slut at all. She
seemed to be doing it just for the money.'

Even as Vanilla Ice and Madonna went their separate ways, Jim Albright too
was beginning to see the flip side of his girlfriend. It was not a view he much
liked. While they both wanted children, the details seemed to keep getting in
the way. There was the thorny issue of a possible pre-nuptial agreement.
Madonna was adamant that they draw one up, but Albright argued that as he
was not, and would never be, financially dependent on her, there was no need.
Nor was he keen on her idea of employing a nanny, believing that they should
bring up any children they might have themselves. At the same time there were
stories swirling around the mass media that Madonna had contracted AIDS,
rumors officially and categorically denied by Liz Rosenberg.

Nonetheless, it must have had the effect of creating further uncertainty in
Albright's mind, especially as he knew that she had had many sexual partners
over the years. Even though she seemed anxious to conceive he continued to
practice protected sex, his concerns only eased when Madonna received a
clean bill of health after taking the obligatory medical prior to starting work
on the film *Body of Evidence* in the summer of 1982.

These differences merely exposed more fundamental issues. Although
they had been together for some months, Albright found himself frustrated
that their relationship seemed to be a one-way street. He lived constantly on
'Madonna time,' his whole world shaped around her strictly organized
regime with its rigid timetables, always reassuring her and bolstering her
battered ego, rarely having the time to enjoy a normal relationship. With the
furor surrounding *Sex* in the fall of 1992, and the critical savaging her erotic
thriller *Body of Evidence* received when it was released the following January,
he felt that Madonna had neither the time nor the emotional strength to
prepare for motherhood.

Albright felt, too, a growing sense of distrust not just about the other men
in her life, but also the women. Virtually everywhere he and Madonna went

the slim, dark-haired figure of Ingrid Casares, the daughter of a millionaire Cuban businessman who first met Madonna at the singer's 1991 New Year's Eve party, would go with them. She was Madonna's shadow, accompanying her and Albright when they went to Florida, Germany, France and Los Angeles together. Like a little lamb – and like Sandra Bernhard before her – everywhere Madonna went, Casares was sure to follow. To Albright, however, she was more than just a shadow; she was an emotional buffer, her presence preventing him and Madonna from growing closer.

At first, Madonna shrugged off accusations from Albright that she and Casares were lovers, saying that, as a friend, she was helping her to overcome her addictions, both to drugs and to her former lover, Bernhard. Later, however, she confirmed to him that they were more than just friends, thereby exposing the unhappy triangular love tangle between Madonna, Sandra Bernhard and their mutual friend, Casares. This perhaps explains, at least in part, the vehemence of Bernhard's scorn towards the singer when their relationship ended. 'I look at my friendship with her as like having a gallstone. You deal with it, there is pain, and then you pass it. That's all I have to say about Schmadonna,' she scathingly remarked.

It was another nightclub owner, John Enos, widely thought to be the subject of the erotic *faux*-'Dear John' letters in *Sex*, whose elusive presence drove a further wedge between Albright and Madonna. On his first visit to Madonna's new home in Miami since she had bought it, Albright found a Blockbuster Video card in Enos's name. When he confronted her about Enos, who runs the Roxbury Club in Los Angeles, she at first denied but then admitted that she was still seeing him. She apologized, promised to be faithful, and for a time their relationship flourished.

Over the months, however, his gradual discovery of her secret friendships with everyone from actors to sports stars, and even a supermodel, sapped his faith in her. While she protested her innocence, he began to grow jealous and suspicious, never quite convinced by her protestations, or sure of her motives. Nor were his anxieties eased when he learned from press reports that she had been seeing some well-known personality before she told him that she had done so. It was partly his own fault. A New York Knicks fan, he had inspired her with his love of basketball, and it was not long before she became fascinated with the sport – and its players. For example, on a flying visit to Arizona she sought out Charles Barkley, then of the Phoenix Suns. In time, her taste for basketball stars would cost her dearly.

Given to jealousy, Albright also found it difficult to watch her performance with the craggy actor Willem Dafoe in *Body of Evidence*, in which they enjoyed wild on-screen sex antics, including a famous scene where she poured hot wax over his naked body. At the same time her growing friend-ship with the Japanese-American model Jenny Shimizu, described by the *Los Angeles Times* as a 'lezbopunk bike-dyke,' with whom she spent time in Paris when she went to see the designer Jean-Paul Gaultier, further added to an increasingly complicated love life. As Albright observes of their time together, 'She'd never been faithful to one man – period. She told me that. She is only loyal to herself.'

For him, though, the most painful time came in November 1993, after he, Madonna, her brother Christopher, the singer Tori Amos and the comedian Rosie O'Donnell, among other friends, had spent Thanksgiving together in the recently acquired house in Miami. They had fun, Madonna and O'Donnell, whom she had met two years earlier during the filming of *A League of Their Own*, keeping everyone amused with their clowning and banter. Beyond that, however, Madonna and her lover were on a high, Albright believing that the worst was behind them. He left the house party early, flying back to New York on his own, but content in the knowledge that their affair was once more back on track. As a result he was devastated to discover later that as soon as he had left, her former lover Tony Ward had joined the house party. Although she dismissed Albright's accusations that she was still sleeping with Ward, their relationship was now broken-backed, though it would drag on for months yet.

It seemed that while she demanded total loyalty from him, she did not feel the same obligation, for it became clear to him that her concern to keep his name out of the media had as much to do with ensuring that her other lovers could not see who she was with at any one time, as it had with protecting him from media attention. As they became increasingly estranged from each other, however, Madonna seemed, perversely, to become more needy of both his time and his affection. Insecure and possessive, she visited him unan-nounced at the Roxbury nightclub in New York where he now worked, checking that he was not flirting with, or even looking at, other women. On nights when he went home to his own apartment, she would call him early in the morning to make sure that he was on his own. Her jealousy reached such a pitch that when she arranged a viewing of her new movie, *Body of Evidence*, for Abel Ferrara, the director of her next film, *Dangerous Game*, and his wife Nancy in a private viewing theater, she afterwards accused his wife of making eyes at Albright in the darkened room.

'She became very, very insecure,' he says. 'She was always saying: "I saw you looking at her, why were you talking to her?" She was always accusing me of cheating on her. I told her that she only had those feelings because that was the life she led.' She left endless messages on his answering machine, their tone by turns humorous, cajoling, wheedling, tetchy or desperate. On one occasion she jokingly threatened to jump from her second-floor hotel balcony if he did not return her call, on another she admitted that she didn't deserve his trust but that she would change and make things right. Endlessly she told him that she loved him, and wanted to have his child.

The picture is of a woman needing love and giving equally of her love, readily falling *in* love and yet unwilling or unable to give of her essential spirit. Here was the contradiction at the sad heart of Madonna's soul, a woman looking for love in all the wrong places. She was not unaware of it. She gave her confused, almost continually heartbroken lover a book, *Love Junkie* by Robert Plunkett, which she felt described something of her emotional condition. The novel is a wry, rather sad tale of a well-to-do if innocent suburban housewife who, following her husband's death, becomes passively involved in the gay scene. The theme of the narrative explores love as something driven by a wistful neediness rather than sexual desire, an aspect of Madonna's personality that her boyfriend truly understood.

'She has a good spirit and a good heart,' Albright observes, 'but there are two sides to her, one of which is loving and caring, the other totally selfish. Madonna's greatest need is for love. So she uses sex as a form of love because of her great desire to feel loved and receive love. Love is Madonna's driving force at every level, from having the fans love her to having the people she sleeps with fall in love with her. She takes the physical act of sex, whether it is with a man or woman, and turns it into love. Madonna feeds on love, she feels starved of love.' He adds, 'Sometimes I feel that she sleeps with someone hoping that something of them will rub off on her; their talent, their wit, their athleticism.'

The tension between them came to a head during her 1993 The Girlie Show Tour, a brilliantly staged burlesque that was a sell-out around the world. At first, things went well between them. She and Albright spoke every day on the telephone, wrote often, and when she made a flying visit to New York to see her throat specialist, they met for dinner in a downtown restaurant. During their cozy chats over the phone she had made it clear that she really did want to have his baby. Organized as ever, she wanted him to fly out to Japan in December, at the end of the tour, so that she could conceive, and she would then take a break from her other commitments to prepare for the child's birth.

There were two problems. The first was that his sister was pregnant and he wanted to be present at the birth, which was likely to coincide with the end of the tour. When he explained this to Madonna, however, she became angry and upset that he was prepared to put his family before her. Secondly, before he saw her, Albright discovered that she had bought a man's suit while out shopping earlier that day. It was not his size, and it was not for him. When he taxed her with this they argued until Albright, angry and frustrated, walked out of the restaurant, leaving her to pick up the tab. A few days later, after she had returned to Europe for the next leg of her tour, he discovered that the suit was for his rival, John Enos.

The argument now continued at long distance, until finally Albright refused to take her calls, even though she would call him up to thirty times an hour. By the time she arrived in Buenos Aires, Argentina, in October, during the South American leg of the tour, Madonna was so distraught that she would no longer perform unless he spoke to her. Still he refused. In desperation Liz Rosenberg, her press secretary, called and pleaded with him to speak to his lover. Again he refused. With the minutes ticking away before the show was due to start, her manager, Freddy DeMann, called Albright and, in a man-to-man chat, convinced him to speak to the singer. She was crying and hysterical, but after they had spoken she calmed down enough to go through with her stage show that night.

On the following day they had a long conversation, in the course of which Albright told her that they were through and that he didn't want to see her any more. He was tired of having his heart broken. Nevertheless, they patched things up over the next couple of weeks, although he did little to help their relationship when he told her over the phone that he had had a brief fling with a girl at the club. Madonna freaked out, furious that he had had the temerity to cheat on her. Now it was her turn to hang up on him. 'I was amazed by her reaction because I had forgiven her umpteen times. She had fucked women, multiple men, the dog in the *Sex* book might have got a lick in, and I go and get a blow job and am man enough to tell her about it,' Albright observes wryly.

Their long-distance relationship continued to limp along, although Madonna became increasingly cool towards him, her reaction to the birth of his nephew Teddy on November 6 nothing if not muted. Since the tour did not finish until just before Christmas, Albright suggested that he fly out to meet her in the Far East. This time it was she who was ambivalent and unenthusiastic, tell-tale signs, if he had needed any, that she had done a complete emotional about-turn: 'There was probably someone else in the background,' he reflects. Then, on her return to America, she was reluctant even to meet him again, but he insisted, telling her that, if they were ending their three-year relationship, they should say goodbye in person.

They met at the beginning of January where it had all begun, on a deserted beach in Miami early one morning. They talked and walked for a while, and then spent the day together before sharing their last night as a couple at her home on Biscayne Bay. Next morning, as he prepared to leave, they shared a long last hug and shed a few tears before he walked out of her life. Like some latter-day Mrs Danvers, Ingrid Casares watched the fading melodrama silently and inscrutably from the shadows.

In New York six months later, Madonna was out running in Central Park when she did a double-take as she passed a fellow jogger. She thought it was Jim Albright or, if not, his brother, for he was the same height and had the same smooth, lightly tanned skin and well-muscled physique. She was intrigued. Shortly after returning to her apartment she asked one of her entourage, Danny Cortese, to do a little detective work and find out who the runner was. Eventually he discovered that he was a fitness instructor named Carlos Leon who worked at the Crunch gym in Manhattan, and she had apparently met him a couple of years earlier at a party. (His version of events is that he first stopped her to advise her on her fitness regime.)

Now even more intrigued, she instructed Cortese to deliver a message to Leon and arrange a meeting by the children's playground in Central Park. It was an appropriate rendezvous. Close up she liked what she saw, once again taken by the remarkable similarities between him and Albright. Furthermore, not only did the two men look alike, but they had similar personalities: quiet, rather shy but fiercely independent, with a clear, if streetwise, sense of morality and considerable dignity. Like Albright, Leon doted on his parents, Maria and Armando, and in time the singer became a frequent visitor to their modest 91st Street apartment. On one occasion she brought her actress friend Rosanna Arquette to join them, everyone tucking into black-eye beans as Cuban music played in the background.

Her new relationship with the sensitive and introverted Leon made a refreshing change from the hectic love life she had enjoyed since she and Jim Albright had parted. Carlos Leon proved himself to be a gentleman, considerate, affectionate and protective. He and Madonna led a quiet life, often walking unnoticed to the cinema in the nearby Lincoln Center, picking up an ice cream or shopping along Amsterdam Avenue, the picture of a normal everyday couple, holding hands in the sunshine. Inevitably, however, Ingrid Casares would be around, ensconced in Madonna's apartment or joining the couple for dinner.

He often brought her gifts of small boxes to add to her trinket collection, and took to putting boxes of candy on her bed – naturally, 'Red Hots' are her favorites. For Valentine's Day in 1995 he gave her a teddy bear and filled a heart with jellybeans and other sweets, much to her amusement and delight.

She was thrilled, too, when he surprised her with the present of a small pedigree dog she had taken a fancy to during a visit to a midtown pet store.

Although he had aspirations to be an actor, Leon found his elevation to instant celebrity hard to take at first – especially the attention of the paparazzi. On one occasion he gave the waiting pack the finger, a gesture that earned him a rebuke from Madonna, the bruising legacy of Sean Penn never far from her thoughts. Nor was he especially comfortable with her starry friends, while Madonna was both careful and watchful of the new man in her life when they were at a glitzy party or other public event. Yet Leon, a jealous man, was often the one looking out for her. He was uneasy when he discovered that Sean Penn was scheduled to present his ex-wife with the award for Most Fashionable Woman of the Year at the 1994 Fashion Music Awards held in New York. While Leon sat in the audience, he was unaware that backstage Sean Penn and John Enos were messing around with each other and Madonna, as Liz Rosenberg looked on with disapproval, conscious that a photograph of their lighthearted fooling could turn the scene into front-page news. At the end of the show Leon went home, claiming he was tired, while Madonna, Sean, the ever-present Ingrid, and others went barhopping. It did seem, though, that Madonna might have turned over a new leaf, especially when she told friends at her thirty-seventh birthday party in August 1995 that she and Carlos were planning to start a family – but after the filming of *Evita*.

That was not, however, the way Jim Albright saw it. While she was filming in Hungary, Madonna phoned him from the set, telling him that he would always occupy a special place in her heart, and thanking him for everything he had been to her. She then went on to complain about Carlos, saying that he was too immature, too much of a macho Latin man, and that their relationship was floundering. When he put the phone down, her former lover had the distinct impression that she wanted to rekindle their affair.

Two weeks later, on April 13, 1996, a news flash announced that Madonna was pregnant. 'It was a shock to me – and to her,' Albright says. 'She definitely would not have called me if she had known that she was pregnant.' Six months later, on October 14, 1996, Madonna, now thirty-eight, gave birth to a 6-pound-9-ounce baby girl in the Good Samaritan Hospital in Los Angeles. She named the baby Lourdes Maria Ciccone Leon, but she was known to everyone as Lola.

Madonna's curly-haired daughter was walking and talking before Jim Albright got to meet her for the first time. 'Beautiful eyes, very smart, just like her mother,' was his verdict when Madonna invited him over. He brought along his nephew Teddy, the youngster whose birth had caused such friction between them. They went into Lola's nursery, once the room she had decked out as a state-of-the-art gym. Madonna put on a record and they joined hands, the four of them dancing round and round to the music – mother and daughter, ex-lover and nephew.

The change in Madonna was striking. Here was a woman who now exuded a tremendous sense of calm, truly someone in touch with herself, with both her spirit and her soul. At long last she seemed to have found what she had been searching for all her life – true, unconditional love. And it had come from inside her.

Chapter Twelve
Me, Myself and I

I F FAXES COULD KILL, then Abel Ferrara was history. He shook his head in disbelief as page after page of handwritten bile spewed out of his machine. After reading just one heavily underscored sample sentence: 'You fucker, you've ruined my fucking career, you scumbag,' the film director got the drift. Then he began to laugh. He showed the pages to his wife, Nancy, then picked up a red pen and circled the words 'I' and 'me' on each page. Soon the fax paper was covered in blotchy red circles, as though suffering from an unpleasant rash. It proved contagious, for Ferrara soon put pen to paper himself, replying in kind to the venomous missives from Madonna, the co-star and co-producer of his latest film, *Dangerous Game*. 'She was so angry about the movie, hysterical, screaming, crying,' recalls Nancy Ferrara, who also appeared in the film. 'The faxes were just nasty, "You fucker, you've fucked my life," that kind of thing. The whole tone was about her, "I" and "me", "I" and "me."'

For once the head of Maverick Films had met her match, coming up against a real live maverick. It proved to be a searing experience for her, emotionally, artistically and financially. Their first meeting had set the tone. She had invited him to watch a rough cut of her latest, as yet unreleased, movie, *Body of Evidence*, in a private viewing cinema in New York in the fall of 1992. After a few minutes he had fallen asleep, snoring loudly through the scenes where Madonna, who plays a sex-driven gallery owner, utters lines like: 'Have you ever seen animals make love?' When he woke up his verdict was not favorable: 'It's such a bad movie. It's terrible, but it's not her fault.' It was a judgment she took to heart.

She took to Ferrara, too, describing him as an 'underground genius.' The provocative director, whose gamey, often indigestible films like *The Driller Killer* and *Body Snatchers: The Invasion Continues*, had for years been providing critics and art-house audiences with food for thought. Madonna, who has been a student of cinema for much longer than she has been interested in music, had admired Ferrara's work from afar, appreciating the European influences in his work, particularly that of the French director Jean-Luc Godard. Grim and often repulsive, Ferrara's films are populated with perverse and often perverted low-life characters who exist in a kind of a depraved purgatory within New York's seedy underbelly. Madonna was

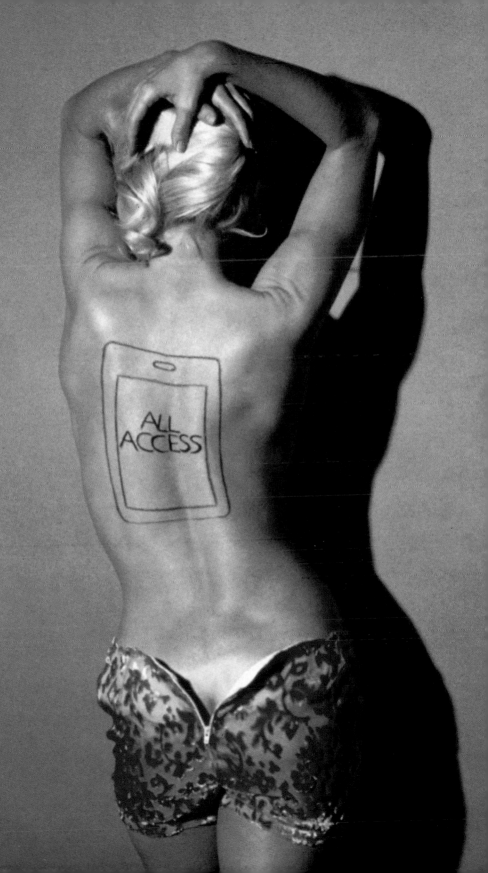

Previous page: A blonde Madonna in a typically suggestive pose

Above: Madonna with New York DJ John 'Jellybean' Benitez, whom she met in 1982. Benitez wrote and produced her first Top 40 hit 'Holiday'. While Madonna was deeply in love with him and talked of marriage, their mutual ambition outweighed their love for each other

Facing page, above: Madonna posing in her provocative 'bridal' outfit, which she wore when she performed 'Like A Virgin', the song that was a US number 1 hit for six weeks. Note the famous 'Boy Toy' belt, now the name of her company

Facing page, below: Madonna and husband Sean Penn, whom she married on her birthday in 1985. It was not long before they were being referred to as the 'Poison Penns'

Above: The success of Madonna's tours in the early 1990s depended upon her power to shock. The overt sexuality increased her popularity for a time, but with the release of her film *In Bed With Madonna*, followed swiftly by her book *Sex*, fans grew tired of this persona

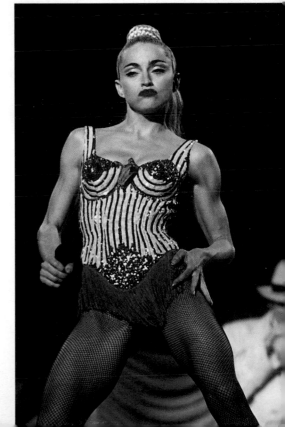

Right: Madonna's hugely successful Blonde Ambition tour, 1990; she was on the road for four months and played in twenty-seven cities worldwide

Above: Madonna began an on-off affair with Warren Beatty in 1989 after he cast her as Breathless Mahoney in the film *Dick Tracy*

Right: Madonna escorted Michael Jackson to the 1991 Oscars — a mutual publicity stunt — and she quickly abandoned him at the post-Oscars party the pair attended

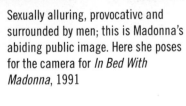

Sexually alluring, provocative and surrounded by men; this is Madonna's abiding public image. Here she poses for the camera for *In Bed With Madonna*, 1991

Left: With boyfriend Tony Ward, who appeared in several of Madonna's videos including *In Bed With Madonna*. He also features in her book *Sex*

Below: Madonna attends Prince's concert with her secret lover and one-time bodyguard Jimmy Albright (*left*). Albright, who bears an uncanny resemblance to Carlos Leon, the father of Madonna's daughter, enjoyed a stormy three-year relationship with the star. They planned to marry, and had even chosen names for their children.

Above: At a time when the world seemed to have had enough of her, Madonna chose 1993 to embark on another world tour – this time it was The Girlie Show

Madonna with San Antonio Spurs basketball player Dennis Rodman, with whom she had an affair in 1994. She was deeply hurt when he published faxes she had sent him in his autobiography

Above: Madonna and Carlos Leon at the première of *Evita*. Madonna had become pregnant by Leon during the shooting of the film and gave birth to a daughter, Lourdes, in October 1996. They met when she was jogging in New York's Central Park and she complimented him on his style of sunglasses

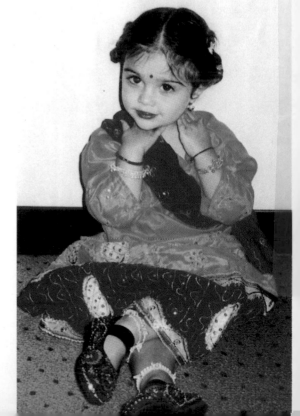

Right: Lourdes Maria Ciccone Leon. The birth of her daughter gave Madonna the chance to give and receive the unconditional love she had been searching for all her life

When most people meet Madonna for the first time they comment on her stature — she is only 5 foot 4 inches tall — and her penetrating hazel eyes. Here she is in Los Angeles, promoting her film *Evita*, in December 1996, just two months after the birth of Lourdes. The cleaned-up image helped win back old fans and gain new ones, as well as bringing her respectability as a singer

Left: Madonna with her younger brother Christopher, to whom she is very close. He has helped with the interior design of her homes, advised on her art collections and assisted in organizing her spectacular stage shows

Below: The singer Sting has been instrumental in guiding Madonna during the last few years. He introduced her to yoga, which she still practices, and it was at a dinner party at his home that she first met an up-and-coming young film director, Guy Ritchie

Facing page: Madonna and long-time friend Ingrid Casares. Unpopular with many of Madonna's entourage, she has been dubbed 'the Shadow'

Married bliss: Madonna holds the hand of her daughter by Carlos Leon, Lourdes, as she walks *en famille* in London in the summer of 2001. Her husband, Guy Ritchie, cradles their son Rocco, at that time not yet a year old

In recent years, Madonna has become close to Stella McCartney (*below*), who designed the wedding dress for her marriage to Guy Ritchie; Gwyneth Paltrow (*left*), also a close friend, was her bridesmaid

Above: Who am I now? The Material Girl starts a craze for wearing slogan tee-shirts, including those printed with 'Mrs Ritchie', the name of her husband's latest film, and the names of her children

Below: Madonna, the all-American girl, riding high in her 2001 Drowned World tour

particularly intrigued by his latest film, *Bad Lieutenant,* the degrading story of a corrupt New York detective, played by Harvey Keitel, on the trail of a gang of thieves who have raped a nun.

Mainstream Ferrara is not, and Madonna was taking a creative risk in agreeing to work with a director variously described as 'talented and fiercely independent,' but also as a 'scuzzmeister,' 'decadent,' or simply an incoherent drunk. She liked the script for his latest film, provisionally entitled *Snake Eyes*, and decided that her new film company, part of her Maverick empire, should part-finance the $10 million budget, though whether this was an act of artistic indulgence or a courageous leap of faith is difficult to determine. For years she had complained that as an actress she was just a brush in the hands of the director who was responsible for painting the resultant picture. Just as she had been in complete control of the text, design, production and photography of her first publishing venture, *Sex*, so she now expected a greater say in the direction and shape of the film her company was funding.

Certainly the original script and casting suited her, allowing her to work with two actors she knew and admired, Harvey Keitel and James Russo, the latter one of her ex-husband's best friends, on a story in which her character, an actress named Sarah Jennings, emerges the winner, a strong woman triumphing over the evil that men do. 'It was a great feminist statement and she [the principal character] was so victorious in the end,' Madonna said of the original script. It was an intelligent screenplay, employing the concept of filming a movie about the filming of a movie, with each actor playing dual roles within the film. The plot is centered on a director, played by Keitel, making a film about a failed marriage, while his own marriage 'off-screen' is falling apart. At the same time Madonna plays a successful actress-cum-mistress in the film within a film, and a whimpering, abused wife who eventually triumphs over the violent verbal and physical interplay between Keitel's director and Russo's actor and pimp husband. 'For an actress the role bore a resemblance to going over Niagara Falls in a barrel,' observed the writer Norman Mailer, who interviewed her, going on to describe Madonna as a rarity among celebrities in that she did not select roles to buttress her status.

The film's eventual title, *Dangerous Game*, was to prove apt, however. She was playing a dangerous game jousting with indomitably cussed individuals like Keitel and Ferrara, for both the film and the process of making it were precisely the opposite of what she had planned. More than that, the movie morphed into a commentary on Madonna herself, becoming a crude, if compelling, biography. 'It's a film about her as much as a film about what we were making because I forced her to confront many of the issues in her life,' Abel Ferrara admits. 'That's why I went with Jimmy Russo as her husband because he's Sean's best friend. But no one even gets it.' Certainly not Madonna, the critics or, for that matter, most of the audience. Some in her circle and those on the film set did appreciate what Ferrara was driving towards in this messy but fascinating work. 'It was a movie about Madonna, we know this,' notes the video producer Ed Steinberg, a friend of the director as well as of the singer. As Ferrara's wife Nancy says of Madonna's place in the film: 'The people who worked for her, they got it.'

In an interesting artistic inversion, the perceived realism of Madonna's documentary, *Truth or Dare*, merely recorded the essential artifice and staginess of her Blonde Ambition Tour, while Ferrara's movie, supposedly an exploration of make-believe, ripped away her carefully contrived mask, the director literally wrenching a draining and difficult performance out of her. She never saw it coming. In the weeks before filming, which took place in the fall and winter of 1992, Madonna, ever the professional, carefully researched her part, visiting a home for battered women and numerous uptown churches, besides the occasion when she went out to get deliberately stoned.

When she arrived on set on the first day of filming she was line perfect and perfectly poised, every inch the star and the successful businesswoman. 'The minute she walked into the room she took control,' recalls Nancy Ferrara, although she adds, 'but in a very positive way.' Aware that, as leading lady she would have an intimate relationship with the director, she went out of her way to befriend his wife, sending Nancy a huge gift package of Dolce e Gabbana lingerie and a bottle of Chanel No. 5 for Christmas. 'She won my heart,' Mrs Ferrara admits.

Within minutes of the start of shooting, however, Madonna suffered a rude awakening. First of all Ferrara threw away most of the script and insisted on improvisation, urging the actors to explore not just the characters they were to play, but themselves. They spent hours discussing motivation, filming their discussions, filming themselves in the process of breaking themselves down. 'I mean, I'm not getting my picture taken by fucking Richard Avedon right now, you know,' a clearly tired and careworn Madonna says at one point in the finished film, the audience uncertain as to whether she is saying that as herself, or in character as the actress Sarah Jennings. The whole process was raw, uncompromising and dark, as much an exercise in group therapy as in shooting a film. A large part of the reason for this was because the movie, exploring themes of personal breakdown, was being shot as the marriages of Abel and Nancy Ferrara and Harvey Keitel and his wife Lorraine were in trouble in real life.

'In the beginning she wanted to read the script, do the lines and that was it. Start at ten, go home at five. Goodbye,' Nancy Ferrara says of Madonna. 'It was not just the lines – the lines were the last and most meaningless thing in this. Abel and Harvey started really to get into the emotion and she was very apprehensive about going forward with that. She really held back a lot, she didn't like it at all. She just never expected that and had never worked that way before. Somewhere in the first three months they broke her down and she got into it.'

Every day became a battle of wills between Madonna and Ferrara, on one occasion ending in a fight. 'She tried to control me but she didn't have a chance,' Ferrara observes. 'I've gone up against the baddest producers and toughest actors and it ain't going to happen. The minute I lose control on the set then I'm useless to them and to her. She tried, she tried the whole time. I fucking hit her on the set even though I promised myself that I wouldn't ever touch her. She made it sound like I almost killed her. I pushed her.'

For Madonna, the whole business was as infuriating as it was traumatic, for the sprawling, incoherent film-making process completely cut across the grain of her well-ordered personality. She complained that her director and fellow actors were drunk on the set, Ferrara often sitting in a corner drinking a glass of wine and letting the movie direct itself, and railed against the laissez-faire attitude during filming, as well as what she saw as the mood of misogyny both in the movie and on the set.

She had reason for complaint. Ferrara laughs knowingly when asked about the story that he picked the ugliest, smelliest film-crew member to simulate having sex with her for a scene that eventually ended up on the cutting room floor. 'Abel is a misogynist,' says his wife. 'He grew up in a house full of women who treated him like a god. He has to have women around him but he hates them. They are a necessary evil.'

At the film's end, her screen character, far from being victorious, is portrayed as defeated, weary and submissive, waiting passively for her violent husband to shoot her in the head. She is everything that Madonna is not. The film, however, is as much an exploration of the singer's own personality as that of her screen character. In a quiet interlude she talks to Keitel about memories of the real rape she experienced in New York years earlier. Her screen husband, Russo, is portrayed as hard-drinking, abusive and out of control, violently cutting off her hair in one scene, eventually killing her. Parallels with Sean Penn and the genuine drama of their marriage breakup are unavoidable. 'I've seen you suck the cocks of CEOs,' Russo yells at her on screen. At a time when, in real life, she was being accused of simply publishing, with *Sex*, pornography for profit, the 'director' Keitel forces her, in her screen-actress persona, to admit that she is 'nothing but a commercial piece of shit.' In another scene Russo says of Madonna's character: 'We both know she's a fucking whore and she can't act.' The very ambiguity of these and other scenes, whether they relate to Madonna or to her character, merely adds to the intrigue; art describing, and often imitating, a celebrity life.

When Madonna saw how the film had been edited, she became almost hysterical, not content with simply sending Ferrara vitriolic faxes, but also screaming her fury at him over the phone. Her own opinion of the film and its director takes no prisoners. In an interview she said: 'He edited out all the brilliant things I said telling Harvey and James's characters to fuck off. He took my words off me and turned me into a deaf mute. When I saw the cut film I was weeping. It was like someone punched me in the stomach. He turned it into *The Bad Director*. If I'd known that was the movie I was making, I'd never have done it. He really fucked me over.'

Although Ferrara was no less scathing about his co-producer – ' She's a fucking jerk. Like we sit around taking out the best scenes in the movie to spite her?' – what is undeniable is that he and Keitel had teased, and sometimes almost bludgeoned, out of her one of the best and most revealing performances of her life. Perhaps that was why she took such exception to a film which, even at this distance, and for all its faults, has at its core a disturbing honesty – the 'ickiness' of life, and particularly her life, laid brutally bare. As Nancy Ferrara coolly and generously observes: 'She looks very vulnerable and that was really pulling her apart. At the end she revealed that when she is not in control, she is not as secure or confident as she would like everyone to think. She revealed something of her humanity. It is one of her best films, fascinating because it says so much about her. That's why she wouldn't endorse it. It was too close to the bone. She hit on all that emotion and couldn't face it.'

Dangerous Game, released in the summer of 1993, marked a critical nadir for Madonna. She had been pounded by the adverse publicity surrounding *Sex*, published in October 1992, had suffered ridicule for her part in *Body of Evidence*, released in January 1993, and now faced up to another sheaf of terrible reviews for her first film as a co-producer. That she disowned her first cinematic baby did little to restore her radical chic – or to help the film's commercial success. It grossed just $60,000 at the box office, one of the biggest flops of the year. She had taken genuine artistic risks in all these projects, revealing herself, personally, as well as physically, only to find herself written off by the critics and her public.

Nor was her musical career any longer in the first flush of youth. Her third single release from the *Erotica* album, 'Bad Girl,' reached a dismal thirty-sixth place in the charts, her lowest ever chart rating. Even friends in the music industry were concerned; as Michael Rosenblatt of Sire Records noted, with considerable understatement: 'It wasn't her high point artistically.' To add insult to injury, the disco diva Donna Summer rejected an approach to cover her selected hits, telling Madonna that she would never give her the rights to sing her songs. It rankled too that, while she was taking on creative challenges and catching considerable critical flak, other singers rode her coattails. She always resented the fact that Janet Jackson seemed to copy her every move, imitating the mood of her pop videos or even using a director Madonna had collaborated with, in this case the photographer Herb Ritts, who had worked on her *Rain* video. Nor, after so many Hollywood mishits, could it help but hurt a little when Whitney Houston hit a double strike with her 1992 film *The Bodyguard*, both the movie and soundtrack single, 'I Will Always Love You,' becoming major hits.

As Madonna licked her wounds, cultural gurus and intellectuals were lining up to write her off. During the conservative Reagan years, so the argument ran, Madonna had reached a natural constituency with her fan base among young women, gays and blacks. Following the collapse of the Berlin Wall, the ending of the Cold War and the arrival of a Democrat in the White House, the world was a different place. It seemed that her time had come and gone.

With her latest projects, *Sex*, the *Erotica* album and now *Dangerous Game*, she had traveled from the mainstream to the margin, and was in danger of being marooned there. Previously cheerleading intellectuals abandoned the artist to a cultural twilight zone, while her own pronouncements, with their artful and knowing references to long-dead European film stars, artists and photographers, went over the heads of her mainstream fans. It appeared that her automatic place on university curricula as an identity who self-consciously defined modern popular culture, a knowing, winking icon of post-modernism, was no longer guaranteed.

The irony was that Madonna, the entertainer who so often excused the far reaches of her behavior as ironic or mocking, was in danger of herself becoming the butt of the joke. A brief but telling exchange with a Hungarian magazine journalist unwittingly caught the irony of her situation. For some obscure reason the journalist, like most of the 1.5 million fans who bought her book, had clearly failed to appreciate that *Sex* had been inspired by the 1933 photo book *Paris de Nuit* by the Hungarian-born French photographer Brassaï, which celebrated the seedier side of Parisian nightlife. 'What was your book *Slut* about?' he asked. Madonna corrected him, pointing out the correct title. 'Not in Hungary,' he persevered. 'Here it was called *Slut*.'

Eastern European journalists aside, it was during this time in her life that Madonna first started thinking seriously about leaving America for good and settling in Europe, actively looking for a suitable house in Britain or on the

Continent. Disillusioned with the constant criticism in her own backyard, she believed a change of scene would help her creatively. At the same time she felt that the Old World was more liberal in its sexual attitudes than uptight Americans. Certainly her more recent work, notably her *Vogue* video and *Sex*, was highly Eurocentric, cherrypicking from German and French cinema of the 1930s, the gay and lesbian scene in Berlin during the Depression, the work of the German photographer Horst P. Horst and the life of Marlene Dietrich. There was a certain irony in this, given that on her first visit to Paris back in 1979 she had not liked the food, the customs or the lifestyle, but instead had presented a stereotype of the typical middle-American abroad.

Even as she considered her future, however, she masked her private misgivings behind a confident public face. Although she admitted to being 'very hurt' by stories saying that she was finished, she retained her sense of humor, lightheartedly suggesting future movie roles with the celebrity interviewer Mike Myers, star of *Wayne's World*, in an interview in June 1993. Her idea was to commission a remake of the Billy Wilder classic, *Some Like It Hot*, casting Sharon Stone in the Marilyn Monroe part and herself not as one of the other two principal characters (played in the original by Jack Lemmon and Tony Curtis), but as the leader of the all-women band; her first action, she said, would be to fire the Monroe character for being unprofessional.

Her humor, allied to her ambition and drive, helped to keep at bay, if not vanquish, the demons that assailed her – the ever-present fear of failure and her horror of becoming mediocre. 'I have an iron will and all of my will has always been to conquer some horrible feeling of inadequacy,' she said. Never prepared to stand still for a moment, she picked herself up, dusted herself down and set to work with the one person she could rely on completely – herself.

Aware that the vultures were gathering, Madonna threw herself with frenzied vigor into organizing, designing and rehearsing the stage extravaganza she called The Girlie Show. She was thrilled, indeed, ecstatic, when the dance legend Gene Kelly visited the rehearsal space she had rented for the show in Los Angeles and shuffled along with her and the other dancers. Even the fact that he wrenched his leg during one sequence could not diminish her delight when he compared her to Marlene Dietrich, whose style she mimicked for the show. 'She was like a kid in a candy store,' her former lover Jim Albright remembers. 'She was so happy and talked about how honored she was to meet him.' Inevitably, the media didn't see it that way. 'Can Gene Kelly Save Madonna's Career?' screamed one tabloid headline.

The singer, her inner doubts only exacerbated by the chorus of often spiteful criticism, spent literally every waking hour arranging the show and the subsequent world tour, feeling, after the events of the last year, that this tour would make or break her career. While her brother Chris designed the sets, she oversaw casting calls and toured strip clubs in Florida looking for girls who could perform on a pole. Madonna, who occasionally visited strip joints in New York with her lesbian friend Ingrid Casares, spotted one girl in the Crazy Horse Club in Miami whose dancing caught her eye. Normally sassy and bold, the stripper was shaking with nerves when she met Madonna. She was hired.

Finding and casting talented dancers was the enjoyable part. The hard work normally started at dawn with a three-hour workout to get herself in shape. Then she would head for the sound studio in Los Angeles to put her dancers through their paces. Ever the perfectionist, she ended up putting in seventeen-hour days, arriving at her Los Angeles home just before midnight for a massage and sleep. In between dance rehearsals – she complained that dancers needed too much mothering – she was involved in meetings to discuss venues, costumes and set design. With 1500 costume changes to be co-ordinated and 300,000 pounds of equipment to be set up for each performance, The Girlie Show was a high-risk, high-cost piece of theater.

It was also a triumph. The sell-out tour, which played on four continents, presented Madonna as a preening harlequin in a show that was mixture of the burlesque styles of *Cabaret* and the *Ziegfeld Follies* combined with the sultry sexual decadence of an upmarket bordello. There was uproar in Puerto Rico when she rubbed that country's national flag between her legs, while in Israel the protests of Orthodox Jews about the show's sexual content forced it to be canceled. During performances in Argentina, Madonna dropped a big hint to Hollywood producers when she sang a few bars of 'Don't Cry for Me Argentina' from the musical *Evita*, a long-discussed film project for which the female lead had still to be cast.

She returned to her home country in triumph, having apparently vanquished her army of critics. The release of her new, highly acclaimed album *Bedtime Stories* – the single 'Take A Bow' put her back at number one in the *Billboard* charts – seemed to confirm that her career was once more on track. She even sniped at the uproar over her previous offerings with the song 'Human Nature,' in which she sang of being 'punished' for telling the world about her 'fantasies.' That she could secure the services of an all-star musical cast, including Sting, Herbie Hancock, Björk and Kenny 'Babyface' Edmonds, merely confirmed her effortless musical ascendancy.

And yet, and yet . . . she was restless, unfulfilled and unhappy. 'She is not good at enjoying success. Its really tough for her,' observes her press secretary, spokeswoman and surrogate mother, Liz Rosenberg. 'She's not good at that.'

While her tour, album and videos were widely praised, this most visual of musical artists was continually frustrated that she had failed to conquer the one artistic mountain that mattered most to her, cinema. As she herself has said; 'I've always seen myself as an actress, first and foremost.'

The bright dawning of her Maverick entertainment empire in 1992 had seemed to bring her what she craved, artistic control and a guaranteed ticket into the elusive world of the movies. Yet after just two disastrous projects, *Dangerous Game* and *Canadian Bacon,* the film arm of her conglomerate was peremptorily closed by her backers, Time-Warner. 'We quickly realized that these peripheral activities were best left alone,' acknowledged Freddy DeMann, at one stroke shattering what was, to Madonna, the artistic raison-d'être for the company; making it less a creative factory in the Warhol mode, more a workbench.

No longer an auteur or a film producer, Madonna was, in the eyes of hard-nosed Hollywood producers, a successful singer but a box-office bomb. Singers like Cher and, for that matter, Whitney Houston had more solid commercial track records in films. Jim Albright witnessed at first hand her anguish as she desperately continued to try to make it on the big screen. 'It's an area that's caused her a lot of pain,' he says. 'She has wanted to take on a lot of roles that haven't been made available to her.' The most galling humiliation came when she lobbied for a starring role in Robert DeNiro's 1995 film *Casino,* the story of the breakdown of the marriage between a former hooker and the manager of a Mafia-run casino in Las Vegas. She loved the script, and feeling she was perfect for the part of the alcoholic wife, spoke to her friend Al Pacino for advice on how to play the role. Then she went into charm mode, taking the film's producers to dinner at a known Mafia restaurant in New York in an effort to convince them that she was perfect for the female lead. It was not to be. She went to an 'awkward' script reading presided over by DeNiro, before finally losing out to *Basic Instinct* star Sharon Stone, who went on to win an Academy Award nomination for her performance. The irony of coming second to Stone, whom she had jokingly cast in her imagined remake *of Some Like It Hot,* was galling.

It was utterly frustrating for Madonna, one moment pondering the delicious career possibilities of running her own film company, the next touting her wares around town in what was little more than a pedigree-cattle market. Moreover, just as her film career seemed to be going nowhere, so too did her personal life. After the breakup of her relationship with Jim Albright in early 1994 her love life became hectic to the point of public ridicule. Jim's passion for basketball had rubbed off on her and she became a fervent New York Knicks fan to the point where she pestered the team for an autographed basketball. She rarely missed a game, usually accompanied by her friend Ingrid Casares, and joining other notables like Ron Perlman, the head of the Revlon empire, and film director Spike Lee – after one game she agreed to appear in Lee's latest movie, *Girl 6*.

Her involvement extended to more than the matches she attended, however, for she became something of a basketball groupie, and took to seeking out the company of several of the big game's stars.

At a New Year's Eve party at her Miami home in 1993, just days before her breakup with Albright, she caroused with Brian Shaw of the Miami Heat, while back in New York she apparently asked Danny Cortese to bring Knicks player Sam Cassals to her apartment.

It was, though, her two-month fling with the outlandish and gangling figure of Dennis Rodman that came close to turning her into a national laughing stock. With his bleached-blond hair, pink-painted nails, numerous piercings and tattoos, Rodman was on the far side of outrageous. On one occasion the man nicknamed 'the worm' called a press conference to announce his wedding and then, after arriving in full wedding drag, told journalists that he was going to marry himself. 'I like a man who is in touch with his feminine side,' Madonna once said – although this probably wasn't what she had in mind.

She had met Rodman at a party, where they exchanged numbers and afterwards carried on a racy correspondence via fax. Once an affair between them had started, she made it clear that she wanted him to leave his girlfriend and father her child, her desire to become a mother by then verging on the desperate. Her body clock was ticking more insistently with every month that passed. 'I think about having children all the time,' she confessed. The eccentric Rodman was ruled out of the equation – and her life – for ever when he published his autobiography where he described their sex life in graphic detail. 'She wasn't an acrobat. But she wasn't a dead fish, either,' he gallantly told *Playboy* magazine.

Just weeks after she and Albright parted, the public caught a glimpse of the turmoil in her life when, on March 31, 1994, she made a now notorious appearance on *The Late Show with David Letterman*. What was shocking and rather sad wasn't the fact that she said the word 'fuck' thirteen times (although many viewers and critics were outraged), or that she constantly tried to bring the conversation back to her sex life, alluding to her relations with basketball players, but that this talented young woman, who had achieved so much in life, was still so pathetically desperate to be the center of attention. Her behavior pointed to an aching void in her life, a deep unhappiness unrequited by success or wealth. 'She is willing to defer everything in the elusive search to be a celebrity,' one Time-Warner executive who knows her well was reported as saying. 'It just feeds on itself. It's like an addiction.'

After the show she left with her girlfriend, Jenny Shimizu, drowning her sorrows over a cup of green tea in a midtown sushi bar. Typically she blamed the fiasco on Letterman, claiming that his staff encouraged her to take verbal liberties. It was not an excuse that washed, or at least not with *New York Post* columnist Ray Kerrison. 'She will do anything, say anything, mock anything, degrade anything to draw attention to herself and make a buck,' he wrote. 'She is the quintessential symbol of the age; self-indulgent, sacrilegious, shameless, hollow.'

Eventually, she was to admit the real reason behind her outburst. 'That was a time in my life when I was extremely angry,' she told *TV Guide* magazine in 1998. 'The press was constantly beating up on me, and I felt like I was a victim. So I lashed out at people and that [Letterman] was one of them. And I am not particularly proud of it.'

For all her success, by mid-1994 she was undoubtedly a damsel in distress. 'Very few people came to my rescue. It was an incredibly eye-opening experience,' she said of this period. So, given that Madonna's life is an almost classic example of a contemporary fairy story, it would not be complete without a couple of knights riding to her rescue. Since, however, this is also a postmodern fairy tale, in which poses are struck and principles deemed passé, it is suitably ironic that the saviors of this icon of aggressively sexy, strong, modern womanhood should be a pair of old-fashioned gentlemen, in the unlikely shape of a cricket-loving English knight and an elderly American writer.

Like a latter-day Don Quixote, the rotund, heavy-jowled figure of Norman Mailer was first into battle, gallantly wielding his literary sword in her defense in a piece in *Esquire* magazine in August 1994. It was a timely reminder to the nation's intellectual and cultural elite that Madonna belonged to the tradition of Andy Warhol, an artist who had examined the void while attempting to push back boundaries and challenge orthodoxies, particularly regarding the eternal themes of sex and love. 'We have among us our greatest living female artist,' Mailer pronounced portentously.

Even as Mailer moved on to tilt at other cultural windmills, Sir Tim Rice, the co-creator of the 1978 hit musical *Evita*, cantered, fully armed, over the horizon. Desperate to be taken seriously as an actress and still smarting from her failed attempt to secure the leading role in *Casino*, Madonna now threw all her chips on one last roll of the dice – an all-out effort to win the lead in the film version of his musical.

When she first met Rice, at a gala dinner in Los Angeles in honor of his composer partner, Andrew Lloyd Webber, her chances of scooping the jackpot looked slim. The project had endured an elephantine gestation period, the planned film of *Evita* trundling through numerous Hollywood studios and gathering a caravan of possible directors, including Oliver Stone, Ken Russell and Glenn Gordon Caron, and actresses, notably Glenn Close, Meryl Streep and Michelle Pfeiffer. (It is worth noting that in the days after the success of *Desperately Seeking Susan,* when Madonna was seen as a solid box-office draw, she had met Oliver Stone, but after a short conversation she realized that she could never work with him.) Yet Madonna, the woman described by the influential film reviewer Roger Ebert as 'the queen of movies that were bad ideas right from the beginning,' was scarcely best placed to scoop a role for which so many first-rate actresses had been nominated, however long she had coveted it. As she tucked into her first course with the dashing Spanish actor Antonio Banderas seated beside her, she launched another charm offensive, chatting animatedly to Rice and the film's producer, the English impresario Robert Stigwood.

So matters stood, until finally, at Christmas 1994, it was announced that the British director Alan Parker, the man behind hits like *Fame, The Commitments* and *Bugsy Malone,* would direct the movie of the musical about the life and times of Eva Perón, nicknamed Evita, the charismatic wife of the Argentinian dictator Juan Perón. Madonna wasted no time in contacting Parker, sending him a four-page letter that outlined why she was perfect for the part, and including with it, for good measure, a copy of her latest video, *Take A Bow,* which drew heavily on Latin-American and Catholic iconography. Ironically, little seemed to have changed since the days when she arrived back from France and sent an equally long missive to Stephen Jon Lewicki for a part in his shoestring movie *A Certain Sacrifice.* Only this time the budget was $55 million and her career in films – as well as the small matter of a $1 million fee – hung on the outcome.

Rice immediately recognized the importance of the movie to the singer, remarking that, 'If this fails she may not have a film career for a while.' So the English lyricist went in to bat on her behalf. It was a sticky wicket. His partner, Andrew Lloyd Webber (now Lord Lloyd-Webber), refused to have her at any price. 'He felt that she had been rude to him so it was a clash of two giant egos,' Rice recalls. 'He was also worried because he didn't think she could sing the part. I felt it didn't really matter although in the end a couple of songs had the notes brought down, which meant they weren't as good.'

As for the film's director and producers, they opted for Michelle Pfeiffer. Even though Madonna had explained to Parker that only she could understand Eva Perón's 'passion and pain,' her screen failures told against her; in short, she was seen as a cinematic kiss of death. 'He was very wary of her,'

Rice tells of Parker, the down-to-earth Cockney director probably bemused when she confided in her letter that fortune tellers had been predicting for years that she would play Evita on screen. 'I can honestly say that I did not write this letter of my own free will. It was as if some other force drove my hand across the page,' she had written.

In truth, the one force that was with Madonna at that critical moment was support from Rice, who felt that, for all her obvious failings, she was perfect for the part. Yet although it would be satisfyingly ironic, in a strictly post-modern kind of way, to be able to say that this cricket-loving, card-carrying Conservative Party member was wholly responsible for restarting her film career, to do so would be slightly wide of the mark. Rice valiantly put forward a strong case, but the fact that Michelle Pfeiffer had just had her second child meant that it would be difficult for her to cope with demanding film shoots in Argentina, Britain and Hungary. As a result, the scales began to tip in Madonna's favor.

Even so, the film's producers checked with Penny Marshall, director of the baseball movie *A League of Their Own*, to find out whether Madonna's star status would throw them any curve balls. 'After all,' said Lloyd Webber, rather prissily, 'there were budgets to consider and a time frame that allowed no room for star temperament or caprice.' Yet despite the fact that Marshall gave her a glowing reference – besides a fine performance in *A League of Their Own*, she had earned the respect of old hands by her efforts to master the intricacies of pitching and hitting a baseball – Madonna understood that she had been chosen by default. 'I knew I was going in with the odds stacked against me,' she said. 'That's an awkward position to be in. You feel everyone's waiting for you to stumble.'

She threw herself into the part with typical energy and dedication, the young woman who had just learned she was worth $100 million as hungry for success as the day she got her first role in *A Certain Sacrifice*. In the months before filming commenced she immersed herself in Eva Perón's life, watching newsreels, reading biographies and learning the tango. Earlier she spent months improving her voice under the tutelage of a leading singing teacher, Joan Lader, before flying to London in October 1995 to record the film's soundtrack with her leading men, Jonathan Pryce as dictator Juan Perón and Antonio Banderas, who played Che Guevara, the Argentinian-born rebel leader who acts in the film as a sardonic narrator. Madonna, already convinced of her empathy with the character she was to play, tried to emulate the heavily Catholic atmosphere of Evita's home country, dimming the studio lights and lighting candles before recordings.

Indeed, the way she identified with Argentina's former First Lady was such that she convinced Parker that she should fly to Buenos Aires to explore the myth of Eva Perón, hiring an Argentinian journalist who introduced her to aged Perónists and others who had known her. Her welcome was hardly effusive, however, whatever she may have hoped for. As she was driven from the airport, she noticed graffiti daubed on walls that read, 'Evita lives, get out, Madonna,' while protesters even burned an effigy of her outside her hotel. It reflected a feeling among many people in Argentina – a deeply conservative, Catholic country with a strong culture of machismo – that the casting of an outrageously sexual pop singer in the role of their revered national heroine was little short of sacrilegious. President Carlos Menem, a lifelong Perónist, even made an address on national television in which he acknowledged that it would besmirch Eva Perón's memory if a woman who was 'the embodiment of vulgarity' were to portray her.

Undaunted, Madonna continued in her mission to understand Eva Perón, while at the same time acting as a kind of unofficial ambassador for the movie. One of her aims was to convince reluctant government officials to allow the film company to use public buildings, notably the Casa Rosada in Buenos Aires, where Eva Perón had addressed her adoring public, as movie locations. It has become part of the Madonna myth that, when the negotiations stalled, she was whisked by boat and helicopter to meet President Menem. Over a flirtatious dinner during which, according to Madonna, the lecherous President spent all evening mentally undressing her, she used her physical allure, her charm and her profound understanding of Eva Perón to convince him to allow filming to take place

As so often with Madonna myths, the reality was rather more prosaic. In the event, the film's producers, the director Parker, British Embassy officials and others held several meetings with Menem and other government dignatories, the discussions not about whether they would be allowed to film but how much it would cost. Indeed Menem, now out of office and currently facing serious corruption charges, had a reputation as a politician who required something rather more tangible than the smile of a beautiful woman in return for his support. In a withering putdown the President, currently married to a former Miss Universe, said later, 'Madonna is not as sexy as she thinks she is. I felt neither fascinated nor even attracted to her.'

But if her rapport with the President was transient at best, her soul connection with Eva Perón grew stronger as she began to inhabit Evita's world and character. Long before shooting started, not only did she take to wearing brown contact lenses that matched the color of Perón's eyes, as well as a porcelain bridge to disguise the gap in her front teeth and a variety of wigs, she also dressed in the same style, wearing anything from colorful peasant dresses to the classic Christian Dior suits from the era of the late 1940s when the New Look had been in vogue. Even Perónists, hostile to her playing the part, were amazed that her look, her mannerisms and even her walk had become uncannily like those of Argentina's former First Lady. Madonna, however, went much further than was strictly necessary to portray her image on screen, adopting Perón's diet and even visiting her grave in the famous La Recoleta cemetery in Buenos Aires.

Ironically, while she superbly imitated Evita's physical appearance and mannerisms in the finished film, as with her previous acting performances, she could only capture her subject's personality as it related to her own. Certainly there were parallels – for a start, both were singers, both were strong, powerful women who made it to the top – but such similarities were never as convincing or compelling in the movie as Madonna liked to proclaim. Nevertheless, she would not be deflected. As she noted in the diary she wrote for the magazine that had virtually become her house journal, *Vanity Fair*: 'I cannot talk about Evita and her life without defending myself.'

Thus Evita was only defined in the film in terms of Madonna, not in relation to her life story or Argentina's history. It was hardly surprising, there-fore, that when President Menem told her over their famous dinner that it was his duty to protect the memory of 'sainted Evita,' Madonna's reply left him somewhat bemused: 'I understand completely because I have the same kind of responsibility to my fans.' She went on to compare her own life to Evita's, saying that they had both come from humble beginnings, had known heartbreak and disappointment, had conducted love affairs in order to achieve their goals, and had become successful and influential women in their own right. 'The bottom line is that we both achieved our objectives for ourselves and for others. Evita elevated the working class and the poor by offering them jobs and equal opportunity, while I gave women the courage to liberate themselves sexually.' It is not the arrogance of this remark that aston-ishes, but the way in which it illustrates Madonna's inability, despite all her pious reading and research, to understand that there was a good deal more to Eva Perón than a simple, and sometimes infantile, desire to shock.

Nonetheless, it cannot be denied that Madonna made a courageous and honest attempt to portray Eva Perón as she genuinely believed her to have been. Indeed, her empathy was such that when she sang the emotional 'Don't Cry for Me Argentina' in a scene shot on the balcony of the Casa Rosada she believed that she felt the spirit of Evita enter her body like a 'heat-seeking missile.' 'She is haunting me, she is pushing me to feel things,' she observed. It is a telling remark, not least because it owes more to Madonna the person than to Madonna the professional actress.

The plain historical reality was rather different from her romantic under-standing. Unlike Madonna – the daughter of a technician who designed tanks, and who enjoyed a middle-class childhood in a whites-only neighbor-hood of middle America – Evita was the illegitimate daughter of a servant who grew up in grinding poverty in the Argentinian countryside, coming to Buenos Aires as an impoverished teenager in the hope of finding work. She lived as a prostitute and worked as a radio actress before meeting and marry-ing a rising politician, Juan Perón, who became the nation's president in 1946. Theirs was a match not of love but of mutual advantage, for together they made a golden couple on the national stage, enhancing Perón's charisma, and thus his power, for which he had an insatiable appetite. With her keen polit-ical instincts Evita succeeded in attracting popular support, notably among the poor, while enjoying a lavish lifestyle funded by money plundered from the country's coffers. Yet, even the millions she and her husband salted away in their Swiss bank account could not help her when she was diagnosed with inoperable ovarian cancer, and she died, aged just thirty-three, in 1952. Denounced after her husband's subsequent fall from power – even their house was demolished – the cult of Evita was born a decade later, her charity work, her empathy with the poor, her glamour and style elevating her to the status of a national saint. Like other stars who died young, nothing in her life became her like the leaving it.

The musical researched, written and composed by Tim Rice and Andrew Lloyd Webber captured the dubious manner of Eva Perón's social climb, the ambivalence of her popular appeal and the emotional ambiguity of her marriage to Juan Perón, while never belittling her undoubted charisma and glamour, or ignoring her longing for mass adulation. At the same time, *Evita* was, after all, initially a stage musical, not a social documentary, and its authors made no secret of having played fast-and-loose with historical events. For example, Che Guevara had been a young medical student in Buenos Aires when Juan Perón came to power but, while he had opposed the new president, he left the country long before Evita's death. Interestingly, Banderas, unlike Madonna in her literal and self-obsessed interpretation of her character, was rather glad that he was given the opportunity to character-ize the revolutionary leader in whatever way he wished: 'It was a liberation for me,' he observed.

Thus, while the other main stars assessed their characters within the constraints of the operatic narrative, Madonna, incapable of understanding Evita other than through the prism of her own psyche, criticized the Rice-Lloyd Webber story as chauvinistic for portraying its subject as a woman who slept her way to the top. 'It's the most obvious and predictable way out, to call a woman a whore and imply that she has no morals and no integrity and no talent. And God knows I can relate to that.' She lobbied to be allowed to portray her character – or rather more accurately, herself – in a more sympathetic light, kinder, more humane, more vulnerable.

Matters came to a head over the lyrics to the one new song Rice had been asked to contribute to the film, 'You Must Love Me.' He wrote it at the urging of both Lloyd Webber and Parker, his collaborator aware that only new songs could give them the chance of an Oscar. Since Rice had already won two Oscars he was not quite so worried as his partner, who had yet to gain one of the coveted awards.

The song, which comes towards the end of the movie as Evita is dying, captures the mutuality of self-interest that drove her and her husband. She recognizes the imminence of her death but still plots with her husband to burnish her image to their advantage, Juan for short-term political gain, Evita in the cause of long-term adulation. The song also highlights both the central thesis and the principal flaw of the musical and the movie – the match between the Peróns was never a love story.

When Madonna saw the lyrics to 'You Must Love Me' she was deeply unhappy, feeling that they were not sympathetic enough either to Evita's character or to her romance with Juan Perón. She therefore wrote changes to the lyrics in her own hand and gave the revised version to Parker, who faxed them to Rice. The lyricist was not amused, sending back a tart fax in which he complained that his song had been changed into a 'sloppy sentimental love song' with 'abysmal and banal lyrics.' For once, Madonna backed down. It was just as well. 'You Must Love Me' went on to win Rice his third Academy Award, the only nomination the film received. Whether the song would have won the Oscar if Madonna had had her way and had changed its tone and form remains an open question.

As hard as Madonna tried to soften Evita's image, the truth is – another irony – that the two women had essential qualities in common: a driving ambition, and a craving for the adoration of the masses. Moreover, although Madonna could not or would not recognize these parallels, the critics did. As the British film critic Alexander Walker perceptively observed of the singer: 'Only film fame eluded her ravenous appetite for mass adulation – and it's this, the very fuel that drove Evita Perón, which the new musical now confers on her. When she said recently that "*Evita* is the first movie big enough to contain me," she was being vainglorious, but she is right.'

There is a final irony. Just as the two women craved and indeed attained the love of the masses, neither Evita in her lifetime, nor Madonna until then, had ever discovered the love of one special person. To put that more accurately, at the time when she was making the movie, Madonna's private life was still unfulfilled. Even the discovery during filming that she was eleven weeks' pregnant was greeted as much with guilt as with joy, for she worried that the constraints of her condition would upset the shooting schedule. Continually nauseous, tired and suffering from stomach cramps, she was pleased when the baby's father, Carlos Leon, arrived from New York with a resupply of her favorite candy. And if the physical demands of the filming schedule were debilitating, just as wearing was the continual speculation about her pregnancy, particularly gossip that she had chosen Leon simply as a convenient sperm donor.

Yet with every day that passed, Madonna was moving away from Eva Perón and closer to the baby growing inside her. 'Dare I say it? I am tired of being her,' she said of Evita, the changes in her physical self presaging the spiritual and emotional transformation she would effect over the coming years.

Of the shadow self with which she had shared her life for the past two years. Madonna observed: 'She was a human being with hopes and dreams and human frailties. I've tried my best. There's nothing more than I can do. It's time to move on to the next chapter of my life.'

Chapter Thirteen
Lady Madonna

FOR NINE DAYS AND NIGHTS they tortured the Jesuit priest, beating him, crushing his legs, and sticking him with needles to keep him awake. Yet, according to eyewitnesses 'scarcely a sigh' escaped Sir John Ogilvie throughout his ordeal, as he continued to refuse to name any of those he had converted to Catholicism during the nine months he had spent in Scotland. Under searching examination 'his patience courage and gaiety won the admiration of his judges' – particularly the Protestant Archbishop Spottiswood. Nevertheless, his fortitude did not prevent him from being condemned as a traitor for his efforts to restore the Roman Catholic faith to Scotland. On March 10, 1615, he was hanged in Glasgow, although he was spared the customary beheading and quartering – that is, his corpse being divided into four and put on public display – and hurriedly buried in the kirkyard of Glasgow Cathedral. Three hundred years later his martyrdom was formally acknowledged when the Vatican sanctioned his canonization.

Today, an austere portrait of Sir John Ogilvie, saint and martyr, in his black Jesuit robes, a halo above his head, hangs in a side room of the Roman Catholic cathedral in Edinburgh, unnoticed and ignored by visitors and worshipers alike. Yet the portrait yields a small but important clue to an understanding of Madonna today. One of the saint's descendants, Isabella Ogilvie, born in 1804, married a Glasgow man, John Ritchie, great-great-grandfather to Madonna's second husband, Guy Ritchie. The woman who has so often railed against the Catholic Church throughout her adult life, now has a saint in her family. Madonna's journey, her artistic and spiritual pilgrimage, has returned her to her roots, traveling from the New World to the Old.

In naming her daughter Lourdes she reminded the public of her Catholic roots as well as her family history – friends had visited the center of Catholic pilgrimage during her mother's illness and prayed for her well-being. The fact that shortly after the birth of her daughter she tried, unsuccessfully, to gain the Pope's personal blessing was a further sign of the elemental place of Catholicism in her psyche, as also was her decision to have Lourdes christened in a Catholic church. The singer whose *Like A Prayer* video outraged the Vatican for its sacrilegious overtones, to the point of threatening her with excommunication, seems now to have become the returning prodigal, a telling testament to the Jesuit saying: 'Give me the child till the age of seven and I will show you the man.' Struggle as she might, she has never been able completely to escape the embrace of the Catholic faith.

More than that, the all-American girl was playing the part of the very model of a conventional wife and mother. The young woman who once berated her lover Dan Gilroy, for having the temerity to call her a 'housewife,' is seemingly now happy to be referred to as 'the missus' by her middle-class British husband, whose hit gangster films have elevated violent homophobia to an art form. Not only did she opt for a traditional church wedding in Scotland, but on most Sundays the couple attend Mass at their local church in London. In her new incarnation she has helped her husband wash his car at weekends, has shopped at the local Tesco supermarket, and sometimes walks arm-in-arm with him to their local pub, the Windsor Castle, for a quiet pint of Guinness. In one self-deprecating TV appearance, Madonna, wearing a pinafore and carrying a feather duster, cleaned and dusted in the background while Ritchie spoke to the camera. As the scene ended, she breathed 'God Save the Queen' in her newly acquired upper-crust English accent. Unsurprisingly, therefore, her decision to move to England permanently has been seen by some commentators either as transparent social climbing, to rub shoulders with British royalty, or as an attempt to wipe the slate clean and make a fresh start.

The woman who once graced the front of *Playboy* is now a *Good House-keeping* cover girl, a mother who extols the virtues of wholesome food, 'tough love,' and a ban on television. At times she sounds just like her father in her denunciation of modern vices: sex and violence on TV, junk food and the lack of a disciplined lifestyle. 'I am much more puritanical than people think,' she says. Madonna, who, as a girl, consciously rebelled against her father and everything he stood for, has now realized, to paraphrase Mark Twain, just how much he has grown up over the last decade. 'It's very amusing that the rebel wants to be a strict, conventional Catholic mother,' says Michael Musto of the *Village Voice*. 'What drives people like Madonna is the need to be validated, to be praised and accepted.'

It seems that Madonna's ever-present alter ego has been transformed from 'Dita Parlo,' the gold-toothed dominatrix of her *Erotica* and *Sex* period, to good old-fashioned Mrs Ritchie – her present name of choice – dutiful wife and mother. Just as she used her Parlo persona to explore the wilder shores of sexual behavior without necessarily owning to those values and impulses herself, so her 'Mrs Ritchie' incarnation can be seen as her way of exploring social conformity without losing her radical chic. Intriguing as ever, she leaves open the question as to whether Mrs Ritchie is the real

Madonna. With her, appearances are invariably deceptive. 'On the one hand, the idea of marriage, and the sort of traditional family life repulses me,' she told the TV presenter Charlie Rose. 'On the other hand I long for it. I'm constantly in conflict with things, because of my past, my upbringing and the journey I've been on.'

'What was I thinking of?' she laughed when, in 1987, her friend Rosie O'Donnell played a clip on her television show of her writhing on the floor in a wedding dress during the first MTV awards in 1984. 'Can you believe that I used to tie a pair of old tights around my hair?' she asked rhetorically when the clip ended. So what was effectively the defining moment of her career was now relegated to the status of a 'TV blooper,' Madonna, demurely dressed in a designer pant suit, conspiring with O'Donnell and her sniggering audience to deny her past self, her music and the radical effect that her earlier personae had had, in terms of both fashion and sexual attitudes, on a generation of teenage girls. Indeed, her public pronouncements over the last few years have consistently denied her earlier creative incarnations while stopping short of renouncing them. 'I don't stay in the same place emotionally and my music reflects that,' she shrugs. Her *Music* video, in which she and two friends go out on the town in a limo, is both an affectionate homage and a farewell to her past; for emphasis, as though any were needed, Madonna's cartoon character kicks over a neon sign that reads, 'Material Girl.'

Beyond these indicators, however, she has embraced musical genres and visual styles she once scorned. At various stages of her career she has championed gays, lesbians, blacks and young women. Her latest album, *Music*, is replete with country-and-western imagery, yet the wide-brimmed hats, rhinestones, denim, cowboy boots and other symbolic paraphernalia are to a considerable extent the trappings of a racist and sexist redneck culture she once loathed. 'Don't ever let me see you wearing cowboy boots and jeans. If you do, don't bother coming over,' she once told her lover Jim Albright, a sentiment she echoed when asked about her supposed 'crush' on the Spanish actor Antonio Banderas, replying that she could never fall for a man who wore cowboy boots.

Indeed, her performance of Don McLean's 1972 classic 'American Pie,' wearing a tiara and with an American flag as a backdrop, seemed to symbolize her social aspirations and cultural conformity, subverting the norm but respecting American tradition. In fact the West she depicts in her work, particularly her video of the hit single 'Don't Tell Me,' which shows her walking down a long dusty road in the semi-desert, is romantically conventional, portrayed as an imaginative frontier, a land of opportunity, a place of escape and freedom. And the mainstream loved it. Scandalously neglected by the music-industry establishment, she has been showered with awards over the last five years, earning a Golden Globe for her performance in *Evita* and a clutch of Grammys for her last two albums, *Ray of Light* and *Music*. Her yearning for respect as an artist, and particularly for her acting, seems to have been transformed into respectability. It is perhaps appropriate, therefore, that one of her most recent screen appearances was a typically humorous, self-deprecating performance in a television advertisement, in which she wets her pants during a hair-raising escape from fans and paparazzi in a fast car. The car is a BMW, *the* status symbol for aspiring white professionals, and Madonna was paid a reported £1 million for appearing in the ad, which was directed by her husband.

Her apparent transformation from post-modern icon to mainstream mother began during her first pregnancy. Just as the death of her mother profoundly dislocated her sense of self, and of herself in relation to her father and family, the church, and society in general, so now, since the birth of Lourdes in 1996, and her son Rocco in 2000, she feels born again, her life anchored by the love she feels for her children. The lost, lonely, unfulfilled yet driven woman floating on the latest cultural currents seems at last to have separated her life from her career, her longing to give and receive unconditional love, that love which she only briefly received from her mother, now assuaged. 'The whole idea of giving birth and being responsible for another life put me in a different place, a place I'd never been before,' she said shortly after the birth of Lourdes. 'I feel like I'm starting my life over in some ways. My daughter's birth was like a rebirth for me.'

The first signs were physical. Not only did she grow her hair and wear flowing Eastern-style robes, she abandoned her three-hour daily workouts, gave her fitness equipment away to charity and took up ashtanga yoga, her friends Sting and Trudi Styler, themselves notable exponents, recommending the husband-and-wife teaching team they employed. Unshowy and down-to-earth, Madonna and her friend Ingrid Casares regularly joined a public class in SoHo, paying $15 a session like everyone else. On one occasion she and Casares were joined by Jim Albright, who immediately noticed the changes in his erstwhile lover. 'She had always had a tight body but now she was much more streamlined, her back was now a perfect "V." Incredibly flexible in a way that she hadn't been before,' Albright remembers.

Yet the changes in Madonna were much more than physical; she was quieter, more relaxed, comfortable in her own skin, no longer the brassy young woman whose every second word was a curse. 'Way back I was loud and, I guess you could say, obscene. Today I use the power of silence,' she says, the performer finally accepting the differences between her creative and personal lives with dignity. Her star quality, instinctively sensed by her first manager, Camille Barbone, but never appreciated or recognized by the singer herself, is now her most potent weapon. No longer the garrulous, rather defensive artist, in interviews nowadays she is 'passively aggressive', rather like a queen granting a supplicant an audience, using the interviewer's nervousness to her advantage.

If she now appreciates the value of silence, time is no longer her enemy. She has been on an artistic treadmill throughout her career, always with places to go, people to see, her disciplined lifestyle not only a mechanism for keeping the negative at bay, but also a nervous addiction. It was 'a great liberating moment to suddenly realize that it's OK when you're not in control of everything. I've been struggling with that for years,' Madonna admits. The coming of Lourdes – Lola – changed all that. She spent time reading to her daughter or making up stories, or lying on the floor playing with toys. 'She's very keen to stimulate Lola's imagination, and they paint together and use PlayDoh,' said her friend, the makeup artist Laura Mercier. 'Between working and being with her daughter, Madonna hardly has any time to herself any more.'

Motherhood certainly suited her. Albright was enchanted by the serene woman he encountered after Lola's birth, observing, 'Madonna has a lot of love inside her so Lola was well taken care of. During my time with Madonna I saw her happy but never as happy as when I saw her with her little girl. She is definitely in love with that child.'

The other passion to take over her life was the study of Kabbalah – a mystical set of Jewish teachings – or at least the version popularized by a former insurance salesman, Rabbi Philip Berg, which she began studying in Los Angeles with Rabbi Eitan Yardeni while she was pregnant with Lourdes. In an attempt to understand her mystical side, Madonna has over the years consulted astrologers and studied Hinduism and Buddhism – her friend Jenny Shimizu gave her spiritual texts to read – and, more recently, yoga, especially for its emphasis on humility, peace, and patience. With the millennium fast approaching, Madonna found herself, like millions of others, looking for an anchor and an explanation for existence. Drawn to the dark mystery of Catholicism, yet repelled by its emphasis on guilt and repression, she found a spiritual resonance in Kabbalah. So too did many of her Hollywood friends, among them Barbra Streisand, Courtney Love, Elizabeth Taylor, Jeff Goldblum, and her one-time lover, Sandra Bernhard, all of them disciples.

Inevitably, there were those who suspected Madonna of simply hitching a ride on the next available bandwagon, like 'lipstick lesbianism' or the fashion for celebrity single mothers. Yet she took her lessons sufficiently seriously to seek the advice of her teacher, Yardeni, on the best day to give birth to her child. He suggested the day of Rosh Chodesh, or new moon, and that was the day she chose to have the baby (which was born by Cesarean section). Indeed she has even taken her daughter along to Kabbalah meetings, occasionally running into Sandra Bernhard, who argues that her own study of the ancient scripts has made her more tolerant and compassionate. Those sentiments do not extend to her view of her former friend, however. 'We recently had a Kabbalah event and Madonna brought her little girl. Smart as a whip. And not impressed with her mother. Kept a healthy distance all night,' Bernhard remarks.

In September 1997 Madonna, hosted a high-powered reception for potential recruits in the courtyard of her Maverick headquarters on Beverly Boulevard, Los Angeles. As her one hundred or so guests drank cocktails and ate latkes and knishes, the singer, wearing a red thread bracelet both to ward off the evil eye and to affirm her kinship with the principles of friendship, spirituality and knowledge, told them about the profound impact her study of the ancient mystical texts had made upon her life. 'I feel like the teaching of Kabbalah embodies modern living. It's all about revealing the God that's in you.'

Kabbalah (the name derives from a Hebrew word for 'tradition,' in turn derived from the Hebrew word meaning 'to receive') is a collection of Jewish mystical writings passed down for generations and based on the Zohar text, a 2,000-year-old tract that purportedly unlocks the code to the Old Testament. Once the preserve of ultra-Orthodox Jewish males, the Kabbalah explains the link between self, God and the universe, emphasizing the need for peace and harmony between the physical and the spiritual. The Kabbalah Centre, an organization with branches all over the world, has elevated a simplified version of the Kabbalah, dubbed 'Kabbalah Lite' and 'McKabbalah' by critics, to cult status in the United States. This has been a cause of concern for many Jewish spiritual leaders; as Rabbi Robert Kirschner complains, 'It is a faddist species of superficial expression of a very significant strain of Jewish religious conviction. It is meant for people who want simplistic answers to the world's problems. There is a real element of escapism and exploitation to it because it exploits people's credulity. People believe if they plug into this system they will have all the answers.' Britain's only woman rabbi, Julia Neuberger, is more succinct: 'I think it's a load of nonsense, but I'm from the liberal, rationalist branch of Judaism.'

Used to criticism, Madonna has persevered with her studies, to such an extent that when I wrote to her about my proposed biography, she sent me a copy of the *Power of Kabbalah* by Rabbi Yehuda Berg, explaining in her covering letter how affected she had been by this fountainhead of wisdom. Just as the picture of the sainted Sir John Ogilvie yields one clue to this complex, self-aware artist, so too did her letter. The subtext was transparent – that she had changed and moved on from her controversial image.

Over kosher cookies in Greenwich Village, a New York rabbi who teaches Kabbalah explained some of its fundamental principles, ideas which help explain Madonna's fascination with these teachings. For the Kabbalah gives a spiritual rationale, a metaphysical context, to the core values and beliefs that have propelled her so far; namely, the virtues of hard work, self-control and the efficient use of time. Thus the Kabbalah teaches how to control rather than react to events and demonstrates, through the notion of the Bread of Shame, how we only appreciate things in life by working for them. At the same time our lives can be enriched by using time productively, distilling a lifetime's experience into a few years. At the heart of these teachings is the move away from the physical to the spiritual, in Madonna's case from material girl to ethereal mother.

Artistically, the change in mood and direction found its fullest expression in *Ray of Light*, released in 1998, her first album in four years, the singer thanking Rabbi Yardeni for 'creative and spiritual guidance' in the cover notes. Madonna, who now publicly styled herself 'Veronica Electronica,' her mystical alter ego, seemed to have come full circle creatively. The rawness and vulnerability of the first songs she penned in the basement of Dan Gilroy's converted synagogue nearly twenty years earlier found a resounding echo in this soul-searching album, which was hailed as her 'most radical, mask-free work.'

She sang about the joy of her daughter's birth, her mother's legacy and the perils of celebrity in a way that was candid and mature, the result of a long journey of the heart. Her lyrics about the high price she paid for celebrity at the expense of her own happiness are matched by reflections on her mother's death, lines she penned during a visit to her father's home. The imagery of decay is a reflection of her persistent nightmares and endless sense of loss, themes she has returned to throughout her songwriting career.

By contrast with her controlling 'Dita Parlo' character, her latest incarnation as 'Veronica Electronica' revealed Madonna in a more nurturing mood, the artist as collaborator rather than diva. Old habits die hard, however. In her joint endeavors there was never any doubt who held the whip hand. When the bedraggled figure of the album's producer, William Orbit, arrived, soaked from a rainstorm, on her doorstep in New York, a plastic bag of tape samples in his hand, it marked the start of fourteen weeks of edgy, creative co-operation to produce *Ray of Light*. The London-born producer, who has worked with Belinda Carlisle and Seal, is known as a scatter-brained genius, and certainly his method of working tested Madonna's patience to the limit. As she admits, 'I am a very organized, methodical person and he had a tendency to get sidetracked by other things. Then we got used to each other's rhythms. I learned to be more open and not such a Nazi.' Even though she has rigorously high standards, a famously short attention span and is a stickler for detail, the two remained friends. 'Madonna's very hands-on and that was a challenge for me. I usually keep the artist away,' says Orbit.

During this incarnation as 'Veronica Electronica' the creative philosophy that inspired her to launch her Maverick company, to nurture and inspire new talent, was clearly apparent. Significantly, she chose material for its power to speak to her about her own life, as much as for its intrinsic creative worth. So, for example, she plucked first-time novelist Jennifer Belle from obscurity, turning her book about a student who turns tricks to pay her way through college, has a distant father and a difficult relationship with her stepmother, and works at the Russian Tea Room in New York to help make ends meet, into a screenplay. Madonna, who worked with Belle on the screenplay, which has yet to be filmed, turned out to be a responsive creative partner, treating the novelist like 'an equal' rather than an employee: 'She would always ask my opinion,' recalls Belle.

For similar reasons, Madonna hooked up with the novelist Kristin McCloy, discussing whether to turn her novel *Velocity*, about the death of a young woman's mother and her subsequent attempt to rebuild a fractured relationship with her father, into a movie. 'It's my life,' observed Madonna. 'In the midst of the tragedy, the character falls in love with someone who is all wrong for her. I can relate to that.' Unfortunately, the project is now the subject of litigation.

She related, too, to making a movie of the dance musical *Chicago* with Goldie Hawn – 'I can do those steps in my sleep,' she boasted – but it was the screenplay by another new writer, Thomas Ropelewski, that caught her eye. His movie, *The Next Best Thing*, is about a single woman in her late thirties who accidentally becomes pregnant by her gay friend. The unlikely couple then decide to raise the child themselves. The movie gave her the chance to work with her friend, the English actor Rupert Everett, riding high after playing opposite Julia Roberts in the hit comedy *My Best Friend's Wedding*, and to play her favorite character – herself. It was also an opportunity to explore a subject central to much of her creative work, namely gender relations in a contemporary setting.

Sadly, like *Shanghai Surprise*, her latest movie, shot in 1999, had an aura of doom around it from early on. Like Sean Penn, Everett is relaxed and assured before the camera. Indeed, so assured was he in making *The Next Best Thing*, that he rewrote much of the script, eventually suing for a writing credit. The film-musical of *Evita* aside, Madonna's last real acting role had been in *Dangerous Game*, a gap of some seven years. Yet, in spite of her lack of recent experience, she was utterly confident in her ability, constantly questioning the veteran John Schlesinger's judgment and direction during shooting, skirmishes which were soon common knowledge beyond the confines of the set.

Eventually, her indomitable self-belief got the better of Schlesinger's vision for the picture. She successfully lobbied for her character, initially a swimming instructor, to become a Californian yoga teacher with a fondness for all things Eastern and, inexplicably, affected an unconvincing English accent. Typically she trained with her own yoga teacher, acting as her assistant in class in order to understand her role better. Her attempt to make her character more like her real-life self was, however, precisely what Schlesinger, who made *Midnight Cowboy* among other highly regarded films, did not want. Of his leading lady the British director observes, 'Madonna likes to create characters with a very definite kind of image and I wanted to soften her quite a lot in this film. I wanted people to forget that she was Madonna.'

With Schlesinger's vision and ideas thwarted – to add to his troubles, he was taken seriously ill at the end of the shoot – Madonna essentially played herself, her absolute self-belief and strength of will, the qualities that have propelled her into the celebrity stratosphere, once again fatally undermining her acting. Released in 2000, *The Next Best Thing* enjoyed only modest success. In one of the kinder reviews, the film critic Stephanie Zacharek complained that, 'She seems wooden and unnatural, and it's tough to watch, because she's clearly trying her damnedest.' Madonna put a brave face on the criticism, but privately she was deeply hurt, especially as the film boasted a solid cast, a first-rate director and a strong idea.

For her, collaboration may have been all very well, but the criticism served to reconfirm her belief that only when she had total control could she truly express herself on the big screen. Over the last two years Madonna has deliberated over whether to become involved in a film of the life of one of her favorite artists, the feminist Mexican painter Frida Kahlo (who died, aged just forty-seven, in 1954), or whether she should buy the rights to Arthur Golden's bestselling novel, *Memoirs of a Geisha*, and turn it into a screenplay. She has also talked of her desire to be a film director. To be director, producer and star, all in one, would indeed bring her total control. Whether or not it would make of her a better, or better-regarded, actress, must for the time being remain unanswered, however.

If, for Madonna, acting in films was all about control, the creative and commercial tension between teamwork and rule by diktat, nurture and authority, 'Dita' versus 'Veronica,' was most clearly expressed in her Maverick empire. The way in which Madonna wooed and won two of her most successful signings, the Canadian singer Alanis Morissette and the British band Prodigy, was testament to her canny business sense and her creative nous. It was also a tribute to her maternal instincts, for when they arrived in New York she personally drove to the airport to pick them up, and spent time with them in the city's clubs and bars. She was particularly drawn to the young Canadian singer, seeing in Morissette's raw rebellion something of herself. 'We had a couple of girlie nights,' recalls Morissette appreciatively, if somewhat cryptically.

Although Prodigy was a different musical proposition, executives from the band's record company were also impressed. 'She attended a meeting early on,' said Richard Russell. 'She was very good. Part of it was just that she was interested enough to turn up and press the flesh, but she also asked what the band were like as artists, what drives them. They were smart questions and they were different to the ones that the chairmen of other labels ask.' Since those signings in the mid 1980s, Madonna has spread her net wide and eclectically, investing in an Asian recording studio, starting a Latin record label, signing a singer from Sweden and a band from Mexico. Not everyone has fallen for the Madonna charm, however, Maverick notably failing to hook the Icelandic singer Björk and Courtney Love.

For a time the incredible success of Morissette's 1995 debut album, *Jagged Little Pill*, which sold 25 million copies worldwide, masked underlying tensions in Madonna's company. In private, she increasingly complained about her manager, Freddy DeMann, saying that he was less concerned with her well-being than with sending her on tours so as to make money from her. Her discontent had first surfaced when her book, *Sex*, was being put together. Madonna clashed with him over his plans to make her tour the *Erotica* album, and she had occasionally griped about DeMann ever since.

Perhaps inevitably, there were other forces at play. In a story as old as rock and roll itself, the singer believed that she could do without her manager, could run her own show and keep the percentage she was paying him. In 1988, after many years together, there was a parting of the ways, although DeMann is rumored to have walked away with a $25 million payoff. Such splits are nothing new in the music business; both The Beatles and The Rolling Stones ended up managing their own affairs, with mixed success. As her former business manager Bert Padell reflects, 'Artists start off as nobodies, then become somebodies and then think they can do it all themselves.' He had suffered the same experience as DeMann when on July 1, 1987, Madonna's one-time secretary, now her new manager, Caresse Henry-Norman telephoned and told him that, also after fourteen years, Madonna no longer required his services. The singer refused to take his calls, and Padell lamented his loss in a poem entitled 'Time for a Change.'

The prosaic reality was that, for Madonna, it was business politics as usual, Maverick's CEO simply tightening her personal control over her company, a case of the captain dropping the pilots. It may have just been coincidence, but her ship began to founder soon afterwards, taking on financial water. There was no escaping the fact that after nearly a decade in business, much of the success of Maverick still rested on Madonna's shoulders, something merely highlighted by the sell-out success of her Drowned World Tour in 2001. With losses of $60 million over the previous two years, heads rolled, the president of Maverick's recording arm and several other executives leaving the company.

With the ousting of the old guard, it seemed that Madonna was increasingly surrounded by 'yes men,' eager to do her bidding, unwilling to challenge her authority. The delicate balance between teamwork and control that had characterized the boom days of her career seemed to have gone. During the mad scramble into the Internet, where music, sports and other stars made millions endorsing products or developing systems, Madonna held back, uncertain about how to deal with this new medium. 'Britney Spears and others were all over the Internet, Madonna was very late out of the blocks,' Bert Padell observes. In the end, though, she had the last laugh, making record-industry history by signing a $42 million deal with the American software giant, Microsoft, to broadcast her performance at London's Brixton Academy in 2000 live on the Internet.

Albright, himself now an Internet entrepreneur, visited her at her New York apartment on Lola's third birthday in October 1999 to make a presentation to Madonna, her new manager Caresse Henry-Norman, and some of her other advisors. While she showed only polite interest in his scheme, of more significance was the fact that also wandering around the apartment that day were Carlos Leon and a British film director named Guy Ritchie. In retrospect, this tableau might have formed the subject of a contemporary version of a Renaissance painting: Madonna, child, and a triumvirate of fathers – real, prospective and possible. It would have been a symbolic moment, had any of them been able to see into the future, the 'significant others' she had encountered during her long search for love present on her daughter's special day.

*

For the first few weeks the birth of Lola papered over the fissures that had begun to appear in the relationship between Madonna and her Cuban lover. As she had confessed to Albright, she had been growing disillusioned with Leon before she became pregnant. During her pregnancy, however, the demands of her shooting *Evita*, the loneliness of hotel life, her loss of confidence and self-esteem as her body changed, meant that when he and, invariably, Ingrid Casares arrived to join her they were welcome faces at a difficult time. When Leon was not with her, Madonna, feeling vulnerable and unattractive, would constantly call him, always fearful that her handsome boyfriend might be seeing someone else. Her obsessive jealousy placed an added strain on the obvious problems that faced an obscure young man of modest means dating one of the world's best-known women.

In the event, the difficulties of her pregnancy – she was constantly tired and often uncharacteristically unwell – were outweighed by the joy of Lola's birth. Madonna and Carlos were delighted with their new arrival, as was everyone else, her New York apartment seeing a constant stream of visitors laden with gifts. Al Pacino brought three teddy bears, the Versaces sent a hand-sewn quilt, her Italian designer friends Domenico Dolce and Stefano Gabbana sent baby clothes, her brother Christopher, Lola's godfather, gave her an inscribed bracelet, while at a baby shower held in Rosie O'Donnell's apartment an assortment of friends and relations gave her clothes and silver jewelry, including a crucifix. The cascade of flowers, clothes and toys from fans was so overwhelming that her staff hired a van to take them to a children's charity.

Determined that no photographer would earn the $350,000 being offered by tabloid editors for the first picture of mother and baby – one enterprising cameraman was caught hidden inside a builder's dumpster outside the building – Madonna, Carlos and their daughter kept a low profile, staying inside the apartment. They had engaged a nanny, but Carlos enjoyed putting the baby down to sleep, and the couple placed matching his-and-hers rocking chairs in Lola's nursery so that they could sit with her.

Inevitably, such domesticity could not last. Soon it was back to work, Madonna giving a grueling series of back-to-back TV interviews at the publicity launch of *Evita* in December 1996, breaking off only to feed Lola. 'I have been so incredibly blessed this past year,' she told the audience after receiving a Golden Globe Award for Best Actress in a Musical at a ceremony in January 1997. With Carlos by her side, she looked every inch the contented celebrity and proudly glowing new mother. 'It was a very jolly evening,' recalls Sir Tim Rice, who was at her table. Doubtless it was, but the happiness, like the brief, peaceful domestic interlude, was destined not to last.

Once the couple had time to draw breath, it was clear to them that the relationship was not working out, that they were more friends than life partners. The fault line in their romance was highlighted by differences over his career. For his part Carlos, uncomfortable in his role as yet another 'Mr Madonna' and hurt by media gibes that he was simply a sperm donor, felt that she could do more to help his budding acting and modeling career – so far all he had managed was bit parts in a couple of movies, including *The Big Lebowski*. As far as Madonna was concerned, she felt that he should stand on his own two feet – as she had had to do.

Difficulties with the chihuahua Carlos had given her symbolized the growing rift. The dog became very jealous of Lola, wetting rugs, gnawing shoes and slippers and even Madonna's bedspread, growling at anyone who smelled of the baby. Even visits to a famous animal psychiatrist, Shelby Marlow, could not cure the dog's jealousy. Finally the couple reluctantly agreed that Chuicita must go for the sake of the baby. It was a heartbreaking decision to say goodbye to their first 'baby,' their failure with their pet anticipating their own problems. In May 1997, just seven months after Lola's birth, Carlos and Madonna parted. 'It was a real relationship,' says Rosie O'Donnell. 'They made a valiant effort to stay together.' Lola, of course, remained with her mother, although Carlos, an adoring father, is a regular visitor.

Jealousy had been an ever-present issue in the relationship. Indeed, the dog's behavior was matched, if not outstripped, by that of Madonna's boyfriend, who was always unsure of her love for him. On one occasion the suspicious Cuban was seen hanging around a downtown restaurant, watching as his girlfriend and Rosie O'Donnell went to dinner in New York. When he was approached by a member of Madonna's staff, he declined to join them and stalked off to his own apartment for the night. A yellow self-adhesive note on the dashboard of Madonna's chauffeur-driven Lincoln Town Car perhaps held a clue to his behavior. It bore just two words: 'Ring Birdy.'

An aspiring screenplay writer, Andrew F. Bird was, all things considered, a very suitable guru for the maternal, spiritual Madonna in her 'Veronica Electronica' phase. The lanky, long-haired young Englishman who stretched his body into impossible shapes during his daily yoga sessions and endlessly broadened his mind with studies in Hinduism, Buddhism and other branches of Eastern mysticism was the right man at the right time. A friend of the film director Alek Keshishian (of *Truth and Dare* fame), Bird first met Madonna in Los Angeles at Keshishian's request while he was trying to sell a screenplay about English gangsters. There was, according to eyewitnesses, an instant magnetism between them. Within weeks Bird, the penniless son of a Midlands accountant who usually slept on friends' sofas, was ensconced in her Los Angeles home while she was recording her *Ray of Light* album. Indeed, he is listed in the album's credits, along with Rabbi Eitan Yardeni, as having provided 'creative and spiritual guidance.'

As the affair progressed, Madonna's appearance, described by some as hippy, although she preferred 'pre-Raphaelite,' seemed to mirror the unkempt grunge look of the would-be screenwriter, who always dressed in black, a newly lit Gitane never far from his lips. Moreover, if her new look shocked those who met her, so did her lifestyle. She really seemed to have gone back to an earlier phase of her life; in late 1997, on the occasions when she visited London, she lived modestly in a rented house on a busy road in Chelsea, happy to visit a local New Age center for yoga classes with other devotees. The gaggle of fans who waited outside the house for a glimpse of her would often be shooed away by Madonna herself, angrily telling them that they were keeping the baby awake. While she was out working Bird stayed at home with Lola, leaning out of the open windows for a surreptitious cigarette, fearful that Madonna would discover that he had broken his promise not to smoke around the baby.

Bird took her to meet his parents at their Warwickshire home, who were charmed by their son's girlfriend, some twelve years his senior. Meanwhile, there was much bemusement, as well as amusement, among both circles of friends at Madonna's latest choice of beau. Yet even though Bird himself was often baffled by the turn of events, they conformed to an established pattern in Madonna's life. She was willing to fall in love, yet unable to sustain her love. Too often this icon of feminine strength and control had been humbled by the frailty of her all-too-human heart. By her own admission she falls in love easily, perhaps too readily, mothering, and very often smothering, the object of her desire. As had been the case with her affair with the young bisexual model Tony Ward, Madonna's maternal instincts were aroused by Bird. She bought him a wardrobe of new clothes and whisked him around the world, and the jobless writer was by her side at her birthday celebration in New York in August 1998.

At the same time, as with her affairs with Jim Albright and others, she wanted Bird to live independently – she gave him cash to rent his own apartment in Los Angeles – but then, insecure and jealous, would call him constantly, worried that he might be seeing another. It was a recipe for a fractured, uneven and trustless romance, and in the end Bird returned to London to try to make a new start, taking a humble job as a doorman at the trendy Met Bar, but at least away from her ceaseless attentions. Once, when

Bird was avoiding her calls, she allegedly phoned the gym he attended in London pretending to be his mother in an attempt to speak to him. Yet he was not always so stand-offish. When she was staying in London in early 1998, Bird arrived at her hotel, Claridge's, in the early hours to see her, his furtive behavior perplexing waiting fans. Of his affair with Madonna, he later admitted that there was a 'deep mutual love . . . a lot of pride had to be swallowed on both sides.'

Then, with their romance up in the air, Madonna discovered that she was pregnant. Even though she had spoken of having more children, she was clear that she wanted a stable relationship, and this was anything but. Several media reports stated that she decided to have an abortion, others that the decision was made for her, when she suffered a miscarriage in the early stages of pregnancy. Whatever the truth or otherwise of these rumors, she remained brutally honest with herself, telling the writer Alan Jackson that she had 'regrets' about the decisions to terminate previous pregnancies. 'You always have regrets when you make those kind of decisions, but you have to look at your lifestyle and ask, 'Am I at a place in my life where I can devote a lot of time to being the really good parent I want to be?' None of us wants to make mistakes in that role, and I imagine a lot of us look at the way our parents raised us and say: 'I definitely wouldn't want to do it quite that way.' I think you have to be mentally prepared for it. If you're not, you're only doing the world a disservice by bringing up a child you don't want.'

For a time the relationship with Bird continued, the couple kept more or less together by transatlantic phone calls and occasional meetings. She even said that she had been inspired to write a song about him, 'Beautiful Stranger,' which contains the (not very original) line, 'You're the Devil in disguise.' Ironically the lyric won her a Grammy Award for the best song written for a motion picture, in this case the comedy film, *Austin Powers: The Spy Who Shagged Me.* By the time she picked up the award in 2000, however, Andy Bird was history.

The affair with Andy Bird had followed a routine familiar to those who knew her well. The deep, unresolved psychological wound of her mother's death established within her a desperate emotional dynamic, in which her unquenchable need for love was matched only by her inability to commit to one person for fear of being hurt. Consciously and unconsciously, she engineered relationships in which she drove away those she cared for and then seized on their bewilderment, anger and frustration as an excuse to move on, an endless merry-go-round of love, jealousy and, ultimately, unhappiness.

Her close friends, who know a Madonna very different from the sexually empowered public persona, have watched, with the helpless anticipation of spectators witnessing an impending car crash, the singer's tortured love life. It has become a fact of her life. It is likely, therefore, that matchmaking was at the very back of Trudi Styler's mind when, in the summer of 1998, she invited Madonna to Lake House in Wiltshire, the listed manor she shared with her husband Sting. Certainly the singer had men on her mind. Or rather, one man, for she called her father in Michigan to wish him happy Father's Day midway through Sunday lunch.

Not that her friends minded. Since her arrival in England, Lake House had become Madonna's home from home, on occasion showing her friends round the mansion, pointing out the 400-year-old tapestries in the King's Room, as well as Sting's impressive recording studio. Since both singers have homes in London and New York (as well as elsewhere) they share similar circles of friends, and even share their domestic staff to keep costs down. They split the cost of flying their New York yoga teacher to Britain, although Madonna complained at paying him when he was not working. In New York they dine together, they have together taken their children to local art galleries, and Madonna has joined Sting's family at his holiday villa outside Florence in Italy. Furthermore, when she decided in 2000 to make London her home permanently, Trudi Styler did much to smooth her path, arranging several social events so that she could meet London artistic society. The fashion designer Stella McCartney, daughter of Sir Paul McCartney, became a fast friend after one such occasion. Again, when she was househunting Trudi Styler recommended a number of suitable houses near her own homes in North London and Wiltshire, although Madonna was aghast at the high prices, losing several prime properties because she thought they were too expensive.

Business of another kind was high on the agenda during the lunchtime discussion. As Sting's butler hovered, the talk was of the indie film Trudi Styler had part-financed and co-produced, *Lock, Stock and Two Smoking Barrels*, a violent story of gambling, gangsters and stolen ganja filmed in the flashy, edgy style of a pop video. The director sitting next to her, Guy Ritchie, and his partner, producer Matthew Vaughn, son of the actor Robert Vaughn, were looking for a record company to produce and market a soundtrack album. Would Maverick be interested? The CEO was indeed enthusiastic, not just about the movie, but about its director. 'I had a whole premonition of my life fast-forward,' she recalls, experiencing the same sensation as when she had first seen Sean Penn on the set of the *Material Girl* shoot. On that occasion she had instinctively felt that she and Penn were going to marry. This time she went, as she put it, 'wobblybonkers.' 'My head didn't just turn, my head spun round on my body,' she recalls of that fateful day. 'I was taken by his confidence. He was very sort of cocky but in a self-aware way.'

He may have been a generation younger and living on a different continent, but in Ritchie she had found another 'cowboy poet,' a character similar to the man she had married thirteen years earlier. The young film director's memory of that first meeting is rather less romantic, however, Ritchie recalling, perhaps whimsically, that it was his partner, Vaughn, who took a shine to Madonna. No matter: eighteen months – and a baby boy – later, he and Madonna were married in a traditional church ceremony, just as she had always wanted.

At the time, though, the only baby on Ritchie's mind was the film he had spent years writing, selling to backers, and finally directing. This was to be his big break, the project on which he had pinned all his hopes. As a result, the meeting with Madonna at Sting's house proved doubly fortuitous, for at her suggestion he and Vaughn flew to Los Angeles to discuss a possible soundtrack deal with Maverick executives. (In the end it was released by Island Records.) Romance came later – although not much later. At the time both had entanglements, Madonna with Andy Bird, Ritchie in a long-term relationship with Rebecca Green, the daughter by his first marriage of the television mogul Michael Green, and then later with TV presenter and former model Tania Strecker. As an added complication, Rebecca Green had helped him produce his first film, a short called *Hard Case*, and had also persuaded her mother and stepfather to put money into his first full-length feature film, *Lock, Stock and Two Smoking Barrels*.

At first sight, Ritchie is an unlikely movie-maker. Born in Hatfield, Hertfordshire, in 1968, he was raised in a well-to-do middle-class family with a proud military tradition and links to the Scottish gentry dating back to the twelfth century. Fascinated from an early age by guns, adventure stories, outdoor pursuits and all things military, it was widely expected that he would become an army officer. Indeed, he had been named for two relations, officers in the Seaforth Highlanders (the regiment in which his family had served for generations), who had been killed in action.

His great-grandfather, Major-General Sir William Ritchie, had been a Gunner Major-General in the Indian Army, while his grandfather, Major Stewart 'Jack' Ritchie, had been posthumously awarded the Military Cross after being killed in action with the 2nd Seaforths while defending British troops during the evacuation from Dunkirk in 1940. His father, John, continued the tradition, being commissioned, as a National Service officer, into the same regiment on the same day as James Murray Grant, the father of the actor Hugh Grant. After completing his service, he had squired numerous glamorous young women around town, finally marrying a model, Amber, and landing a job in the advertising industry, in which he would eventually be responsible for the famous Hamlet cigar campaign. When Guy was five his parents divorced, his mother later marrying Sir Michael Leighton, the eleventh holder of a 300-year-old baronetcy.

Although his mother moved into the Leighton family estate, Loton Park near Shrewsbury, Guy only spent a few months there, for he was farmed out to a succession of private schools. 'He went to the local school for a few weeks but he certainly wasn't brought up here, by no stretch of the imagination,' says Sir Michael, who divorced Guy's mother in 1980. He remembers his stepson as a promising clay-pigeon shot with a flair for art and an interest in the natural world. For his part, John Ritchie remembers of his son that 'he wanted to be a gamekeeper, or continue the family tradition and go into the army.'

Certainly he was no academic, not least because his severe dyslexia proved a considerable handicap, and he left the last of the ten or so private schools he attended aged just fifteen, with one GCSE qualification in film studies to his name. 'Education was lost on me,' he once said. 'I may as well have been sent out in a field to milk cows for ten years.' He later claimed that he had been expelled from his £4,275 ($6,000)-a-term Standbridge Earls School near Andover in Hampshire – which specializes in teaching children with learning difficulties – for taking drugs. His father disputes this, recalling that his son was caught cutting lessons and entertaining a girl in his room.

From then on the young Guy Ritchie worked in a series of menial jobs, as a laborer, barman, van driver and messenger. Moving to London, he took to dabbling in drugs, affecting a Cockney accent and hanging out with an exotic mix of louche private-school friends and working-class wideboys in the pubs and bars of Soho, Notting Hill and the East End. 'He seems to have acquired his working-class accent quite deliberately,' says his uncle, Gavin Doyle. 'He was always a well-spoken boy.' In one episode, apparently a row over a gambling debt, he acquired a scar on his face after a close encounter with a knife. He once said, 'I've lived in the East End for thirty years and let's just say I've been in loads of mess-ups and I've lost a lot of money on cards.' Wary of the mesh of fact and fantasy in his story, cynics muse that the injury was more likely the result of falling off a horse and landing on his silver spoon – quite apart from the fact that 'thirty years' would mean that he had moved to the East End when no older than five.

Certainly he had a safety net. His father, a friend of the film directors David (now Lord) Puttnam and Alan Parker, used his contacts to help him secure a job with a Soho-based film company, where he cut his teeth on a series of pop videos and promos. He found that the film world was not dissimilar to the military life familiar to his family; the camaraderie and banter, long periods of boredom punctuated by frantic activity, and detailed planning followed by rapid improvisation. Shrewdly following the primary rule for first-time writers – write about what you know – his script for *Lock, Stock and Two Smoking Barrels* was based on an exaggerated version of the underworld stories he had soaked up while carousing around London.

Given the values of his then future bride, it is something of an irony that the movie is a hymn to homophobia and choreographed violence, a self-enclosed, amoral world in which men are macho and women absent, a kind of downmarket gentleman's smoking club in celluloid. Indeed, during her 2001 Drowned World Tour, Madonna took a sly sideswipe at the boorish male milieu described by her husband's films when she chanted, 'Get your tits out for the lads.' Nonetheless, the film is redeemed by a swaggering, self-deprecating sense of humor, never taking itself too seriously. With witty references to classic movies like *The Italian Job*, and the style of a lads' night out, Ritchie's film captured a mood in modern Britain, earning a cult status in his home country even as it slid, almost unnoticed, past bemused American audiences.

One American was very impressed, however, for Madonna had grown keen to develop her relationship with Ritchie. She continued to see in him many of the qualities that had attracted her to her first husband. Ritchie, to her, was Sean Penn with a twist. Like Penn, he came from a prosperous family, and yet cultivated a bad-boy image that was interesting enough to intrigue without ever becoming too dangerous. For while he considers himself 'media friendly,' Ritchie has an aggressive streak, like the Californian actor, famously brawling in the fashionable Met Bar with Madonna's former lover, Andy Bird, and later earning a police caution for kicking a fan outside the house he and Madonna rented in Notting Hill. It is noticeable, too, that during her Drowned World concert tour in 2001 she dedicated a song to her new husband, calling him 'the coolest guy in the universe' – precisely the same words she had used when describing Sean Penn.

An artist, a writer and, most importantly, a successful film director, it is no great surprise that Ritchie's talent and chosen career were immediately attractive to Madonna. She saw in him the qualities so often ascribed to her: 'He's a risk taker and he's got a hungry mind,' she noted. Nor was he afraid of hard work, another quality he shares with her. The Ritchies, like the Fortins and Ciccones, are from a class of people who place a premium on endeavor and self-improvement. As Colonel William MacNair, historian of the Ritchie family, observes, 'Guy is from a family within a class who naturally wanted to better themselves, producing the academics, engineers, and military men who scattered around the globe, forming the backbone of the British Empire.'

Unlike so many of her previous boyfriends, Ritchie had made his own luck, and earned his success. 'Guy works almost as hard as Madonna does,' her friend Rupert Everett remarks. 'That's a good thing for her, definitely a change for her, because he's definitely not a boy toy. He has got a serious career going so he's dealing with his own stuff.'

If his independence, and his indifference to her iconic status and ambition proved attractive, his stubborn focus on his career hindered their developing romance. It was very much an on-off relationship, neither willing to give up their home turf, Madonna arguing that she had to stay in America so that Carlos Leon could have access to Lourdes. 'I wanted to rip his head off sometimes,' she says of Ritchie, referring to the frustrating first year during which they were reduced to calling each other or writing letters, she on location, filming *The Next Best Thing*, he promoting his debut movie and working on a sequel, *Snatch*, starring Brad Pitt.

That he was involved in a year-long relationship with the TV presenter Tania Strecker, whom he had known for fourteen years, hardly helped. 'He was the love of my life,' she says, the leggy, six-foot blonde blaming the diminutive singer for her eventual break up with Ritchie. For while he was seeing Strecker, at that time a recovering alcoholic, he was also quietly showing Madonna around London when she was in town, accompanying her on househunting expeditions and taking her out for dinner. When they were apart, Madonna reverted to characteristic behavior, calling him endlessly, demanding to know where he had been and who he was seeing. During one dinner with Trudi Styler, Sting and others in New York in late 1999, she was physically restrained from phoning Ritchie by other guests, who suggested that her behavior was likely to drive him away. Indeed, like several of her other lovers, he became so exasperated by her insistent phoning, especially when he was carefully editing his latest film, that he refused to return her calls. There were, too, other occasions, so Strecker claims, when Madonna called while he was with her.

As the millennium came to an end, Madonna was the first to give way, agreeing that she should live permanently with Ritchie in London. As she told one friend, the writer Ingrid Sischy, 'I picked up my life and my daughter and everything and I rented a house in London and moved there. And that's really when our relationship started to work. But it was a huge sacrifice for me.'

Nevertheless, she put a brave face on it, deciding to record her latest album, *Music*, in London with Mirwais, an unknown French producer, and putting her daughter's name down for the Lycée Français in South Kensington – 'because I'm half French' – and considered sending her to the exclusive Cheltenham Ladies' College as her senior school. Her previous lukewarm comments about her newly adopted homeland – 'I'm sure Britain is beautiful somewhere, I've just never found it' – were forgotten amid the swooning media coverage of her decision to live in Britain.

'Veronica Electronica,' it seemed, had been superseded by a new alter ego, 'Lady Madonna.' In her latest incarnation, she was immediately installed as the new queen of British society, no charity gala, no award ceremony, no social event complete unless graced by 'Her Madge–esty.' It was not long before she was dining with Prince Charles at his country home, Highgrove in Gloucestershire, discussing the dubious joys of jet lag with the heir to the throne. 'I'm an Anglophile,' she now declared, citing William Shakespeare and Sid Vicious as examples of eminent Englishmen she admired, apparently without irony. Her old friend Ed Steinberg, who produced the video for her first single all those years ago, saw in her a desire to go upmarket, to win the hearts and minds of her new British constituency. 'She now has English aristocracy on her mind and she wants to change her image. She wants to become a lady now and forget about the past.'

Amidst all the turmoil and change in her private life, in the winter of 2000 Madonna discovered that she was pregnant once again. This time, however, there was no question that she would have her baby. Even so, her uncertainty about her relationship with the child's father was hardly helped on Valentine's Day, just a few weeks into her pregnancy. She was crestfallen when she discovered that a wonderful arrangement of tiger lilies, her favorite flowers, had been sent by a business associate rather than her lover. It was only after an assistant called Ritchie to remind him of the significance of the day that he bought her a modest bunch of blooms. 'They looked like he had picked them up from a petrol-station forecourt,' recalls one former member of staff, who was there when Ritchie arrived with the wretched bouquet. After a brisk exchange, the couple left for dinner in silence.

While Madonna confessed that, after years of searching, she had found her 'soulmate,' there seemed to be a marked reluctance on Ritchie's part to commit to a woman ten years his senior. The fact that his other lover, Tania Strecker, was still in the background only complicated these delicate matters of the heart. 'I'm not saying the last time we [that is, she and Ritchie] met because that's a bit of a sore one – not for me but for her,' Tania Strecker has said. 'She is frightened of me.' The implication is clear; he was still seeing Strecker after he had taken up with Madonna.

In February 2000, however, as Strecker's relationship with Ritchie petered out, Madonna and her lover deliberately adopted a higher public profile. They attended the *Evening Standard* Film Awards together, were seen out at numerous fashionable restaurants, and even took Lola to see the children's movie *Toy Story* 2. At the same time, Madonna made it clear that the other new love of her life, her infatuation with Britain, was only skin deep, for she flew back to Los Angeles to prepare for the birth of her second child, taking a swipe at her new home country's 'old and Victorian' hospitals before she left.

Her medical caution was justified. Unlike the first time she gave birth, when she had joked that she was going for a cosmetic nose job as she was being wheeled into surgery for a Cesarean operation, this time there was a degree of genuine concern about her second child's birth. Months before, she had been diagnosed with a condition known as placenta previa, in which the placenta covers the birth canal, cutting off the baby's blood supply and greatly increasing the risk of hemorrhage for the mother. As a result, she had made arrangements to have another Cesarean once her unborn child had gone to full term. With a month to go everything seemed fine. Then, on the evening of August 10, Madonna felt unwell, and as a precaution asked a member of her staff to drive her to Cedars-Sinai Hospital in Los Angeles. On the way she rang Guy Ritchie, who was at a private screening of his new movie, *Snatch*, elsewhere in the city. By the time he arrived specialists monitoring her condition had realized the gravity of the problem and decided that immediate surgery was necessary.

By then Madonna was losing blood fast and, according to at least one report, was close to going into shock. With Guy Ritchie holding her hand and whispering words of comfort, she was sedated and wheeled into surgery where, at 1 am on the morning of August 11, 2000, she gave birth to a 5-pound 9-ounce baby boy, Rocco John Ritchie. Because he was jaundiced – normal for premature births – he was placed in an incubator, where he remained for the next five days, Madonna taking him to her Los Feliz home in time for her forty-second birthday. To Ritchie, it seemed the right moment to make an honest woman of her. On her return home, Madonna discovered a crumbled paper bag by the side of her bed. She was about to throw it away, 'Then I noticed something in it, a little box,' she recalls. Inside was a diamond ring. 'Then I saw a card. In it was a really sweet letter that he wrote to me about everything we've been through, my birthday and the baby and how happy he was.' The film producer Erin Berg, a friend of Ritchie's, later told the world that the couple were to marry before Christmas. 'He just wants them to be a family,' said Berg. 'He has been over the moon since the birth of his son. The man is gushing.'

With her forthcoming marriage announced, Madonna threw herself into planning the event with her customary energy and focus. Once more Trudi Styler was on hand when her friend was considering the religious side of her wedding, and she recommended that she should talk through the issues with Canon John Reynolds, who had blessed her own marriage to Sting in 1992. The clergyman, whose parish covers Sting's home at Lake House in Wiltshire, was telephoned by Madonna from Los Angeles shortly after the birth of Rocco. 'She wanted to discuss the ecclesiastical options with me,' the canon remembers, adding that, 'She was very friendly and asked intelligent, pertinent questions.'

He was not the only one to voice his admiration, for the world was once more infatuated with the talented Mrs Ritchie-to-be. Just weeks after giving birth, Madonna was managing to juggle motherhood, run an entertainment empire, mastermind the worldwide launch of her *Music* album, plan her wedding, pick up two music awards at an MTV ceremony, plan two concerts in New York and London in November 2000 – and get herself into a pair of low-slung hipsters. She was a living, breathing tonic for every woman over the age of forty. Her two invitation-only concerts were a chance for the glitterati to pay homage to someone who was almost a latter-day version of the Madonna: icon, mother, mogul, superstar, corporation – oh, and a singer, too.

While in New York the concert was billed as the return of the home-coming queen – 'It's great to be back,' she told her fans – in Britain she was embraced as an honorary Brit, as English as fish-and-chips, warm beer and cricket. That the staging, designed by her friends Domenico Dolce and Stefano Gabbana, for the short six-song set resembled a trendy Texan hoedown, and that the songs were as American as mom's apple pie, mattered not in the least.

The christening of Rocco, followed on the next day by her wedding, both in the far north of Scotland, merely confirmed her effortless social ascendancy. In the event, the wedding, held just before Christmas on Guy Ritchie's thirty-second birthday, although eagerly anticipated by millions, managed to remain completely private. Memories of the fiasco on the clifftop at Malibu were still painful for Madonna. It would not be repeated. The couple's choice of the grand but remote Skibo Castle outside the quiet town of Dornoch, the kind of place where the purchase of a new car is hot gossip, was about as far removed from Hollywood glamour as it is possible to be. Yet there was a fitting symmetry about the decision, not just for Ritchie, whose Scots ancestry and links with the Seaforth Highlanders made the north of Scotland an appropriate choice, but also for Madonna. After all, it was her immigrant Ciccone forebears who had labored in the steel mills of Pennsylvania for the Scots-born tycoon Andrew Carnegie, the man who, in 1897, had restored Skibo, by then a crumbling ruin, to its former glory. It seemed fitting, therefore, that a descendant of the men who had helped make Carnegie's fortune should now reign supreme, if only for a few days, over his former domain. It was a point that would not have been lost on Tony Ciccone, who, like his father and brothers, had worked for a time in the steel mills in order to fund his education.

Even though the castle had been recommended by friends – Sting and Trudi Styler have a home near by, and the actress Catherine Zeta-Jones calls it 'the most romantic place on earth' – the couple flew north to make the final arrangements a couple of weeks before the wedding. As they looked around Dornoch Cathedral, chosen as the setting for Rocco's christening, Madonna could not help but burst into song. This time it was not 'Good Golly Miss Molly,' the tune with which she had once regaled her college friends in a church in Ann Arbor, but 'Ave Maria,' the sound echoing through the near-empty cathedral, an impromptu rendition watched only by a couple of tourists – and a local journalist. At the christening ceremony itself, held on December 21, it was Sting, one of Rocco's godfathers, who regaled the congregation with the same piece, watched by the tearful parents, as well as Madonna's father and Ritchie's parents and a clutch of the couple's best friends, including her business associate Guy Oseary (another of Rocco's godparents), Donatella Versace, who designed the £10,000 – reportedly – cream silk christening gown, Trudi Styler (another godparent), who also read a hymn, Madonna's sister Melanie, Ingrid Casares, actress friends Gwyneth Paltrow and Debi Mazar, and Rupert Everett, whose arrival, like that of many of the guests, was delayed because of fog. His endeavors perfectly fitted with Madonna's Kabbalah philosophy: 'We wanted to find a place that was really hard to get to, because when people have to work to get somewhere, you know they really want to be there,' she said.

After the thirty-minute ceremony the trio posed briefly, albeit regally, for photographers, Madonna, veiled and with her hair swept back in a bun, looking like a cross between her Evita persona and a minor member of the royal family. That photocall, however, was the only morsel thrown to the ravenous media, whose representatives descended upon Dornoch in droves, for after it the couple retreated to the well-guarded seclusion of their castle redoubt. No thudding helicopters this time to ruin the big day, only the noisy protests of paparazzi photographers being flushed out of the undergrowth on the 7,500-acre estate by the security team Ritchie had engaged.

On the following day, a lone piper broke the silence as Lourdes led the wedding party through the castle's great hall, lit with hundreds of sputtering candles, scattering rose petals as she went. Here, too, there was another significant difference between Madonna's first and second weddings. For her marriage to Penn, she had wanted her ensemble to have a 'Grace Kelly feel.' This time, at this altogether more grownup event, she had the real thing, for she wore the same Cartier tiara that Princess Grace had worn for the wedding of her eldest daughter, Caroline.

Guy Ritchie, wearing a kilt of Hunting Mackintosh plaid, and Madonna, in a strapless ivory gown designed by her maid of honor, Stella McCartney, took their vows before the Reverend Susan Brown, watched by her father and Ritchie's best men, Matthew Vaughn and nightclub owner Piers Adam. Many commentators had wondered whether the feminist icon would promise to 'love, honor and obey,' but in fact the couple had written part of their vows, which included the words, 'cherish, honor and delight in family.'

Once they had taken their vows, they swapped specially designed rings, after which the Reverend Brown presented the newlyweds with a twin pack of toilet paper, her traditional wedding present, explaining the symbolism thus, 'Two rolls together reminding them that their marriage should be strong and long.' On the following day the newlyweds left the castle for a brief honeymoon at Lake House, where their romance had started, Madonna reflecting on a ' truly magical, religious experience.'

Now that she had officially become Mrs Ritchie, Madonna delighted in her new persona, signing her name and even changing her credit cards to reflect her new status. If not truly domesticated – 'I don't have the cooking gene,' she jokes – her life seemed redolent of home, hearth and family, echoing an observation her father-in-law had made, 'She is a delightful and talented person and quite homely.'

Is this then the same performer – and catalyst for changes in attitudes over two decades – who sold over 100 million records, scored more number-one hits than The Beatles and Elvis Presley, and energized, enthralled and enraged a generation? As one of Guy Ritchie's gangland characters might say, has she gone all girlie on us?

Well, in a word yes. Through her personality and her performances, the last year has seen Madonna reveal and explore the duality of what it is like to be female; from mother to murderess, passive victim to cold predator, woman as creator or devourer, capable of changing swiftly from men's prey to praying mantis.

The lyrics of her 2001 single 'What It Feels Like For A Girl' capture the innate tension in a modern woman, expected simultaneously to display both strength and weakness. The violence of the song's accompanying video, directed by her husband, reflected the singer's anger, not just at the balance, or lack of it, between the sexes, but at how women are prisoners of their hormones, victims of their biology. It was no coincidence that she wrote the song while she was pregnant with Rocco and when her future with Ritchie was far from assured. The video, she says, 'shows my character acting out a fantasy and doing things girls are not allowed to do. This is an angry song.' So angry and violent, indeed, that MTV banned the three-minute film, which shows Madonna driving round in a souped-up car, with a senile old woman in the passenger seat. She robs a man at a cash machine, sets fire to a filling station as a male gas attendant lies prone on the floor, drives through a boy's hockey match and aims a gun at two cops – when she pulls the trigger it is seen to be a water pistol. In the final scene, Madonna drives the car at full speed into a lamppost, presumably killing both her and her passenger.

For a woman who has always eschewed violence, both in her personal and her artistic life, the *What It Feels Like For A Girl* video was a radical departure. While critics rather patronizingly pointed to Ritchie's fascination with violence, and to Madonna's need to compete with the chainsaw-wielding extremes of pop sensation Eminem, as the reasons behind her change of heart, the reality is that the video and the iconography of her Drowned World concert, is entirely consistent with the themes that she has been exploring for the last twenty years, namely the relationship between the sexes, the ambiguity of gender, and the unresolved conflict, for women in a patriarchal society, of being fully female and sexual while exercising control over their lives. Artistically, too, it was a logical development from the *Substitute for Love* video she made in 1998, which attracted controversy for its use of images of the hounding of Diana, Princess of Wales, by a predatory, male-dominated mass media. Woman as victim then, woman as avenger now.

Vengeance upon men was a theme she explored further in the Drowned World concert tour of 2001, Madonna in one scene shooting her male tormentor, in another, dressed as a vengeful geisha, taking a sword to her aggressor; images of battered women assailed the audience from video screens. The audience saw a Madonna transformed from 'Mrs Ritchie,' earth mother, nurturing wife, spiritual seer, into a contemporary pop version of Puccini's operatic heroine Turandot, wreaking her revenge on the world of men. Thus her carefully cultivated 'Mrs Ritchie' persona is as deceptive as it is beguiling. In many respects the changes in her personal circumstances, her willingness to lead a life rather than pursue a career, have given her the stability and impetus to take on new artistic challenges and renew her assault on society's sensibilities.

Indeed, her first full-length feature-film collaboration with her husband, a remake of *Swept Away*, a 1975 film by the Italian director Lina Wertmüller, gives an indication of the direction of her future career, and her concerns. Although Ritchie was keen on making an historical epic in the style of Ridley Scott's *Gladiator*, it seems that his wife had other ideas, not least because Wertmüller's interests and concerns neatly dovetail with Madonna's. While Italians accuse her of being too feminist and Americans see her as too sexist, Wertmüller, as a feminist director, has continued to break taboos in order to examine the politics of gender, role reversal, and the subordination of women.

If Wertmüller's aims sound familiar, so too is Madonna's role as the lead in *Swept Away*, in which she plays a rich Italian socialite who is shipwrecked while on a yachting holiday, ending up on a remote island with a Marxist sailor. He becomes the master, she the slave, not only because he is stronger, but because he knows how to survive. Yet the underlying message is that women can be victims of sexism even when they have escaped established 'female' roles. That the character played by Madonna, Rafaella, is rich and independent means that she is further victimized because she does not fit the traditional, stereotyped male view of what a woman should be and how she should act.

When filming starts, what will test Ritchie's directorial abilities – and indeed his marriage – will be whether he is able to succeed where many of his predecessors have so signally failed; that is, whether he can control Madonna's natural inclination to make her characters more glamorous and sympathetic, so that the audience view her, Madonna herself, in a more winning light. For the truth is that the bleeding of her personality into her performances, so effective in her songwriting, her videos and her concerts, has been the fatal flaw in her career as an actress. She has wooed Oscar, but has yet to win him.

It also remains to be seen whether motherhood and marriage, and the gradual teasing away of her life from her career, can replace her almost visceral need for mass adulation, and for love. Totally in control of her career, so often out of control in her love life, Madonna is a prisoner of her biology and background, themes that she has explored again and again. Indomitable in public, insecure in private, the paradoxes at the heart of her personality have propelled her forward, this blonde's ambition powered by that insatiable need to be adored. For the last twenty years we have shared her artistic journey and her personal pilgrimage as she has exchanged one mask for another, from 'Dita Parlo' to 'Veronica Electronica,' to 'Lady Madonna' and 'Mrs Ritchie.' In a sense, she has been continually revealing, yet always concealing.

So where does she go from here? The banal question merits only an equally banal answer: Who knows? She goes where we go, a cultural bloodhound always on the scent of the fresh, the cool and the credible. That is part of her excitement and appeal, at once the ambitious all-American girl, the clinical corporate chief, the loyal friend, the uncertain lover, and the restless, life-enhancing force of nature, continually challenging, provoking and enchanting.

As she herself says, 'It feels to me that I'm slowly revealing myself, my true nature. It feels to me like I'm just getting close to the core of who I really am.'

Her journey has only begun.

Madonna: Discography, videos, film and theater, tours

12-inch vinyl, cassette and CD maxi-singles chronologically

1982 Everybody; Everybody (Instr.) (12-ins vinyl only)

1982 Everybody (Dub) (UK 12-ins)

1983 Burning Up; Physical Attraction (12-ins vinyl only)

1983 Lucky Star (Full Length); I Know It (UK 12-ins)

1983 Holiday (Full Length); Think Of Me (UK 12-ins, also limited edition with poster)

1984 Borderline (New Mix); Lucky Star (New Mix)

1984 Borderline (US Remix); (Dub Remix); Physical Attraction (UK 12-ins)

1984 Like A Virgin (Ext. Dance Remix); Stay (Extra limited edition with poster in UK)

1984 Material Girl (Ext. Dance Remix); Pretender (LP)

1985 Angel (Ext. Dance Mix); Into The Groove (Single)

1985 Angel (Ext. Dance Mix); Burning Up (Mix) (UK 12-ins, also issued with poster sleeve)

1985 Dress You Up (12-ins Formal Mix); (Casual Instr. Mix); Shoo-Bee-Doo (LP)

1985 Dress You Up (12-ins Formal Mix); (Casual Instr. Mix); I Know It (UK 12-ins, also limited edition with poster sleeve)

1985 Gambler (Ext. Dance Mix); (Instr.); Nature Of The Beach (UK 12-ins, 'Nature' performed by Black 'n' Blue)

1985 Crazy For You (UK, 45-rpm 12-ins single)

1985 Into The Groove; Everybody; Shoo-Bee-Doo (UK 12-ins, also limited edition with poster)

1986 Cosmic Climb (Ext. Dance Mix); (Ext.); We Are The Gods (subtitled 'The Early Years')

1986 Live To Tell (LP); (Edit); (Instr.)

1986 Open Your Heart (Ext.); (Dub); White Heat

1986 Open Your Heart (Ext.); (Dub); Lucky Star (UK 12-ins)

1986 Papa Don't Preach (Ext. Remix); Pretender

1986 Papa Don't Preach (Ext. Remix); Ain't No Big Deal; Papa Don't Preach (LP) (UK 12-ins, also limited edition with poster)

1986 True Blue (Color Mix); (Instr.); Ain't No Big Deal; True Blue (Remix/Edit)

1986 True Blue (Ext. Dance); Holiday (Full Length) (UK 12-ins)

1987 La Isla Bonita (Ext. Remix); (Ext. Instr.)

1987 Causing A Commotion (Silver Screen Mix); (Dub); (Movie House Mix); Jimmy, Jimmy (US cassette single, first copies in longbox)

1987 Causing A Commotion (Silver Screen Mix); (Dub); (Movie House Mix); Jimmy, Jimmy (US cassette single)

1987 Causing A Commotion (Silver Screen Mix); (Movie House Mix); Jimmy, Jimmy (Fade) (UK 12-ins)

1987 The Look Of Love; Love Don't Live Here Anymore; I Know It (UK 12-ins, also limited edition with poster)

1987 Who's That Girl (Ext.); (Dub); White Heat (LP) (CD & cassette single)

1987 Who's That Girl (Ext.); White Heat (LP) (UK 12-ins, also cassette maxi)

1988 Cosmic Climb; We Are The Gods; Wild Dancing (Wild Dance Mix) (subtitled 'The Early Years'; in USA issued as poster sleeve & picture disk)

1989 Cherish (Ext.); (7-ins); Supernatural (UK 12-ins)

1989 Dear Jessie (LP); Till Death Do Us Part (LP); Holiday (12-ins) (UK 12-ins, cassette maxi & picture CD, also limited edition with poster sleeve. CD reissue 1989)

1989 Express Yourself (Non-Stop Express Mix); (Stop & Go Dubs) (UK 12-ins, also issued as picture disk showing nude Madonna)

1989 Express Yourself (Non-Stop Express Mix); (Stop & Go Dubs); (Local Mix); The Look Of Love (LP) (CD & cassette single)

1989 Keep It Together (12-ins Remix); (Dub); (12-ins Ext. Mix); (12-ins Mix); (Bonus Beats); (Instr.) (**From here on, all maxis also released on CD.** The CD maxi-single includes 'Keep It Together' [Single Remix], but omits the [Dub] and [Bonus Beats] versions)

1989 Like A Prayer (12-ins Dance Mix); (12-ins Ext. Remix); (Churchapella); (12-ins Club); (7-ins Remix/Edit); Act Of Contrition

1989 Like A Prayer 1 (12-ins Ext. Remix); (12-ins Club); Act Of Contrition (UK 12-ins, also issued with poster sleeve)

1989 Like A Prayer 2 (12-ins Dance Mix); (Churchapella); (7-ins Remix/Edit) (UK 12-ins)

1990 Hanky Panky (Bare Bottom 12-ins Mix); (Bare Bones Single Mix); More (LP)

1990 *The Holiday Collection*: Holiday (LP); True Blue (LP); Who's That Girl (LP); Causing A Commotion (Silver Screen Single Mix) (UK CD/mini LP)

1990 Justify My Love (Orbit 12-ins Mix); (Hip Hop Mix); (The Beast Within Mix); Express Yourself (1990 Remix – Long) (CD and cassette maxi-single includes 'Justify My Love' [Q-Sound Mix])

1990 Justify My Love (Orbit 12-ins Mix); (LP); Express Yourself (1990 Edit) (UK 12-ins, also limited edition on pale blue vinyl)

1990 Justify My Love 1 (Orbit 12-ins Mix); (Hip Hop Mix); (The Beast Within Mix); Express Yourself (1990 Remix, Long) (UK CD maxi-single)

1990 Justify My Love 2 (Hip Hop Mix); (Q-Sound Mix); (The Beast Within Mix) (UK CD maxi-single) 1990 Vogue (12-ins); (Bette Davis Dub); (Strike-A-Pose Dub) (**From here on, all maxis are also available on cassette.** Cassette and CD maxi-singles include 'Vogue' [Single])

1990 Vogue (12-ins); Keep It Together (12-ins Remix) (UK 12-ins, CD & cassette maxi-single)

1990 Vogue (12-ins); (Strike-A-Pose Dub) (UK 12-ins, also limited edition with poster)

1991 Rescue Me (Titanic Vocal); (Lifeboat Vocal); (Houseboat Vocal); (S.O.S. Mix) (CD maxi-single includes 'Rescue Me' [Single Mix])

1991 Rescue Me (Titanic Vocal); (Lifeboat Vocal); (Houseboat Vocal) (UK 12-ins)

1991 Rescue Me 1 (7-ins Mix); (Titanic Vocal); (Demanding Dub) (UK CD & cassette maxi-single)

1991 Rescue Me 2 (Lifeboat Vocal); (Houseboat Vocal) (UK CD & cassette maxi-single)

1991 Crazy For You (Remix); Keep It Together (Special Remix); Into The Groove (Shep Pettibone Remix) (Remix for UK)

1991 Get Down; Get Down (Ext. Mix) (subtitled 'The Early Years'; issued in UK as picture disc)

1992 Erotica (Kenlou B-Boy Mix); (Jeep Beats); (Madonna's In My Jeep Mix); (WO 12-ins); (Underground Club Mix); (Bass Hit Dub)

(**From here on, all maxis are issued on Maverick/Sire label.** The CD maxi-single includes 'Erotica' [LP Edit] and [Masters At Work Dub], but omits [Bass Hit Dub]. A CD, entitled *Erotic*, was included with the *Sex* book, it contained versions of 'Erotica'.)

1992 Erotica (LP); (Instr.); (Radio Edit) (UK 12-ins, also limited edition with poster)

1992 Erotica (Orbit Max); (Kenlou B-Boy Mix); (Underground Club Mix); (Orbit Dub); (Madonna's In My Jeep Mix) (UK CD & cassette maxi)

1992 Deeper And Deeper (Shep's Classic 12-ins); (Shep's Deep Makeover Mix); (Shep's Deep Beats); (David's Klub Mix); (David's Deeper Dub); (Shep's Deeper Dub) (CD maxi-single includes 'Deeper and Deeper' [LP Edit], [Shep's Fierce Deeper Dub], and [David's Love Dub], but omits [David's and Shep's Deeper Dubs])

1992 Deeper And Deeper (Shep's Classic 12-ins); (Shep's Deep Makeover Mix); (David's Klub Mix); (David's Love Dub); (Shep's Deeper Dub) (UK 12-ins)

1992 Deeper And Deeper (LP); (Shep's Deep Makeover Mix); (David's Klub Mix); (Shep's Classic 12-ins); (Shep's Fierce Deeper Dub); (David's Love Dub); (Shep's Deep Beats) (UK CD & cassette maxi-single)

1992 Michael Jackson: In The Closet: (Cm) (Tum) (Tmd) (K 12-ins) (Mixes Behind Door 1, Madonna as the Mystery Girl)

1992 Michael Jackson: In The Closet: (Tm) (Fsm) (Tmof) (Tud) (Mixes Behind Door 2, Madonna as Mystery Girl)

1993 Bad Girl (Ext. Mix); Fever (Ext. 12-ins Mix); (Shep's Remedy Dub); (Murk Boys' Miami Mix); (Murk Boys' Deep South Mix); (Oscar G's Dope Dub) (CD maxi-single includes 'Bad Girl' [Edit] and 'Fever' [Hot Sweat 12-ins], but omits 'Fever' [Shep's Remedy Dub] & [Oscar G's Dope Dub])

1993 Bad Girl (LP); Erotica (William Orbit 12-ins); (William Orbit Dub); (Madonna's In My Jeep Mix) (UK 12-ins, also limited edition with poster)

1993 *Erotica*: Bad Girl (Extended Mix); Erotica (Kenlou B-Boy Instr.); Erotica (Underground Tribute); Erotica (Wo Dub); Erotica (House Instr.); Erotica (Bass Hit Dub)

1993 *Keep It Together* (Remixes): Cherish (Ext.); Keep It Together Dub; Keep It Together (Bonus Beats); Keep It Together (Instr.) (Includes 7 mixes of the title track: 12-ins Remix, Dub, 12-ins Extended Mix, 12-ins Mix,

Bonus Beats, Instrumental, & Original Version)

1993 Rain (Radio Remix); (LP); Up Down Suite (Non-LP Track); Waiting (Remix) (Also CD maxi-single)

1993 Rain (Radio Remix); Up Down Suite (Non-LP Track); Waiting (Remix) (UK CD maxi-single)

1993 Remixed *Prayer* EP: Like A Prayer (12-ins Dance Mix); (12-ins Extended Mix); (Churchapella); (12-ins Club); (7-ins Remix); Express Yourself (Non-Stop Express Mix); (Stop & Go); (Local Mix) 1993 This Used To Be My Playground (Single); (Instr.); (Long) (UK 12-ins)

1993 Fever (Hot Sweat 12-ins Mix); (Ext. 12-ins Mix); (Shep's Remedy Dub); (Murk Boys' Miami Mix); (Murk Boys' Deep South Mix); (Oscar G's Dope Dub) (UK 12-ins, CD includes [LP] but omits [Oscar G's Dope Dub])

1994 I'll Remember (Guerilla Beach Mix); (LP); (Guerilla Groove Mix); (Orbit Alternative Mix) (US 12-ins)

1994 I'll Remember (LP); (Guerilla Beach Mix); (Orbit Mix); Why It's So Hard (Live From The Girlie Show Tour) (CD maxi-single)

1994 Secret (Junior's Sound Factory Mix); (Junior's Sound Factory Dub); (Junior's Luscious Club Mix); (Junior's Luscious Club Dub); (Allstar Mix) (CD maxi-single includes 'Secret' [Edit], [Junior's Luscious Single Mix] and [Some Bizarre Mix], but omits [Junior's Sound Factory & Luscious Club Dubs])

1994 Secret (Junior's Luscious Single Mix); (Junior's Extended Luscious Club Mix); (Junior's Luscious Dub); (Junior's Sound Factory Mix,); (Junior's Sound Factory Dub) (UK CD maxi-single)

1994 Secret (LP Edit); Let Down Your Guard (Rough Mix Edit); Secret (Instr.); (LP) (UK CD maxi-single)

1994 Take A Bow (InDaSoul Mix); (LP); (Silky Soul Mix); (InDaSoul Instr.); (Instr.) (Also CD maxi-single)

1994 Take A Bow (Edit); (LP); (Instr.) (UK CD maxi-single)

1994 Bedtime Story (Junior's Sound Factory Mix); (Junior's Sound Factory Dub); (Orbital Mix); (Junior's Wet Dream Mix) (Junior's Wet Dream Dub)

1994 Bedtime Story (LP Edit); (Junior's Wet Dream Mix); (Junior's Dreamy Drum Dub); (Junior's Sound Factory Mix); (Junior's Single Mix) (Also CD maxi-single)

1995 Oh Father; Live To Tell (Live Edit from Ciao Italia Tour); Why's It So Hard (Live from The Girlie Show Tour) UK CD maxi-single, also limited edition with four postcards)

1995 Bedtime Story (Junior's Sound Factory Mix); (Junior's Sound Factory Dub); (Orbital Mix); (Junior's Wet Dream Mix) (UK 12-ins, also limited edition with hologram foil sleeve)

1995 Bedtime Story: (1) Bedtime Story (Junior's Single Mix); Secret (Some Bizarre Mix); (All-star Mix); (Some Bizarre Single Mix) (2) Bedtime Story (LP); (Junior's Wet Dream Mix); (Junior's Dreamy Drum Dub); (Orbital Mix); (Junior's Sound Factory Mix) (UK double CD limited edition in box with lyric booklet)

1995 *Into The Groove*: Into The Groove; Everybody; Shoo-Bee-Doo

1995 Like A Virgin (Ext. Dub); Stay

1995 Live To Tell (LP); (Edit); (Instr.)

1995 Lucky Star (US Remix); I Know It

1995 Material Girl (Jellybean); Pretender

1995 *Open Your Heart*: Open Your Heart (Ext.); Open Your Heart (Dub); White Heart (LP)

1995 *Papa Don't Preach*: Papa Don't Preach; Ain't No Big Deal; Papa Don't Preach (LP)

1995 Who's That Girl (Ext.); White Heat (LP) (US cassette single. UK CD & cassette had bonus track: 'Who's That Girl [Dub])

1995 You'll See (LP); (Instr.); (Spanish); Live To Tell (Live From Who's That Girl Tour) (Also CD maxi-single)

1995 You'll See (Edit); Rain (LP); You'll See (Instr.) (UK CD maxi-single)

1995 Human Nature (Runway Club Mix); (I'm Not Your Bitch Mix); (Runway Club Mix Radio Edit); (Bottom Heavy Dub); (Howie Tee Remix); (Howie Tee Clean Remix); (Radio); (Love Is The Nature Mix) (Also CD maxi-single)

1995 Human Nature (Human Club Mix); (Runway Club Mix); (Master With Nine Sample); (I'm Not Your Bitch Mix) (UK 12-ins)

1995 Human Nature 1 (LP); Bedtime Story (Junior's Sound Factory Mix); (Orbital Mix) (UK CD maxi-single)

1995 Human Nature 2 (Radio Edit); (Human Club Mix); (Chorus Door Slam With Nine Sample); (I'm Not Your Bitch Mix) (UK CD maxi-single)

1996 One More Chance (LP); You'll See (Spanish); (Spanglish) (UK limited edition with poster sleeve)

1996 *Wild Dancing*: Wild Dancing (Original); (Dance Mix) (Madonna sings back-up vocals only)

1996 You'll See (LP); (Instr.); (Spanish); Live To Tell (Live from WTG Tour) (Also CD maxi-single)

1996 Love Don't Live Here Anymore (Soulpower Radio Remix Edit); (LP Remix Edit); (Soulpower Radio Remix); (LP Remix) (UK CD maxi-single)

1996 Another Suitcase In Another Hall; Don't Cry For Me Argentina (Miami Mix Edit); You Must Love Me; Hello And Goodbye (UK CD maxi-single, also limited edition with 3 film prints in standard jewel case)

1996 You Must Love Me (Video); Rainbow High (LP); You Must Love Me/I'd Be Surprisingly Good For You (Orchestra) (Warner Bros UK CD maxi-single)

1996 Don't Cry For Me Argentina (Miami Mix, Alt Ending); (Miami Spanglish Mix); (Miami Mix Edit); (Miami Dub Mix); (Miami Mix Instr.); (Miami Spanglish Mix Edit) (US CD maxi-single)

1996 Don't Cry For Me Argentina; Santa Evita; Latin Chant (Warner Bros. UK CD single)

1997 Don't Cry For Me Argentina (Miami Mix Edit); (Miami Spanglish Edit); (Miami Mix); (LP) (Warner Bros. UK CD single)

1997 *Rescue Me* (Alternate Mix): Justify My Love (Q-Sound Mix); (Orbit 12-ins Mix); (Hip Hop Mix); Express Yourself; Justify My Love (The Beast Within Mix); Rescue Me (Single Mix); (Titanic Mix); (Houseboat Vocal); (Lifeboat Vocal); (S.O.S. Mix)

1998 Ray Of Light (LP); (Sasha UltraViolet Mix); (William Orbit Liquid Mix); (Victor Calderone Club Mix) (CD maxi-single)

1998 Ray Of Light (12-ins Single) (UK 12-ins)

1998 The Power Of Goodbye; Mer Girl

1998 *Power Of Goodbye* (Remix EP): (LP); (Dallas's Low End Mix); (Luke Slater's Super Luper Mix); (Luke Slater's Filtered Mix); (Fabian's Good God Mix) (Australian version had the same track listings)

1999 Frozen (LP); (Stereo MC's Mix); (Extended Club Mix); (Meltdown Mix – Long) (Also CD maxi-single)

1998 Frozen (Extended Club Mix); (Stereo MC's Mix); (Meltdown Mix – Long) (UK 12-ins, CD maxi-single had bonus tracks [LP] & [Widescreen Mix])

1998 Ray Of Light (LP); (Sasha Ultra Violet Mix); (William Orbit Liquid Mix); (Victor Calderone Club Mix) (US CD maxi-single)

1999 Nothing Really Matters (LP); (Club 69 Vocal Club Mix); (Club 69 Future Mix); (Club 69 Phunk Mix); (Club 69 Speed Mix); (Kruder

& Dorfmeister Mix); (Vikram Radio Mix); (Club 69 Future Mix); (Club 69 Radio Mix) (US CD maxi-single)

1999 Nothing Really Matters (LP); (Club 69 Radio Mix); (Club 69 Vocal Club Mix); (Club 69 Phunk Mix); (Vikram Radio Dub); (Kruder & Dorfmeister Mix) (US limited-edition, double 12-ins single)

1999 Beautiful Stranger (LP); (CC Mix); (CR Mix) (From soundtrack of *Austin Powers 2: The Spy Who Shagged Me*)

2000 Music (HQ2 Club Mix); (Groove Armada 12-ins Mix); (Calderone Anthem Mix); (LP); (Deep Dish Dot Com Mix); (Young Collective Club Remix) (US double 12-ins)

2000 Music (HQ2 Club Mix); (Calderone Anthem Mix); (Deep Dish Dot Com Mix); (Groove Armada Club Mix); (Young Collective Club Remix); (HQ2 Radio Mix); (Calderone Radio Edit); (Deep Dish Dot Com Radio Edit); (Groove Armada 12-ins Mix) (US CD maxi-single)

2000 Music (Deep Dish Dot Com Radio Edit); (LP); (Groove Armada Club Mix); (Gab12-ins Mix) (UK, also issued as picture disk)

2000 American Pie (LP); (Vission Radio Mix); (Calderone Filter Dub Mix); (Vission Visits Madonna (One of Madonna's two musical contributions to *The Next Best Thing* Original Sound Track. This remake of the Don McLean classic features a filter dub mix by Victor Calderone)

2000 American Pie Pt.1 (LP); (Calderone Filter Dub Mix); (Calderone Vocal Dub Mix) (UK CD maxi-single, includes an exclusive vocal dub mix by Victor Calderone)

2000 American Pie Pt.2 (LP); (Richard Vission Radio Mix); (Vission Visits Madonna) (UK CD maxi-single)

2000 American Pie Pt.3 (Calderone Vocal Club Mix); (Calderone Extended Vocal); (Vission Visits Madonna); (Vission Radio Mix); (LP) (UK CD maxi-single)

2000 American Pie Remixes (Richard Hampty Version); (Richard Hampty Version Radio Mix); (Victor Calderone Vocal Club); (Victor Calderone Extended Vocal Club Mix); (LP) (Japanese CD maxi-single)

2001 Don't Tell Me (Timo Maas Mix); (Tracy Young Club Mix); (Vission Remix); (Thunderpuss' 2001 Hands In The Air Anthem); (Victor Calderone Sensory Mix); (Vission Radio Mix); (Thunderpuss' 2001 Hands In The Air Radio) (Double 12-ins set & CD maxi-single, issued as EP for Japan)

2001 Don't Tell Me (Thunderpuss' 2001 Hands-In-The-Air Anthem); (Timo Maas Mix); (Victor Calderone Sensory Mix); (Tracy Young Club Mix); (Thunderpuss' 2001 Tribe-A-Pella) (UK CD maxi-single)

2000 Don't Tell Me Pt.1 (Radio Edit); (Cyber-Raga); (Thunderpuss Club Mix) (UK CD maxi-single includes exclusive [Thunderpuss Club Mix] not released in USA)

2000 Don't Tell Me Pt.2 (LP); (Vission Remix); (Thunderpuss Radio Mix (UK CD maxi-single)

2000 Don't Tell Me Pt.3 (Radio Edit); (Cyber-Raga); (Thunderpuss Club Mix); (Vission Remix) (UK CD maxi-single)

2001 Don't Tell Me (Remixes) (Timo Maas Remix); (Thunderpuss Mix); (Victor Calderone Mix); (Richard Humpty Vission Mix (UK CD maxi-single)

2001 What It Feels Like For A Girl (Paul Oakenfold Perfecto Mix); (Richard Vission Velvet Masta Mix); (Calderone & Quayle Dark Side Mix); (Tracy Young Club Mix); (Above & Beyond 12-ins Club Mix); (Tracy Young Cool Out Radio Mix); (Richard Vission Velvet Masta Edit); (Above & Beyond Club Radio Edit); (Spanish) (US CD maxi-single)

2001 What It Feels Like For A Girl (LP); (Calderone & Quayle Dark Side Mix); (Above & Beyond Club Mix); (Paul Oakenfold Perfecto Mix); (Richard Vission Velvet Masta Mix) (Special UK limited edition contained poster and was packaged in cardboard sleeve)

7-inch vinyl, cassette and CD singles from USA and UK chronologically

1982 Everybody (3.19 Remix) / (4.42 Dub) (UK single)

1983 Holiday (Edit) / I Know It

1983 Holiday / Think Of Me (UK single)

1984 Borderline / Think Of Me (Also issued with poster sleeve in USA)

1984 Borderline / Holiday (USA: Back-To-Back Hits)

1984 Borderline (Edit) / Physical Attraction (UK single)

1984 Lucky Star (Edit) / I Know It (LP)

1984 (1) Borderline (Edit) / Physical Attraction 2) Holiday (Edit) / Think Of Me (UK special shrink-wrapped double-pack of 7-ins singles plus special sticker)

1984 Like A Virgin / Stay (Also issued with silver cover in USA)

1984 Like A Virgin / Lucky Star (USA: Back-To-Back Hits)

1985 Material Girl / Pretender (UK single, also limited edition with poster sleeve)

1985 Crazy For You / No More Words (Issued on Geffen label; B-side performed by Berlin)

1985 Crazy For You /Gamblers (USA: Back-To-Back Hits)

1985 Crazy For You / I'll Fall In Love Again (UK single, picture sleeve; B-side performed by Sammy Hagen)

1985 Angel (Remix) / (Edit)

1985 Angel / Material Girl (USA: Back-To-Back Hits)

1985 Angel (Fade) / Burning Up (Remix) (UK single)

1985 Dress You Up / Shoo-Bee-Doo

1985 Dress You Up / I Know It (UK single)

1985 Into The Groove / Dress You Up (USA: Back-To-Back Hits; also later 'Backtrax' reissue as 3-ins CD single)

1985 Into The Groove / Shoo-Bee-Doo (UK single, also issued as heart-shaped picture disc & 2 stickers)

1985 Gambler / Nature Of The Beach (UK single; B-side by Black 'n' Blue; also issued with poster sleeve)

1986 Papa Don't Preach (LP) / Pretender (Also CD & laser disk singles with bonus track 'Papa Don't Preach')

1986 Everybody / Papa Don't Preach (USA: Back-To-Back Hits)

1986 Papa Don't Preach (LP) / Ain't No Big Deal (UK single)

1986 True Blue / Ain't No Big Deal (Also US limited edition on blue vinyl)

1986 True Blue (Remix) / Holiday (Edit) (UK single)

1986 Open Your Heart / White Heat

1986 Open Your Heart / Lucky Star (UK single)

1986 Holiday / True Blue (UK reissue of 7-ins singles)

1986 Live To Tell (Edit) / (Instr.)

1986 Live To Tell / True Blue (USA: Back-To-Back Hits)

1987 La Isla Bonita (LP) / (Instr. Remix)

1987 La Isla Bonita / Open Your Heart (USA: Back-To-Back Hits)

1987 Who's That Girl / White Heat
(From now on, all singles were also issued as cassette singles)

1987 Causing A Commotion / Jimmy, Jimmy (UK single, also limited edition shrink-wrapped with button badge)

1987 Causing A Commotion / Who's That Girl (USA: Back-To-Back Hits)

1987 The Look Of Love / I Know It (UK single)
1989 Like A Prayer (7-ins) / Act Of Contrition (Also 3-ins CD single)
1989 Like A Prayer (7-ins) / Oh Father (Edit) (USA: Back-To-Back Hits)
1989 Express Yourself (7-ins Remix) / The Look Of Love (LP) (Also issued as a CD 3-ins single. UK, also limited edition had working zipper over inner picture sleeve)
1989 Cherish (7-ins) / Supernatural
1989 Cherish (Fade) / Express Yourself (7-ins Remix) (USA: Back-To-Back Hits)
1989 Oh Father / Pray For Spanish Eyes (LP)
1989 Dear Jessie / Till Death Do Us Apart (UK single, also as picture disk)
1989 Like A Prayer (7-ins) / (7-ins Fade)
1990 Keep It Together (Single Remix) / (Instr.)
1990 Vogue (Single) / (Bette Davis Dub)
1990 Vogue (Single) / Keep It Together (Single Remix) (UK single)
1990 Vogue / Keep It Together (USA: Back-To-Back Hits; also later 'Backtrax' reissue as 3-ins CD single)
1990 Hanky Panky (LP) / More (LP)
1990 Justify My Love / Express Yourself (Shep's 'Spressin' Himself Re-Remix)
1990 Justify My Love / Rescue Me (USA: Back-To-Back Hits; also later 'Backtrax' reissue as 3-ins CD single)
1991 Rescue Me (Single) / (Alt. Single Mix)
1991 Rescue Me (7-ins Mix) / Spotlight (LP) (UK single)
1991 Crazy For You (Remix) / Keep It Together (7-ins Remix) (UK single of 7-ins singles)
1992 This Used To Be My Playground (Single) / (Long)
1992 This Used To Be My Playground (Single) / Hanky Panky (USA: Back-To-Back Hits; also 'Backtrax' reissue as 3-ins CD single)
1992 Erotica (LP) / (Instr.) (All singles issued on Maverick/Sire label from now; also 3-ins CD single)
1992 Deeper And Deeper (LP); (Instr.) (3-ins CD single)
1992 I'll Remember (LP) / Secret Garden (LP) (UK issue)
1993 Bad Girl (Edit) / Fever (Also 3-ins CD single)
1993 Bad Girl (Edit) / Erotica (William Orbit Dub) (UK single)
1993 Rain (Radio Remix) / Waiting (LP) (Also 3-ins CD single)
1993 Rain (Remix) / Open Your Heart (LP) (UK single)
1993 Fever (LP) / (Remix) (UK single, also limited edition of picture disk with numbered insert)

1994 I'll Remember (LP) / Secret Garden (LP) (Also 3-ins CD single)
1994 Secret (LP) / (Instr.) (Also 3-ins CD single)
1994 Secret / Let Down Your Guard (Rough Mix Edit) (UK single)
1994 Take A Bow (LP) / (In Da Soul Mix)
1994 Take A Bow (LP) / (Instr.) (US 3-ins CD single and UK single)
1994 Bedtime Story (Album Edit) / (Junior's Single Mix) (UK single)
1995 Bedtime Story (LP) / Survival (LP) (Also 3-ins CD single)
1995 Human Nature (Radio) / Sanctuary (LP) (Also 3-ins CD single)
1995 You'll See (LP) / (Instr.)
1995 You'll See (LP); Live To Tell (Live From Who's That Girl Tour) (US 3-ins CD single)
1996 Love Don't Live Here Anymore (Soulpower Radio Remix) / (Album Remix)
1996 One More Chance / Vèras (Spanish version of 'You'll See') (UK single)
1996 You Must Love Me (LP) / Rainbow High (LP) (Also 3-ins CD single)
1996 Don't Cry For Me Argentina / Santa Evita (UK single)
1998 Frozen (LP) / Shanti / Ashtangi (LP) (Also 3-ins CD single)
1998 Ray Of Light (LP) / Has To Be (Non-Album Track) (Won the 1999 Grammy for Best Dance Recording, and was nominated for Record Of The Year; also 3-ins CD single)
1998 The Power Of Goodbye / Mer Girl (Also 3-ins CD single)
1998 The Power Of Goodbye / Little Star (UK single)
1999 Nothing Really Matters (LP) / To Have & Not To Hold (LP) (Also 3-ins CD single)
2000 Music (LP) / Cyber-Raga (Non-Album Track) (Also 3-ins CD single)
2000 Drowned World / Substitute For Love (UK single)
2001 Don't Tell Me (LP) / (Thunderpuss 2001 Hands In The Air Radio Edit)

Vinyl, cassette and CD albums chronologically

1983 *Madonna:* Lucky Star; Borderline; Burning Up; I Know It; Holiday; Think Of Me; Physical Attraction; Everybody (Also issued as 8-track, cassette album & CD)
1984 *Like A Virgin:* Material Girl; Angel; Like A Virgin; Over And Over; Love Don't Live Here Anymore; Dress You Up; Shoo-Bee-Doo;

Pretender; Stay (Also issued as 8-track, cassette album & CD; UK version included 'Into the Groove')

1984 *Revenge Of The Killer B's:* Ain't No Big Deal (Warner Bros: only one Madonna track)

1985 *Vision Quest* (Soundtrack): Crazy For You, Gambler (Geffen: only two Madonna tracks)

1986 *True Blue:* Papa Don't Preach; Open Your Heart; White Heat; Live To Tell; Where's The Party; True Blue; La Isla Bonita; Jimmy, Jimmy; Love Makes The World Go Round (Also issued as 8-track, cassette album & CD)

1987 *Who's That Girl* (Soundtrack): Who's That Girl; Causing A Commotion; The Look Of Love; 24 Hours (Duncan Faure); Step By Step (Club Nouveau); Turn It Up (Michael Davidson); Best Thing Ever (Scritti Politti); Can't Stop; El Coco Loco (Coati Mundi) (Also issued as 8-track, cassette album & CD. Madonna selected the soundtrack; but only performed four songs; other singers are attributed)

1987 *You Can Dance:* Spotlight; Holiday; Everybody; Physical Attraction; Over And Over; Into The Groove; Where's The Party ('Spotlight' was only unreleased song: cassette & 8-track included bonus dubs of 'Spotlight', 'Holiday', 'Over and Over' and 'Into the Groove'. CD omitted 'Spotlight' bonus, but included the other three, plus 'Where's the Party')

1987 *Who's That Girl:* Who's That Girl?; Causing A Commotion; The Look Of Love; 24 Hours; Step By Step; Turn It Up; Best Thing Ever; Can't Stop; El Coco Loco (So So Bad) (Also issued as 8-track, cassette album & CD)

1987 A *Very Special Christmas:* Santa Baby (A&M: only one Madonna track)

1989 *Like A Prayer:* Like A Prayer; Express Yourself; Love Song; Till Death Do Us Part; Promise To Try; Cherish; Dear Jessie; Oh Father; Keep It Together; Spanish Eyes; Act Of Contrition (Also cassette album & CD)

1989 *The Early Years:* Wild Dancing (Ext.); Time To Dance (Ext.); On The Street; We Are The Gods; Cosmic Climb; Time To Dance; Cosmic Climb (Ext.); On The Street (Ext.); Wild Dancing; Time To Dance (Instr.) (UK issue)

1989 *Best Of & Rest Of Madonna Vol. 1* (UK CD; 5 tracks from *The Early Years* & interview)

1989 *Best Of & Rest Of Madonna Vol. 2* (UK CD; 10 tracks from *The Early Years*)

1990 *The Immaculate Collection:* Holiday; Lucky Star; Borderline; Like A Virgin; Material Girl; Crazy For You; Into The Groove; Live To Tell; Papa Don't Preach; Open Your Heart; La Isla Bonita; Like A Prayer; Express Yourself; Cherish; Vogue; Justify My Love; Rescue Me (Also issued as double-length cassette album, digital compact cassette & CD. Also issued as *The Royal Box* with either cassette or CD of the LP, plus *The Immaculate Collection* video, eight postcards & a poster)

1990 *I'm Breathless:* Songs From And Inspired By The Film *Dick Tracy:* He's A Man; Sooner Or Later; Hanky Panky; I'm Going Bananas; Cry Baby; Something To Remember; Back In Business; More; What Can You Lose; Now I'm Following You, Part I; Now I'm Following You, Part II; Vogue (Also cassette album & CD)

1991 *The Immaculate Conversation:* UK Interview (Cassette album only)

1991 Michael Jackson: *Dangerous:* In The Closet (One track; Madonna as Mystery Girl; also cassette album)

1992 *Erotica:* Erotica; Fever; Bye Bye Baby; Deeper And Deeper; Where Life Begins; Bad Girl; Waiting; Thief Of Hearts; Words; Rain; Why's It So Hard; In This Life; Did You Do It?; Secret Garden (Two versions issued: the *Clean Version* omitted 'Did You Do It?'; also cassette album & CD)

1992 *Barcelona Gold:* This Used To Be My Playground (Only one Madonna track; also cassette album & CD)

1994 *With Honors* (Soundtrack): I'll Remember (Maverick: only one Madonna track)

1994 *Just Say Roe:* Goodbye To Innocence (Sire: only one Madonna track)

1995 *Bedtime Stories:* Survival; Secret; I'd Rather Be Your Lover; Don't Stop; Inside Of Me; Human Nature; Forbidden Love; Love Tried To Welcome Me; Sanctuary; Bedtime Story; Take A Bow (Also cassette album & CD)

1995 *Something To Remember:* I Want You; I'll Remember; Take A Bow; You'll See; Crazy For You; This Used To Be My Playground; Live To Tell; Love Don't Live Here Anymore; Something To Remember; Forbidden Love; One More Chance; Rain; Oh Father; I Want You (Orchestral) Also cassette album & CD)

1995 *Inner City Blues: The Music Of Marvin Gaye:* I Want You (Motown: only one Madonna track)

1996 *Evita – Highlights:* Requiem For Evita; Oh! What A Circus; On This Night Of A Thousand Stars; Eva And Magaldi / Eva Beware Of The City; Buenos Aires; Another

Suitcase In Another Hall; Goodnight And Thank You; I'd Be Surprisingly Good For You; Peron's Latest Flame; A New Argentina; Don't Cry For Me Argentina; High Flying, Adored; Rainbow High; And The Money Kept Rolling (In And Out); She Is A Diamond; Waltz For Eva And Che; You Must Love Me; Eva's Final Broadcast; Lament (Also cassette album & CD)

1997 *Carnival (Rainforest Foundation Concert):* Freedom (Victor: only one Madonna track)

1998 *Ray Of Light:* Drowned World / Substitute For Love; Swim; Ray Of Light; Candy Perfume Girl; Skin; Nothing Really Matters; Sky Fits Heaven; Shanti / Ashtangi; Frozen; Power Of Goodbye, The To Have And Not To Hold; Little Star; Mer Girl (Won the 1999 Grammy Award for Best Pop Album. Japanese CD had two extra tracks; also cassette album & CD)

1999 *Austin Powers 2: The Spy Who Shagged Me:* Beautiful Stranger (Soundtrack; only one track. Madonna plays: Seductress on video only)

2000 *Music:* Music; Impressive Instant; Runaway Lover; I Deserve It; Amazing; Nobody's Perfect; Don't Tell Me; What It Feels Like For A Girl; Paradise (Not For Me); Gone (Won the 2001 Grammy Award for Best Recording Package; also cassette album & CD. CD has bonus track 'American Pie')

2001 *In The Spotlight With Madonna:* Interview 1; Interview 2 (An enhanced audio CD with regular audio tracks and multimedia computer files. These are unauthorized interviews with Madonna; also contains a 100 page booklet)

2001 *Madonna (Remaster):* Lucky Star; Borderline; Burning Up; I Know It; Holiday; Think Of Me; Physical Attraction; Everybody; Everybody; Burning Up (12-ins); Lucky Star (New Mix) (Original release: 1983. Includes bonus 'Burning Up' and 'Lucky Star [Ext. Dance Remixes] previously unavailable on CD)

2001 *Like A Virgin (Remaster):* Material Girl; Angel; Like A Virgin; Over And Over; Love Don't Live Here Anymore; Dress You Up; Shoo-Bee-Doo; Pretender; Stay (Original release: 1984. Includes bonus 'Like A Virgin' and 'Material Girl' [Ext. Dance Remixes] previously unavailable on CD)

2001 *True Blue (Remaster):* Papa Don't Preach ; Open Your Heart ; White Heat; Live To Tell ; Where's The Party; True Blue; La Isla Bonita; Jimmy, Jimmy; Love Makes The World Go Around; True Blue (The Color Mix); La Isla Bonita (Extended Remix) (Original release: 1986. Includes bonus 'True Blue' and 'La Isla Bonita' [Ext. Dance Remixes] previously unavailable on CD)

2001 *Complete Madonna Interviews* (Interviews only, no music)

2001 *The Complete Audio Biography* (3-CD Set) (Comprises a 2-CD narrative written by Martin Harper and read by Sian Jones. The third CD has an interview with Madonna)

2001 *The Early Years: Give It To Me:* Give It To Me; Shake; Get Down; Time To Dance; Wild Dancing; Let's Go Dancing; We Are The Gods; Cosmic Climb; On The Street; Oh My!

Music videos

1982 *Everybody* (Director: Ed Steinberg. From: *Madonna*)

1983 *Burning Up* (Director: Steve Barron. From: *Madonna*)

1984 *Borderline* (Director: Mary Lambert. From: *Madonna*)

1984 *Holiday #1* (Director: Unknown. From: *Madonna*. Low-budget, not released)

1984 *Lucky Star #1* (Director: Arthur Pierson. From: *Madonna*)

1984 *Like A Virgin* (Director: Mary Lambert. From: *Like A Virgin*)

1984 *Like A Virgin* (Director: Mary Lambert. MTV *Video Music Awards*)

1984 *Lucky Star #2* (Director: Arthur Pierson. From: *Madonna* – extended version)

1985 *Material Girl* (Director: Mary Lambert. From: *Like A Virgin*)

1985 *Crazy For You* (Director: Harold Becker. From: *Vision Quest* – original motion picture soundtrack)

1985 *Into The Groove* (Director: Susan Seidelman. From: *You Can Dance* – made with film clips from *Desperately Seeking Susan*)

1985 *Dress You Up #1* (Director: Danny Kleinman. From: *Like A Virgin*)

1985 *Dress You Up #2* (Director: Danny Kleinman. From: *Like A Virgin* – extended with introduction and different angles)

1985 *Gambler #1* (Director: Harold Becker. From: *Vision Quest* – original motion picture soundtrack)

1985 *Gambler (The Virgin Tour Live)*

1985 *Like A Virgin (The Virgin Tour Live)*

1985 *Over And Over (The Virgin Tour Live)*

1986 *Live To Tell* (Director: James Foley. Includes film clips from *At Close Range*)

1986 *Papa Don't Preach* (Director: James Foley. From: *True Blue*)

1986 *True Blue* (Make My Video Contest winner; Madonna does not appear)

1986 *True Blue* (Director: James Foley. From: *True Blue* – European version)

1986 *Open Your Heart* (Director: Jean-Baptiste Mondino. From: *True Blue*)

1987 *La Isla Bonita* (Director: Mary Lambert. From: *True Blue*)

1987 *The Look Of Love* (Director: James Foley. From: *Who's That Girl?*, made with film clips)

1987 *Causing A Commotion* (MTV Video Music Awards)

1988 *Into The Groove (Ciao Italia – Live)* (Used to promote the commercial video)

1989 *Like A Prayer* (Director: Mary Lambert. From: *Like A Prayer*)

1989 *Make A Wish* (Two-minute Pepsi commercial, broadcast worldwide March 2)

1989 *Express Yourself* (MTV: *Video Music Awards*)

1989 *Cherish* (Director: Herb Ritts. From: *Like A Prayer*)

1989 *Express Yourself* (Director: David Fincher. From: *Like A Prayer*)

1989 *Oh Father* (Director: David Fincher. From: *Like A Prayer*)

1989 *Dear Jessie* (Director: Unknown. From: *Like A Prayer*. Released outside USA; animations only, Madonna does not appear)

1989 *Papa Don't Preach* (Warner, laser disc only)

1990 *Vogue* (Director: David Fincher. From: *I'm Breathless* – music from and inspired by *Dick Tracy*)

1990 *Vogue* (MTV: *Video Music Awards*)

1990 *Vote!* (For 'Rock the Vote' campaign – broadcast October 22 to November 6)

1990 *Justify My Love* (Director: Jean-Baptiste Mondino. From: *The Immaculate Collection* – sold as first-ever video single)

1991 *Like A Virgin* (Director: Alek Keshishian. From: *Like A Virgin* – made with clips from *Truth Or Dare*)

1991 *Holiday #2* (Director: Alek Keshishian. From: *Like A Virgin* – made with clips from *Truth Or Dare*)

1992 *This Used To Be My Playground* (Director: Alek Keshishian. From *Barcelona Gold*; includes clips from *A League Of Their Own*)

1992 *Erotica* (Director: Fabien Baron. From: *Erotica*)

1992 *Deeper And Deeper* (Director: Bobby Woods. From: *Erotica*)

1993 *Bad Girl* (Director: David Fincher. From: *Erotica*)

1993 *Fever* (Director: Stephan Sednaopi. From: *Erotica*)

1993 *Rain* (Director: Mark Romanek. From: *Erotica*)

1993 *Bye Bye Baby (Live From The Girlie Show Tour)* (Used in Australia to promote the single, which was not released in USA or UK)

1994 *I'll Remember* (Director: Alek Keshishian. Includes film clips from *With Honors*)

1994 *Secret* (Director: Melodie McDaniel. From: *Bedtime Stories*)

1994 *Take A Bow* (Director: Michael Haussman. From: *Bedtime Stories*)

1995 *Bedtime Story* (Director: Mark Romariek. From: *Bedtime Stories*)

1995 *Human Nature* (Director: Jean-Baptiste Mondino. From: *Bedtime Stories.*

1995 *I Want You* (Only briefly released to promote *Inner City Blues: the Music of Marvin Gaye*)

1995 *You'll See* (Director: Michael Haussman. From: *Something to Remember*)

1996 *Love Don't Live Here Anymore* (Director: Jean-Baptiste Mondino. From: *Something To Remember*)

1996 *You Must Love Me* (Director: Alan Parker. From: *Evita: the complete motion picture soundtrack*; includes film clips)

1996 *Don't Cry For Me Argentina* (Director: Alan Parker. From: *Evita* – made with film clips)

1997 *Another Suitcase In Another Hall* (Director: Alan Parker. From: *Evita* – made with film clips. Not released in USA)

1997 *Buenos Aires* (Director: Alan Parker. From: *Evita* – made with film clips. Not released in USA)

1998 *Frozen*

1998 *Ray Of Light* (Won the 1999 Grammy for Best Short Form Music Video)

1998 *Drowned World/Substitute For Love* (Not released in USA)

1998 *The Power Of Goodbye*

1999 *Nothing Really Matters*

1999 *Beautiful Stranger* From soundtrack of *Austin Powers 2: The Spy Who Shagged Me*. Plays: Seductress on video only)

2000 *American Pie* (From the soundtrack of *The Next Best Thing*. Included on DVD)

2000 *Music* (Also released as DVD)

2000 *Don't Tell Me* (Also released in US as enhanced CD-single in Jan 2001)

Films, videos and TV programs

1972 [untitled] Super-8 film project in which an egg is fried on Madonna's stomach (Director: Unknown; running time unknown; unrated)

1980 *A Certain Sacrifice* (Director: Stephen Jon Lewicki; unrated (18 in UK in 1992); 60 mins. As Madonna Ciccone; plays: Bruna)

1983 *Vision Quest* aka *Crazy For You* (Director: Harold Becker; R; 105 mins. Plays: cameo)

1984 *Madonna* (Director: Steve Baron; Mary Lambert; video; 17 mins)

1984 *American Bandstand* (Hosted: Dick Clark; TV; 60 mins)

1985 *Desperately Seeking Susan* (Director: Susan Seidelman; PG-13; 104 mins. Plays: Susan)

1985 *Live Aid* (TV; runs 960 mins. Performs at JFK Stadium)

1985 *The Virgin Tour – Live:* Dress You Up; Holiday; Into The Groove; Everybody; Gambler; Lucky Star; Crazy For You; Over And Over; Like A Virgin; Material Girl (Director: Danny Kleinman; video; 50 mins)

1986 *Shanghai Surprise* (Director: Jim Goddard; PG-13; 90 mins. Plays: Gloria Tatlock)

1987 *Who's That Girl – Live in Japan:* Open Your Heart; Lucky Star; True Blue; Papa Don't Preach; White Heat; Causing A Commotion; The Look Of Love; Medley: Dress You Up/Material Girl/Like A Virgin; Where's The Party; Live To Tell; Into The Groove; La Isla Bonita; Who's That Girl; Holiday (Director: Mitchell Sinoway; video; 92 mins)

1987 *Rolling Stone Presents Twenty Years of Rock & Roll* aka *Rolling Stone: The First Twenty Years* (Director: Malcolm Leo; unrated; 97 mins; archive footage)

1987 *Who's That Girl* (Director: James Foley; PG; 92 mins. Plays: Nikki Finn)

1988 *Bloodhounds of Broadway* (Director: Howard Brookner; PG; 93 mins. Plays: Hortense Hathaway)

1988 *Ciao Italia – Live from Italy* Director: Egbert van Hees; video; 100 mins)

1990 *Blonde Ambition World Tour Live:* Express Yourself; Open Your Heart; Causing A Commotion; Where's The Party; Like A Virgin; Like A Prayer; Live To Tell/Oh Father; Papa Don't Preach; Sooner Or Later; Hanky Panky; Now I'm Following You (Parts I & II); Material Girl; Cherish; Into The Groove; Vogue; Holiday; Keep It Together (Director: David Mallet; video; 112 mins)

1990 *Blonde Ambition – Japan Tour 90:* tracks as above (Director: Mark Aldo Miceli; video; 105 mins)

1990 *Dick Tracy* (Director: Warren Beatty; PG; 103 mins. Plays: Breathless Mahoney)

1990 *Dick Tracy: Behind the Badge, Behind the Scenes* (TV)

1990 *The Immaculate Collection:* Lucky Star; Borderline; Like A Virgin; Material Girl; Papa Don't Preach; Open Your Heart; La Isla Bonita; Like A Prayer; Express Yourself; Cherish; Oh Father; Vogue; and Vogue (From The 1990 MTV Awards) (Various directors; video; 60 mins)

1991 *Truth or Dare* Outside USA aka *In Bed with Madonna* (Director: Alek Keshishian; R; 114–120 mins)

1991 *National Enquirer: The Untold Story of Madonna* (Good Times)

1991 *Women in Rock* (Atlantic Video)

1991 *Justify My Love* (Warner Music Video; 13 mins)

1992 *A League of Their Own* (Director: Penny Marshall; PG; 117–128 mins. Plays: Mae 'All-The-Way-Mae' Mordabito)

1992 *Blast 'Em* (Director: Joseph Blasioli; approx. 90 minutes; PG – documentary on paparazzi includes Madonna)

1992 *Oscar's Greatest Moments: 1971 to 1991* (Director: Jeff Margolis; video)

1992 *Shadows and Fog* (Director: Woody Allen; PG-13; 86 mins. Plays: Marie the Strongman's Wife)

1993 *Body of Evidence* aka *Deadly Evidence* (Director: Ulrich Edel; R; unrated version on video; 101 mins. Plays: Rebecca Carlson)

1993 *Dangerous Game* (Director: Abel Ferrara; R; 108 mins. Plays: Sarah Jennings)

1993 *The Girlie Show – Live Down Under:* Erotica; Fever; Vogue; Rain; Express Yourself; Deeper And Deeper; Why's It So Hard; In This Life; The Beast Within; Like A Virgin; Bye Bye Baby; I'm Going Bananas; La Isla Bonita; Holiday; Justify My Love; Everybody Is A Star/Everybody (Video)

1993 *Madonna Exposed* (Good Times)

1995 *Blue in the Face* (Director: Paul Auster; Wayne Wang; R; 83–95 mins. Plays: Singing Telegram)

1995 *Four Rooms* (Director: Allison Anders; Alexandre Rockwell; R; 98 mins. Plays: Elspeth in *The Missing Ingredient*)

1995 *The History of Rock 'N' Roll; Vol. 10* AKA *Up From the Underground* (Video; 60 mins)

1996 *Evita:* A Cinema In Buenos Aires; 26 July 1952; Requiem For Evita; Oh What A Circus; On

This Night of A Thousand Stars; Eva And Magaldi / Eva Beware of the City; Buenos Aries; Another Suitcase In Another Hall; Goodnight And Thank You; The Lady's Got Potential; Charity Concert / The Art of the Possible; I'd Be Surprisingly Good For You; Hello And Goodbye; Peron's Latest Flame; A New Argentina; On the Balcony of the Casa Rosada 1; Don't Cry For Me Argentina; On the Balcony of the Casa Rosada 2; High Flying; Adored; Rainbow High; Rainbow Tour; The Actress Hasn't Learned the Lines (You'd Like To Hear); And the Money Kept Rolling In (And Out); Partido Feminista; She Is A Diamond; Santa Evita; Waltz For Eva And Che; Your Little Body's Slowly Breaking Down; You Must Love Me; Eva's Final Broadcast; Latin Chant; Lament (Director: Alan Parker; PG; 134 mins. Plays: Eva Perón)

1996   *Girl 6* (Director: Spike Lee; R; 108 mins. Plays: Boss #3)

1997   *Happy Birthday Elizabeth: A Celebration of Life* (Director: Jeff Margolis; TV)

1998   *Oprah Winfrey Show* (Director: Joseph C. Terry; TV; 60 mins)

1998   *Behind the Music* aka *VH1's Behind the Music* (Director: David Greene; TV)

1998   *Ray Of Light* (Limited-edition video single of the Grammy winner)

1999   *Madonna: The Video Collection 93–99*: Bad Girl; Fever; Rain; Secret; Take A Bow; Bedtime Story; Human Nature; Love Don't Live Here Anymore; Frozen; Ray Of Light; Drowned World/Substitute For Love; The Power of Goodbye; Nothing Really Matters; Beautiful Stranger (Directors: various; PG-13; 67 mins. Promoted as her 14 favorite music videos; *Drowned World/Substitute For Love* was previously unreleased in the USA)

2000   *Music* (Director: Jonas Åkerlund; video; 10 mins)

2000   *The Next Best Thing* (Director: John Schlesinger; PG-13; 108 mins. Plays: Abbie Reynolds)

2000   *In the Life* (TV; episode # 7.4; May)

2000   *Music* (DVD video single with two slightly different versions)

2001   *Don't Tell Me* (CD Maxi-Single [enhanced]; for PC or Mac)

2001   *Drowned World Tour 2001* (Director: Hamish Hamilton; TV)

2001   *Star* (Director: Guy Ritchie; 7 mins. Plays: Star [uncredited])

2001   *The 43rd Annual Grammy Awards* (TV)

2001   *What It Feels Like for a Girl* (Director: Guy Ritchie; video; 5 mins. Plays: The Chick)

Theater

Goose and Tom-Tom by David Rabe. Lincoln Center Theater workshop, 1987. Played: Lorraine.

Speed-the-Plow by David Mamet. Produced by the Lincoln Center Theater at the Royale Theater, Broadway, 1988. Played: Karen.

Tours

1985   The Virgin Tour

1987   Who's That Girl? World Tour

1990   Blonde Ambition World Tour

1993   The Girlie Show World Tour

2001   Drowned World Tour

Index

Index